SMART CARDS
Seizing Strategic Business Opportunities

SMART CARDS
Seizing Strategic Business Opportunities

THE SMART CARD FORUM

EDITED BY CATHERINE A. ALLEN & WILLIAM J. BARR

WITH RON SCHULTZ

Chicago • London • Singapore

© Richard D. Irwin, a Times Mirror Higher Education Group, Inc. company, 1997

All rights reserved. No part of this publication may be
reproduced, stored in a retrieval system, or transmitted,
in any form or by any means, electronic, mechanical,
photocopying, recording, or otherwise, without the prior
written permission of the publisher.

This publication is designed to provide accurate and
authoritative information in regard to the subject matter
covered. It is sold with the understanding that neither the
author nor the publisher is engaged in rendering legal, accounting,
or other professional service. If legal advice or other expert
assistance is required, the services of a competent professional
person should be sought.

From a Declaration of Principles jointly adopted by a Committee
of the American Bar Association and a Committee of Publishers.

Times Mirror
Higher Education Group

Library of Congress Cataloging-In-Publication Data

Smart cards : seizing strategic business opportunities / by the Smart
  Card Forum ; edited by Catherine A. Allen and William J. Barr.
      p.   cm.
   Includes bibliographical references and index.
   ISBN 0-7863-1108-8
      1. Smart card industry. 2. Smart cards. I. Allen, Catherine A.
   II. Barr, William J. III. Smart Card Forum.
   HD9696.S583U67   1997
   332.7'6—dc20   96–41903

Printed in the United States of America
1 2 3 4 5 6 7 9 0 DOC 3 2 1 0 9 8 7 6

*This book is dedicated to the innovative staff
and members of the Smart Card Forum
who have helped launch an industry*

PREFACE

Two billion smart cards are expected to be in circulation by the year 2000. By then, over 25 percent of United States households will be using a smart card to make payments, to access information from computers or television sets, or to store healthcare information. The advantage of the smart card over the familiar magnetic stripe plastic card with regard to security and multiple applications will drive its acceptance.

"Smart cards" are now widely used in Europe, Asia, and South America for making electronic cash, debit and credit payments, for medical information and insurance, and for frequent user points in loyalty programs. Stored value or electronic cash and debit applications are part of the emerging banking infrastructure in China, Viet Nam, and South Africa. The launch of the VISA Cash card in Atlanta during the recent Olympics left that city with a modernized electronic cash society.

Recognizing the advantages of smart cards, consortia of banks, telecommunications companies, transit authorities, the federal government and MasterCard and Visa International are developing "smart card" programs and projects.

The Smart Card Forum—established in 1993 by Citicorp, Bellcore, and the Financial Services Division of the Treasury Department to facilitate extensive adoption of smart card technologies in North America—is responsible for much of the industry's growth. The Forum has conducted research showing that consumers and merchants alike are highly receptive to smart card usage. Market trials further demonstrate that consumer interest is far less at issue than the cost of infrastructure development.

Yet, given this reality, acceptability, and potential, few executives are equipped to make the critical strategic business and investment decisions rapidly emerging smart card technology will demand. They recognize the phrase "smart card" but have little understanding of what this new technology and its related applications can mean for their organizations, commercial or governmental.

Smart Cards: Seizing Strategic Business Opportunities addresses the issues of launching innovations within organizations and relates how this has been done successfully.

After reading this book executives should be able to create a business model for the introduction of a variety of smart card applications. They should be able to define their markets, and identify potential partners and their capabilities. They will be able to make reasonable financial projections, develop market trial implementation plans, avoid legal regulatory hurdles and make sound vendor assessments.

Smart Cards: Seizing Strategic Business Opportunities was written by leading experts drawn from the Smart Card Forum—now grown to comprise more than 230 corporations and government entities.

The book starts with a short scenario of how an average American family might find itself using smart cards, daily and pervasively, within just two years. It then proceeds to an overview of smart card history, development, technology, and potential. All readers will benefit from the basic definitions and background presented in the first six chapters.

Some readers may then want to concentrate on learning more about the use of smart cards in their specific fields such as: financial services, transportation, healthcare, or education, and will go directly to the entries focusing on these specialties, and then read other material selectively. Others will undoubtedly read the entire book in sequence. The choice is yours.

You will find that much of the book's special-subject content has been written as stand-alone material. From chapter to chapter, you might find the same basic material interpreted slightly differently as perspectives change and authors' individual opinions are expressed. We feel this diversity of outlook adds to the value of this presentation and have avoided trying to force the authors into rigid editorial conformity.

Catherine Allen
William J. Barr
Ronald Schultz

ACKNOWLEDGMENTS

We wish to thank the many people who have made this book a reality. First and foremost, Ron Schultz, for his humor and persistence in pulling this book together from the various authors.

We thank Jim Keefe, our editor at Irwin Professional for his enthusiasm and guidance, John Burke, Senior Partner at Foley, Hoag and Eliot for his knowing and incisive legal counsel, and our agent Susan Schulman for her direction and efforts.

We would also like to thank the staff of the Smart Card Forum, Bob Gilson, Linette Trabulsy, and Pat Morley, and the Forum's Board for their unwavering support and dedication to this project.

Last, we want to recognize the two mentors who have significantly influenced the smart card industry and the creation of the Forum: Colin Crook, Senior Technology Officer, Citicorp and George Heilmeier, President of Bellcore. These men have supported the formation of the Forum and industry through their vision, counsel, and resources.

FOREWORD

I really want to use a smart card. Here's just one reason why. It was a hot summer day as I drove through Santa Cruz yesterday. Thirsty, I stopped at a Safeway to buy a cold soft drink. Seeing long checkout lines I focused on the three vending machines out front. One machine was being serviced, the second wouldn't handle bills—I had no change, and the third rejected every $1 bill I had even ones that looked mint-fresh to me. I next went to a Costco and had the same experience. I never did get a drink. The current payment systems prevented commerce from happening.

Sony has an observation that when a technology can make a tenfold improvement it opens big new market opportunities. That tenfold leap can be in any dimension including cost, speed, size, capacity, or portability. PCs had it. Cellular phones had it. Personal digital assistants (PDAs) didn't have it—until the current Pilot from US Robotics. Smart cards themselves are ten times smaller than a Pilot and ten times lower in cost.

Does this prove smart cards will happen? No, it suggests opportunity that the industry must find how to capitalize on.

Smart cards are part of the new interest in "wearable" computing. That's computing power so cheap and small it's always with you. This is achieved by jettisoning the input and output devices and focusing on the essence of computing, memory, and processing. Input and output, the monitors, keyboards, and printers are computing's legacy to the physical world. They add huge bulk compared to the processing itself. Smart cards use input/reader devices that can take many forms—grey boxes in retailers, vending devices, wireless phones, PCs, set top boxes, and kiosks are just a few. Someday no physical contact with the reader will be needed. The wearable computing will identify your presence as you approach, opening doors, turning on room lights, unlocking your car, giving you access to the high-speed toll lane.

In a world moving towards one-to-one marketing, smart cards hold the capability to customize and better serve our individual needs. The smart card can carry information that is only yours—your emergency health information, biometrics such as voice prints and fingerprints, or information on your travel preferences. Smart cards can provide more privacy and security in accessing payments and information services.

Central to the history of computing has been the battle for momentum between centralized and decentralized computing. By centralized I mean server- and telecommunications-based computing. Decentralized means local processing-based computing.

The two camps are not true enemies, in fact often the best solution by far is a combination of both centralized and decentralized.

At the same time, in each era of computing one of the two leads in the mind and imagination of the world. For much of the PC era decentralized was ascendant. The PC was viewed as a revolution against centralized computing. Now the internet has made centralized models where the action is.

My point is that the smart card industry must pick paths that can succeed in an internet-based world. Many of the uses for smart cards currently being tried can be replicated by centralized computing. The internet is doing things that had been viewed as uses of smart cards.

Smart card promises are yet to be implemented to their fullest extent and I believe the eventual implementation will revolve around a central question: Where and when will the greatest deployment successes occur?

- Telecommunications. Smart cards began with telephone cards in Europe as ways to eliminate fraud and reduce costs of replacing vandalized terminals. Wireless technologies are using smart cards for secure access and payment because of the portability across nations. What is important about the telecommunications industry is their access to users (phone service and cardholders) and control over potential readers (payphones, screen phones, cellular phones, etc.) For this reason, telecommunications applications and companies will be in the forefront of successful applications.

The multiple application capabilities of smart cards could not only provide security and payment capabilities but greatly enhance my life with preferred long distance provider details, frequently-called numbers, my "to do" list, and cellular phone activation on one card.

The chapter on Telecommunications will give you a preview of some of the potential.

- Education. The combination of centralized (access to databases, authorization) and decentralized needs (security, identification) make smart cards attractive to this market. The majority of card systems going onto campuses today include multiple technologies (magnetic stripe, microprocessor chip, bar code) for multiple applications. Students can use a smart card to buy books and meals, pay tuition, make phone calls, use library and athletic facilities, register for courses, and gain entry to their rooms. Universities and corporate campuses have the ability to mandate cards as well as numerous readers on or near campus. In the case of the University of Michigan, retailers surrounding the campus area were eager to add point of sale readers to capture the student and faculty market.

The Education chapter addresses some of the issues in market rollout.

FOREWORD xiii

- Security. Smart cards, with their ability to store biometrics, PIN numbers, encryption algorithms and engines, public and private key technologies, are ideal for security applications. Security on the Internet, security on ATMs, secure access to home banking, secure access to buildings, rooms, computers, and files—the potential in this area is enormous.

Computer, set top box, PDA, and screen and cellular phone device manufacturers are currently exploring or implementing smart card readers for security purposes. Even the digital cash software providers are moving to include smart cards for portability and security. Security experts favor the card solution because of problems with hackers and viruses.

- Medical. The ability of large hospitals, HMOs, insurance companies, and other healthcare providers (or the government for that matter) to mandate the use of cards and readers for their providers creates another potentially high success environment. The cards could carry emergency medical identification insurance and payment applications as well as record visits, treatments, and prescriptions in patient care. The idea of not having to fill out long forms in the doctor's waiting room is very attractive.

Privacy will be a major concern here and access to entire record databases. The sections on regulations and privacy as well as the Healthcare chapter cover these issues quite well.

- Financial Services and Electronic Benefits Transfers. Banks and ATM networks control customer access as well as devices and have the opportunity to help "make the market" happen. This is especially true in light of the federal mandate to make all government payments electronic by the year 1999. This will require cards in a larger portion of the population's hands and the mandate for ATMs and POS terminals in some areas to accept EBT. Smart cards make sense not only because of the enhanced security but also their ability to house multiple applications. Several states have issued RFPs to combine EBT with drivers licenses—another factor in mandating cards and readers.

There are a number of other areas where high market potential exists—in vending, in government services, in entertainment parks, in airports, and in shopping malls—all places where user acceptance of cards and the potential for control or influence over readers exist.

I may not know where the greatest smart card deployment successes will come from, but I do know they are coming. And now there's a book to help executives understand the issues surrounding successful implementation of smart cards in a variety of industries.

This book was edited by Bill Barr of Bellcore and Catherine Allen of The Santa Fe Group. They were co-founders of the Smart Card Forum. The book was authored by experts in the field who are also members of the Smart Card Forum. I believe this book is a great contribution to the industry. It combines dispassionate as well as passionate viewpoints on the industry and helps readers focus on the actual questions. I encourage you to use this as your "primer" for smart cards and to get active, as I have, in the Smart Card Forum and in the industry.

Scott Cook
Chairman, Intuit, Inc.
November 1996

CONTENTS

PART ONE

Smart Cards Technology Overview 1

1 Overview of Smart Cards and the Industry 2
2 Components of the Business Proposition: The Consumer Demand Proposition 21
3 Worldwide Developments and Player Motivations 44
4 Shifting Boundaries 57
5 Leveraging New Business Opportunities and Differentiating Your Products and Services 79
6 Smart Cards and Electronic Commerce 90

PART TWO

Overview of Applications 111

7 Financial Services 112
8 Telecommunications and Information Services 128
9 Healthcare and Smart Card Technology 151
10 Smart Cards In Government 169
11 Transportation 177
12 Travel and Entertainment 199
13 Retailing and Electronic Coupons 209
14 Education 224

PART THREE

Overview of Technology Issues 235

15 A Smart Card Primer 236
16 Security, Privacy, and Smart Cards 248

APPENDIX

About the Smart Card Forum   265

Glossary   279
Smart Card Resource List   295
Smart Card Forum Deliverables   298
Bibliography   299
Index   303

SMART CARDS
Seizing Strategic Business Opportunities

PART ONE
Smart Card Technology Overview

Smart Cards will become an everyday expression in the next 12 to 24 months if the explosion of trials, applications, industry announcements, and media coverage are any barometer of this emerging technology.

The first section of this book is strategic in nature, providing readers with a context for understanding what the technology is; what applications are available; who the players are and what motivates them; what the legal/regulatory issues are; and how smart cards and other emerging technologies, such as the Internet, interact.

The issues discussed in Part One are the topics of debate in the Smart Card Forum Working Group meetings, industry conferences, and corporate strategy sessions. We have framed them for you as they are today, but you will see how fast new innovations are appearing, and how quickly things are changing. The number of trials is increasing at exponential rates. Recent announcements by IBM and Mondex International have changed the playing field once again.

The chapters are written by experts in this industry. The book is a collaborative effort—significant in the fact that competitors are bound by a common interest and motivated to work together to launch this industry.

CHAPTER 1

Overview of Smart Cards and the Industry

Catherine A. Allen
The Santa Fe Group

Jeffrey Kutler
American Banker

A LOOK AT SMART CARDS IN 1998

Steve and Laura Cook seem the typical, middle American, mid-fortyish couple. They live in a suburb, work in the city, and have a son, Jack, 18, who just went off to college.

Their household has three bedrooms, two and a half baths, three televisions (two with VCRs), three telephones (not counting the cellular in Steve's car), two desktop computers (not counting the one Jack uses at school) with printers and modems, and a laptop computer that Steve travels with.

Less obviously, the Cooks also depend on an entire range of microprocessor components every day to run their alarm clocks, air-conditioning, kitchen appliances, lighting systems, doorbells, intercoms, garage-door openers, trains, planes, and automobiles.

Now in 1998, microprocessors are showing up in a new format—on plastic cards. Between them, Steve and Laura have 12 payment cards and 10 identification cards—credit, ATM, oil company, retail and grocery store, health insurance, video rental, employee ID, and their driver's licenses. As old cards have expired in recent months, they have been replaced with cards carrying microcomputer chips, known as smart cards because of their digital intelligence and memory capacity.

Although smart cards are relatively new to the United States, Laura saw many of them during a 1996 business trip to Europe. In both France and England, she bought cards from news dealers for use in the public telephone systems. The cards came with a stored value—equal to what she paid for them—and the value was debited with each call.

Steve Cook also knows a bit about smart cards because he has been carrying one for almost two years. His employee identification card is a smart card. He uses it to open the gate at his office parking lot and, once inside the building, to enter secure areas such as the computer room. Like conventional cards, Mr. Cook's card has his picture on it, which verifies his identity for normal purposes. But a digital version of that picture is stored within the chip to deter tampering.

The chip greatly multiplies the information capacity of the magnetic stripes used for several decades on cards—so much capacity that it stores a digital version of Mr. Cook's hand print. When he wants to enter the restricted computer center, Mr. Cook puts his card up against a chip reader and his hand into a scanning device. When the two match, the door unlocks.

At college, Jack Cook is seeing more of the smart card's potential. He was issued one on his arrival, and he can't live without it. It is the key to his tuition account with the bursar's office. It is his library card. He can put stored value into the chip—just like in the European phone systems—and use the card in place of cash for purchases in the bookstore, in vending and laundry machines, parking meters, and at a few retail stores in town that have hooked into the system. It is also his ID card and stores information for use by Student Health.

"Cool," says Jack. "I can't wait for the whole world to work like this." It may only be a matter of time. A stored-value demonstration project that banks staged during the 1996 Atlanta Olympics left that city with a modernized electronic cash economy inspiring others to move in the same direction. Throughout the country, institutions and government agencies, technology companies and entire industries are increasingly intent on harnessing the power of the chip card.

In the Cooks' suburb and the city where they work, the telephone company is installing its first smart card phones. Libraries, having already automated their card catalogues, are converting to a smart card system for borrowers. Doctors and hospitals are storing medical records on smart cards and preparing to issue smart ID and account cards to patients. The bridge authority is planning a smart card system to collect tolls without requiring vehicles to stop, and the metropolitan bus system is installing fare boxes with chip card readers.

1998's not a brave new world. It's the world we've always known, but with more power—and value—in the hands and pockets of the people carrying a new generation of plastic card.

JUST WHAT ARE SMART CARDS?

Now that we've forecast smart card usage in the near future, let's look more closely at what a smart card is and does. Similar in size and shape to a credit card, a smart card stores and processes information on an integrated microprocessor chip located within it.

There are two basic kinds of smart cards. An "intelligent" smart card contains a central processing unit—a CPU—that actually stores and secures information and makes decisions, as required by the card issuer's specific application needs. Because intelligent cards offer a read/write capability, new information can be added and processed. Monetary value, for example, can be added or debited as required.

The second type of card is often called a memory card. Memory cards are primarily information storage cards that contain stored value which the user can "spend" in a pay phone, retail, vending, or related transaction. Many of today's telephone cards in Europe and Asia are memory cards.

The intelligence of the integrated circuit chip in both types of cards allows them to protect the information being stored from damage or theft.

Cards can be contact or contactless or a combination of the two. As the storage capacity of cards increases and costs decline, smart cards will be able to handle voice, video, and other processing capabilities—making them the most portable computers—the "computer in the pocket."

A BRIEF HISTORY OF SMART CARDS

In 1971, Ted Hoff, a scientist at Intel Corp. in California, succeeded in assembling a computer on a tiny piece of silicon. On that chip, smaller than a fingertip, was more computing power than could be drawn from ENIAC, the 18-ton, room-size electronic brain that had ushered in the commercial computer era exactly 25 years previously.

The birth of the chip began a microelectronic revolution that appears endless, offering ever broadening possibilities for harnessing technology to everyday tasks and conveniences, at ever more affordable prices.

Because the chip can possess all the technical attributes of a computer—memory, logic, intelligence, processing power—its use on the smart card promises to become the ultimate in minitechnology, the most portable and practical of the electronic systems that have become so indispensable in our lives and modern society.

The smart card, like the chip itself, began to take shape in the creative mind of an inventor, and is every bit as much a work in progress. When Intel and other leading-edge companies were still struggling to create a market for the computer on a chip, Roland Moreno, a Frenchman, began to contemplate the implications of microelectronics. In 1974 he obtained the first patents for the chip on a card. Just two decades later, more than 20 million bank cards and millions more telephone calling cards in France affirmed his vision.

CHAPTER 1   Overview of Smart Cards and the Industry   5

What Moreno wrought has impacted relatively limited parts of the world—so far. But the chip card's vast and wide-ranging potential was so obvious to more than 230 companies worldwide that they joined to explore and develop it in a collective body called the Smart Card Forum. The Forum's progress, ideas, and outlook form the core of this book, at a time when many forces are converging to suggest that Moreno's invention is about to explode into public awareness as a mass-distributed technology.

RATES OF CHANGE

The vectors of technology and economics converge in the computer chip according to Moore's Law, a formulation named for Intel founder Gordon Moore. In the 1970's he postulated that the chip would double data-processing performance rates about every 18 months, while prices declined by a similar factor. Microchip manufacturers focused their research and development on the components of more conventional computing devices. These became compact enough to sit on a desktop—today's personal computers are thousands of times more powerful than ENIAC was—and eventually came in the form of laptops and hand-held "personal digital assistants" like the Apple Newton or Sony Magic Link. Moore's Law continues to hold up, despite experts' presumption that it can't go on forever.

But Moore's Law applied more slowly in the smart card area. The chip on a plastic card posed special challenges. To assure compatibility with, and seamless migration from, existing payment systems, the chip would have to be encased snugly within the standard card's thickness. It would also have to be durable enough to withstand the wear and tear of two, three, or more years of repeated usage, including insertions into specially equipped card-reading terminals.

By 1996, the manufacture of specialized chips for plastic cards had become a sizable business, particularly to supply the pioneering applications in France and a few other countries. But the most advanced card chips held only 8K, or 8,000 bytes (characters), of memory at a time when the capacity of chips for computer assemblies was climbing well into the millions.

However, Moore's Law is working its inexorable magic on card chips. Some with 64K or 256K are already in the pipeline, and megabyte chips are probably no more than a couple of years away.

WHY THE CHIP?

Even in their relatively elementary stages, cards with chips constituted a major technological advance over the preceding magnetic stripe technology, which the bank credit card industry adopted, ironically, just as the first Intel chips emerged in the 1970s. That pre-existing standard was based on magnetic tape—the same commodity on which audio cassette recordings are produced. The tape can be seen on the back of any bank card and is known in the trade as a magnetic stripe. It holds two or three tracks of basic data, typically the cardholder's name, account number, card expiration date, and perhaps a personal identification number (PIN) or other security check.

The magnetic stripe's capacity is no more than a few hundred characters of data, well below the thousands that a chip can hold. To understand the difference: Three hundred characters are about what you see in this paragraph. Eight thousand bytes, or the memory on an 8K memory chip, is more than 1,000 words, or six to seven typed pages of information. At 256K we have the equivalent of a magazine; at multiple megabytes we get into the realm of books and even encyclopedias.

Chips' advantages over magnetic tape begin with their data capacity. It makes possible higher levels of security than simple PINs, and allows businesses to provide far more than a simple credit or payment service. In fact, several offerings can be combined into a "multi-application card" that might include banking, a stored-value payment system for mass transit, parking meters, or vending machines, and a frequent-travel or frequent-shopper rewards program—all tracked on the chip.

Beyond that, chips don't wear out as easily as magnetic based cards through contact or friction, are not susceptible to damage when they pass through magnetic fields, and are far more difficult to compromise or counterfeit.

Perhaps the chip card's most significant advantage is its higher level of security. Not only are chip cards more tamper-resistant and difficult to replicate than mag stripe, the chip has the capability of containing encryption technologies like public and private keys that allow high levels of transmission and storage security—so much so that smart cards have been used by the United States to secure and deploy atomic bombs.

If these advances and advantages are so obvious and clear—Roland Moreno and his followers have been spreading the message for years—then why has it taken so long for the smart card to take hold?

By the standards of technology diffusion, smart cards may not be taking long at all. After the invention of the telephone, it took almost 100 years until it could be found in virtually every U.S. household—and in many countries the penetration rate is still well below that. Decisions made by MasterCard and Visa suggest that as many as 500 million or more bank-issued cards worldwide will have chips early in the next century. By then, banking applications will likely be catching up to others that got underway sooner on college campuses, in mass transit and telephone networks, and in airline frequent-traveler programs.

The United States is also having to play catch-up with other parts of the world—for understandable reasons that may help explain why the smart card was slower to take off in this biggest and most advanced of national economies. While the U.S. banking and bank card businesses were big and influential enough to have spurred the global adoption of chip cards with an early endorsement, these organizations had little reason or incentive to do so.

Despite the technology's attractions, the economics, as presented by advocates in the 1970s and 1980s, did not add up. Chip cards offered to solve a problem that the U.S. credit card industry, which then accounted for 75 percent to 80 percent of the worldwide market, did not have. The American card groups had at their disposal a superior and low-cost telecommunications infrastructure. This allowed them to authorize and verify cardholder transactions quickly and cheaply through a low-cost telephone connection into an electronic database. Additionally, the credit and debit card programs being promoted as replacements for cash and checks appeared more profitable than stored value or electronic purse applications.

WHY FRANCE?

France, by contrast, faced telecommunications problems that the new card technology could readily solve. Authorizations of card transactions were far more expensive than in the United States—assuming the availability of a telephone connection. The smart card could hold sufficient data for a transaction to be authorized at the point of sale without requiring an on-line telephone inquiry. The cardholder's identity could be verified using an embedded PIN code.

Soon after Moreno began marketing his invention, the French government launched a campaign to upgrade its telecommunications infrastructure and promote the development and export of high technology. The smart card played to both national strategies. France's domestic telecommunications are now among the most sophisticated in the world; its public telephones operate with prepaid, stored-value chip cards instead of coins; and most French households are equipped with "Minitels" or other dial-up terminals, many of them compatible with smart cards and accessing numerous interactive and information services ranging from travel ticketing to home banking.

Meanwhile, a decision by the French banking industry, with government encouragement, to embrace smart cards, turned the country into a showcase for the technology and gave card manufacturers like Gemplus, Bull, Soliac, and Schlumberger a base for international expansion.

With marketing, education, and improved economics, the smart card made significant inroads in several other European countries, including a stored-value cash replacement system called Danmont in Denmark, and the

German national health insurance program. Several Asian countries—notably Japan and Singapore—and developing Eastern European nations are creating entire new payment systems with smart cards at their core instead of currency and checks.

In 1995, MasterCard and Visa chose Australia for the most significant early tests of their smart card approaches. Though competitive, the two groups agreed to a common technical standard for credit and debit applications that they negotiated with a third association, Europay International, and named EMV. Agreeing to such a technical baseline, which is likely to influence all transactional uses of chip cards, is expected to exert the same promotional impact on smart cards as worldwide adoption of the magnetic stripe did on credit cards.

With Visa and several of its member banks, First Union, Nations and Wachovia, issuing smart cards in conjunction with the Atlanta Olympics, and with North American trials of the Mondex electronic cash system from the United Kingdom also underway, the technology has rebounded from the earlier objections of American banks.

WHY THE INTEREST IN SMART CARDS NOW?

The dramatic growth of interest in smart card technology and related applications over the past eighteen months is attributed to several factors:

1. *Bank associations are delivering technical specifications.* Europay, MasterCard, and Visa have jointly created the so-called "EMV" specifications to eventually permit interoperability among chip-based payment cards for credit and debit applications. Without common technical standards, an array of incompatible systems would proliferate—building serious barriers to both consumer and merchant acceptance.

2. *Card costs are declining and price/performance ratios are improving.* As with computer-based applications of the silicon chip, technology innovations continue to result in steady price declines and significant performance upgrades.

3. *Market experience is accumulating.* Live, in-market card initiatives continue to accelerate around the world. In the financial services area, electronic purse schemes have been introduced in over 30 countries. These programs, addressing a wide variety of local business and cultural needs, generally seek to capitalize on chip-based "stored value." Here, cash value stored *in the card itself* (or in a terminal or other electronic device) can be used to purchase products and services by electronically transferring the value from buyer to seller. A proliferating array of programs in other financial service segments, telecommunications, health care, retail, transportation, and educational applications are increasing consumer familiarity with the actual benefits and risks of specific chip card usage.

4. *Competitive challenges threaten control of traditional markets and longer-term capability to enter new markets.* The advent of the chip, in conjunction with the convergence of communications, computing, and information/entertainment technologies, stands to redefine the competitive landscape of many industry sectors. For instance, some of the European bank networks have launched electronic purse programs partially to prevent competitive non-bank programs from fragmenting the market and weakening customer relationships. Moreover, organizations recognize that a "wait-and see" attitude towards adopting new technologies can seriously compromise longer-term competitive viability.

5. *Networks/systems are being developed for electronic/remote access to products/services.* New electronic markets are emerging rapidly. The rise of the Internet is the most well-known example of this. However, there are many others, including proprietary home/remote banking networks, and wireless systems, such as digital cellular and digital satellite-based systems. Smart cards are being considered as access keys as well as for payments on these emerging systems.

6. *The ability of magnetic stripe technology to support the future performance requirements of card systems is increasingly being questioned.* In some cases, chip card applications could have been accomplished using a magnetic stripe. However, a chip is used to provide flexibility in cost-effectively introducing new applications. Examples of this include the Shell Smart loyalty program launched by Shell UK, and the German Government's Health Card program. The security issues with magnetic stripe cards are also mitigated by the chip technology.

In addition to these generalized trends, some very specific changes have taken place. Both MasterCard and Visa have taken strong and visible positions supporting smart card technology for payment applications. The Smart Card Forum in the United States, and similar organizations in a number of European and Asian countries, emerged to form a consensus about standards and infrastructure needs.

A number of large banks in the United States and abroad—Citibank, Chase, Wells Fargo, Nations, Wachovia, Huntington Banc Shares, Hong Kong Shanghai, Barclays, Bank of Montreal, Toronto Dominion Bank—have announced trials. National and state governments have begun to implement smart card based programs in electronic benefits transfer, healthcare, driver licensing, and transportation.

Electronic purse trials worldwide have tripled over the past year, with projections for growth in telecommunications, transportation, and healthcare

EXHIBIT 1–1

Organizations Should Think about Smart Cards As:

- Payment vehicles
- Access keys
- Information managers
- Reward cards
- Customized delivery systems

---

arenas being quite optimistic. Banks, however, are only one of the players providing electronic purse or stored value systems. ATM networks, governments, telecommunications companies, and others interested in delivering information, communications, and entertainment to the home are looking for ways to enable those transactions with payments via a card or software on-line.

The focus of many of these industry players centers around five categories of applications enabled by smart card technology which suggest how organizations should regard smart cards.

1. Smart Cards as Payment Vehicles The technology enables credit and debit transactions to occur in a much safer and fraud resistant environment. Electronic purse or stored value cards are viewed as new revenue streams where float, unclaimed value, and transaction fees contribute to business cases. Credit lines on stored value cards and insurance for lost or stolen cards are two other potential revenue opportunities for payments cards. Electronic benefits are being paid out via smart cards, as well.

2. Smart Cards as Access Keys Smart cards are a portable computer technology that facilitates encryption (public and private keys), authorization, authentication and information processing, and storage which enable the secure delivery of financial transactions and information in on-line and off-line environments. Today, smart cards are used for physical access to buildings, computer centers, and computers themselves. Increasingly, they are used for access to networks and software programs. The security and payment application capabilities of smart cards makes them ideal for Internet access and home banking services. Providers of entertainment services via satellite or cable are using smart cards for access as well as programming and payments.

3. Smart Cards as Information Managers Cards today hold between 1K to 16K of memory and processing capability. This capability is expected to grow dramatically in the next two years. A 64K is already in prototype. Integration of operating system capabilities like JAVA on the chip will expand the capability to where applets (mini-applications) can be downloaded via PCs, ATM's, or even pay phones to alter or enhance applications on the card. Recent Smart Card Forum consumer research shows strong interest in managing account information, frequently called phone numbers, loyalty points, transactions, and other relevant "emergency" information via a portable smart card. Corporate treasurers are looking to smart cards to help track projects and expenses.

4. Smart Cards as Marketing Tools Customized database marketing, electronic coupons, loyalty programs, gift certificates, and discounts can be administered via smart cards. The use of graphics and limited editions make the cards "collectibles" that can be tied to other promotions such as movies and sporting events The Jacksonville Jaguars created marketing interest in "sets" of cards for all ten games of the 1995 season.

5. Smart Cards as Customized Delivery Systems As processing and memory capabilities of cards increase, screen sets and other brand and individualized information and accounts can be stored on the card or used as pointers to other programs on-line.

The business opportunities generated by smart cards will be hindered only by lack of creativity and innovation on the part of businesses issuing those cards and managing the systems. Exhibit 1–2 shows smart card's role in an evolving distributed computing environment.

EXHIBIT 1–2

Smart Cards in Evolving Computing

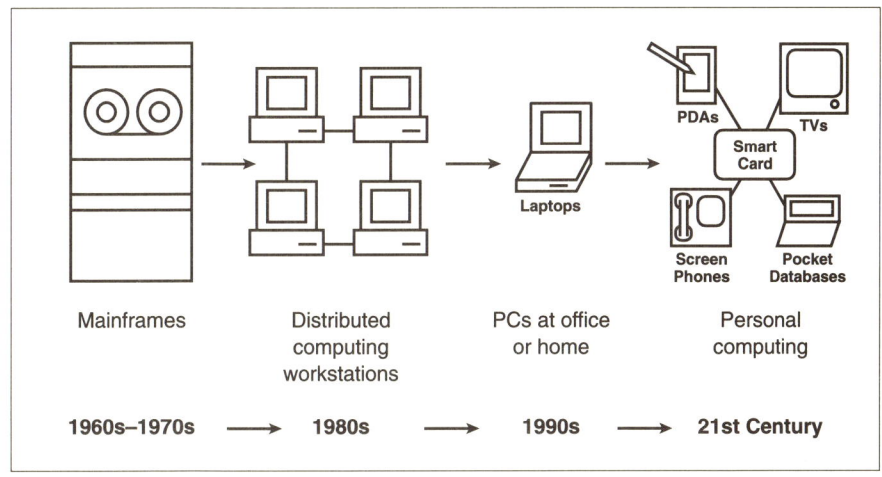

WHERE NEXT?

This is still just the beginning. For all the arguments in their favor, smart cards have much to prove. The United States, in particular, must create an infrastructure for producing and issuing the cards, and a point-of-sale terminal network able to read and update the chip data. The economics of adapting old transaction systems and producing new ones are increasingly favorable, and technology suppliers are gearing up for anticipated demand. But the aggregate financial commitment, in the United States and elsewhere, will be significant—$10 billion according to some industry research projections.

As described in the chapters that follow, numerous companies, industries, financial and educational institutions, and various types of government agencies are working feverishly to probe the technology's limits and get the most out of it.

One lesson already learned, and demonstrated in the formation of the Smart Card Forum and the EMV standardization process, is that progress will require collective discussion, and action. No one company can optimize smart cards unilaterally, and even industry-wide coordination through, say, a banking or retailing trade association, will fall short of the mark. For the smart card is not a commodity or product in itself, except when it might be bought from a kiosk or a vending machine for a specific purpose. One of these limited-application cards may function no differently from another; it may provide a desired and easily perceived convenience to the purchaser, with no obvious product differentiation and no further "value added" benefit. The real business opportunities lie in enabling secure, convenient and quick transitions via a portable device.

At its full potential, the chip in the card is an enabling technology, an opener of doors, and more than likely, an eradicator of traditional business categories or boundary lines.

It used to be said that computers could never become so "smart" that they would dominate the human sphere—the nightmare of HAL in the story "2001: A Space Odyssey"—because the machines could only be as smart as their programmers and programming allowed. It's not quite that simple. Artificial intelligence has given some machines the capacity to learn from experience, at least in a rudimentary fashion.

But it is indisputably true that the smart card, which descends from the same lineage that produced artificial intelligence and other computer advances, will be limited only by the human ingenuity and creativity applied to it.

INTEREST IN MULTIPLE APPLICATION SMART CARDS

A number of industry players, such as those in financial services and telecommunications, are interested in multiple application smart cards. These industries have found many challenging questions in launching these cards, including:

- How can smart cards include multiple brand logos without confusing the consumer?
- Who is liable for lost and/or stolen cards and how are they replaced?
- Who provides customer service and how is it made seamless to the consumer?
- How are applications developed, certified, installed, and upgraded?
- How are privacy, accuracy, and security insured?
- How are revenues shared?

One of the best examples of a multi-application smart card in the United States is at Florida State University. This program has placed a state-run college in the unaccustomed role of card issuer and business manager, a cost-cutting move responding to cutbacks in government funding. Far from a mere identification device, the FSU card also provides key-access to secure buildings, tracking of tuition and financial aid accounts, secure and authenticated access to the Internet, discount long-distance calling, banking services, and stored-value payments in machines, at campus stores and libraries, and at participating off-campus merchants. The university necessarily entered into alliances to make the whole package work—alliances essential to tapping the enabling technological power of the chip, and creating a business model.

Consumers' desire to carry fewer cards holds significant business opportunities and risks. These issues will be addressed throughout this book in more detail and represent the defining elements for the future success of this technology.

THE COLLECTIBLE MARKET FOR SMART CARDS

With the launch of VISA Cash stored value cards at the 1996 Atlanta Olympics, the potential for collectible smart cards in the United States was inaugurated as well. Even prior to the games, smart cards issued from vending machines at the Card Tech/Secure Tech conference in Atlanta in May reportedly brought the three participating banks—Nations, Wachovia, and First Union—four million dollars in float-based revenue on the cards' face value.

Collectible cards, while new to the U.S., have been traded in Europe and Asia for some time. The concept started with chip-based telephone and payment cards in Europe and Japan. Collectors would buy cards singly, in packages and in "sets." The cards are more valuable if not used—making float and unclaimed value or slippage (as in the travelers check business) a very attractive business proposition for issuers.

Reportedly, Nippon Telephone and Telegraph has 40 percent unclaimed value on phone stored value cards they issue. An optical technology card worth $5 issued by Nynex at the 1992 Democratic Convention in New York for use in payphones is now worth $2500.00 according to collectors. Many organizations in the United States are creating collectible cards with superb graphics. The National Football League's Jacksonville Jaguars, with First Union and Schlumberger, created graphics for cards usable at ten home games that create a puzzle when complete.

According to an *American Banker* interview of Murray Church, publisher of *Money Card Collector,* 40 percent of sales of the Olympic cards are going to international collectors. Three dealers—Kars Unlimited, B&B Fone Cards, and Promotions and International Cash Cards—are distributing the smart stored value cards worldwide. Collectible cards in mint condition retail for $8 above face value. Resale values are highest on limited edition items, especially low numbers, with unspent cash. Pretrial cards, employee cards, and special event cards are even more prized. "When was the last chance you got to collect a whole new form of money?" Church asks in a comment on collectible cards.

The Olympic VISA Cash cards are the tip of the iceberg. The collectibles market is expected to grow exponentially in the United States. In Europe, France Telecom has kiosks on the streets of Paris to sell their stored value phone cards. There are at least three catalogs and several major trade shows in Europe and Asia for collectible cards. In the United States, there is a major phone card trade show where smart cards are beginning to appear.

The cards with the best graphics, often artists' series, are the most popular with general collectors, while numbered and special events cards are favored by the serious collector.

This collector phenomenon is just part of the innovative, market-driven components of smart cards and also part of the fun!

THE SMART CARD FORUM

The Smart Card Forum was established in 1993 by Citicorp, Bellcore, and the U.S. Treasury Financial Management Services Division to accelerate the widespread acceptance of smart cards that support multiple applications in North America. The concept was to bring together, in an open environment, leading business and technology executives from the public and private sector to promote interoperability across applications and technologies and to facilitate market trials.

Membership in the Forum has grown rapidly to over 230 corporate and government entities from the U.S., Canada, South America, and Europe. Education, business proposition development, and public policy initiatives have become additional goals of Forum members as pilot projects emerge.

A number of compelling reasons have driven Forum participation and interest in smart card technology:

- Convergence of information technologies is creating new business opportunities spurred by electronic delivery.
- Increased competition, from non-traditional industry players as boundaries between information and payment technologies blur, is causing traditional providers of these services to look for ways to enhance and retain customer relationships.
- Costs of smart cards and readers are declining as functionality and capabilities increase. Enhancements to card security, processing power, and storage create opportunities for multiple application cards.
- Regulatory bodies are increasingly concerned about consumer issues related to stored value and healthcare information cards.
- International standards for payments and telecommunications are emerging to eliminate the risks of interoperability.
- Growth of pilot projects worldwide for stored value, loyalty, college, and security applications is making smart card investments a reality, not a future event.

Forum members recognize that there are several elements necessary to succeed in deployment of smart cards. These include a critical mass of cards supporting applications of interest to consumers, merchants, and organizations that wish to issue or accept cards. They also include an infrastructure developed through alliances, interoperability of standards and processes, consumer trust in the institutions issuing the cards, and potential long-term economies of scale coupled with flexible organizations. Exhibit 1–3 lists these and other elements essential for implementating smart card pilots.

EXHIBIT 1-3

Elements Essential to Smartcard System Implementation

- Critical mass of cards in use
- Multiple applications of interest to consumers
- Merchant business proposition
- Infrastructure developed through alliances to accept cards
- Common technology that resists fraud
- Brand identification/consumer trust
- Marketing capability to launch cards
- Market preemption to set de facto standards
- Involvement of a high-volume/low-value application, e.g., transit or payphones
- Potential for long-term economies of scale

The listed elements have spurred growth in the Smart Card Forum's influence and membership. The Forum and its members have made smart cards a household word in North America and created new business opportunities for a number of industry players. It is the authoritative voice for this emerging technology. Part IV and the Appendix provide more detailed information on the Forum and its deliverables.

TECHNOLOGY, COMPLEXITY, AND INNOVATION

Two major factors—rapid technological innovation and complex business environments, especially for those industries impacted by technological change—are driving organizations to alter the way they do business, develop new products and services, and bring them to market.

Smart card technology and the potential it offers for creating new business opportunities is an example of this phenomenon. Not only are traditional competitors learning to work together in industry groups like the Smart Card Forum, but they are forming alliances to develop the infrastructure for smart cards and to create new applications for their customers.

Colin Crook, Senior Technology Officer of Citicorp, puts the situation in context: "The role of technology in shaping our world—from influencing market behaviors affecting consumer attitudes and capabilities—cannot be overstated. Gone are the days when a static view of the world was sufficient in charting corporate strategies. Past organizational models must be replaced with fundamentally new operating models that account for today's fast and unpredictable shifts in technology and business."

Technology is driving massive industry changes, creating new paradigms in which non-traditional players compete and competitive advantage depends mainly on marketing, brand identification, and new delivery systems targeted to convenience-oriented consumers.

Nowhere is this more apparent than in the converging financial, information, and entertainment services arenas. Consumers are becoming more demanding in terms of convenience, security, time savings, and value. Loyalty to businesses is less of a factor, especially when better customer service is offered elsewhere. Demographics are driving this demand. Dual career families, families with small children, and single people, all need help in managing day-to-day chores. Consumer interest in, and acceptance of, technology-based products and services that address these needs for security, value, and convenience are growing. Exhibit 1–4 illustrates the diversity of industries converging in their interest in meeting the needs of consumers at home or wherever they may be.

EXHIBIT 1-4

Industry Convergence

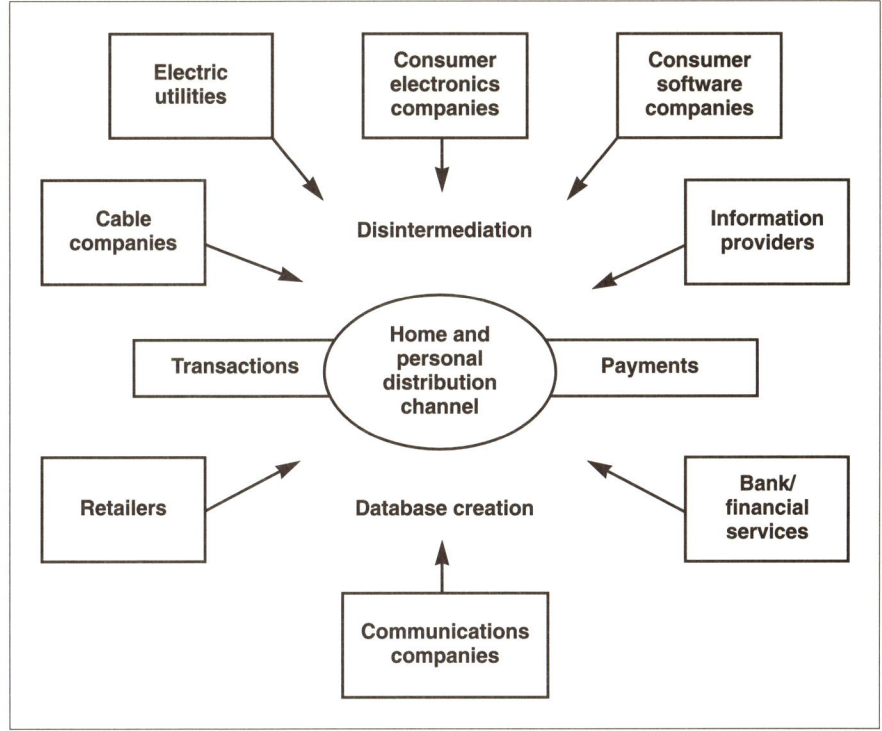

As companies try to manage new innovations and emerging businesses in this complex competitive market, concepts such as flexibility, adaptability, time to market, customized marketing, and customer service come forward. Companies planning to implement smart card based applications face an even more complex environment, because of the rapid changes in technologies, standards, and players. The critical point for these companies is that change is constant and savvy players will be ready to adapt. By way of illustration, here are some examples of changes, some mentioned previously, within the smart card industry in the past 12 months:

- Release of Europay/MasterCard/Visa (EMV) specifications for international debit and credit card payments via chips.
- Announcement of Visa and MasterCard applications co-residing on the same terminal in a New York City trial by Citibank and Chase.

- Work between SUN, chip manufacturers and banks to put JAVA on a chip to manage applets.
- Increased interest, led by U.S. firms, in multiple application cards.
- Monthly announcements of smart card-based pilot project worldwide.
- Mondex announcing Internet access with their smart card and Cybercash and DigiCash announcing smart card interfaces with their software.
- Acquisitions and alliances related to smart cards announced by large players such as Mondex, AT&T, American Express, MicroCard Bull, Schlumberger, Gemplus, and Siemens.
- Increased interest and focus on microprocessor card production by Motorola, Thomsen, Phillips, and Intel.
- Availability of terminals that can read chips as well as mag stripes.
- Announcement of increased state and federal government smart card initiatives, including software rollout of 12 million MARC cards for military personnel and six state RFPs for multiple application cards.
- Ten thousand smart card terminals per month going into China to create a national infrastructure for the Golden Card electronic purse and identification project.
- Increased regulatory interest and decisions related to stored value cards, i.e., Regulation E and FDIC regulation proposals.

These recent events illustrate the speed and seriousness of companies and governments addressing smart card based applications and issues. In response, banks like First Union and Wells Fargo and companies like Schlumberger have been able to bring smart card projects to market in less than six months. American Express' stored value business unit has a mandate to bring stored value products from concept to market in two months.

The idea of bringing innovations to market quickly is not new, but technology is driving the velocity and intensity of that change and introduction of smart card pilot projects are a good example of that phenomenon. As Jim Manzi, former president and CEO Lotus Development Corporation, comments, "The importance of information technology in a competitive economy is not in cost reduction, but in innovation, new products, and processes. A model of competitiveness based on innovation has become absolutely crucial in a world in which market cycles—which used to be 5 to 10 years in the making—now come and go in 12 to 18 months."

SMART CARDS AND INNOVATION

One of the most exciting components of smart card technology is the seemingly unlimited innovative ideas and applications the technology offers, especially as processing and memory capabilities increase.

New start-up companies are emerging around security and encryption applications, operating systems and graphics for collectible cards. Examples are Integrity Arts, Five Paces, UBIQ, and Santa Fe Smart Card Graphics. Alliances are forming to exploit new business opportunities in vertical markets—Verifone and CommerceNet, NBS Technologies, Bull CP8, Sallie Mae, Huntington Bancshares, and Battelle.

As this book illustrates, the technology creates new business opportunities revolving around payments, security, access, loyalty, information management and customization of customer services. The portability, durability, and graphics potential on the card as well as storage capacity on the chip will allow for the integration of voice, data, video, and graphic arts.

The fact that consumers and merchants are familiar with, and positively motivated to use, card technologies will facilitate the adoption rates of the technology and related applications.

What is important to issuers and industry players is to not think traditionally about their industry, products, or services as enabled by smart cards. The technology is breaking down barriers between industry segments and how services and products are delivered. Smart cards are part of a much larger global industry trend to electronic delivery and commerce. Their customer acceptance and portability enable new ways of thinking about how business can be conducted.

The following are some examples of innovations underway or in pilot that involve smart cards:

- Using smart cards to promote the state and its technology leadership (State of Utah).
- Pulling coupons off TV ads with an RF device and smart card and redeeming those coupons at retail outlets via a reader (Smart TV).
- Putting multiple applications targeted to the frequent traveler on one card for convenience (American Airlines, American Express).
- Putting collectors' editions of stored value cards with artists' graphics into sets (Jacksonville Jaguars, Danmont, VISA Cash Olympics Cards).
- Using smart cards as programming screens and payment cards for television (UBI and Sky TV).

The industry is in a nascent stage—the innovative applications and creative mind sets of individuals will make smart cards mainstream. Industry players are beginning to respond to this need for innovation by changing the way they think about, and do, business. Examples of some of the innovative approaches beyond smart card start-ups and alliances include:

- Creating cross-business teams to leverage multiple applications within the organization and to reduce infrastructure costs.
- Participating in industry organizations such as the Smart Card Forum and Federal Smart Card Users Group where cross-industry workgroups focus on issues, business case elements, and new applications.
- Using brainstorming, creativity workshops and other "intuitive" approaches to new business and new product development for smart cards.
- Exploring new ways of thinking about competitive market places by working with entities like the Santa Fe Group and the Institute for the Future.
- Forming interdisciplinary teams (marketing, legal, finance, engineering, operations) for smart card deployment within the company.
- Talking to existing pilot operations, merchants, customers, vendors, etc. regularly. The industry is moving so quickly that it is critically important to stay abreast of marketplace changes. The Smart Card Forum, Card Tech/Secure Tech Trade Shows, industry newsletters and pilot visits help companies keep their finger on the smart card pulse.

CONCLUSION

Smart cards are a reality, not a technology looking for an application. This book will provide executives with the context, resources, and framework they need to understand this emerging technology and the business opportunities it provides.

Companies looking to implement new smart card-based businesses or use smart cards to enable other businesses and delivery systems will need to be adaptive, innovative, and first-to-market. This book will supply you with the tools to leverage smart card technology to meet those needs successfully.

CHAPTER 2

Components of the Business Proposition
The Consumer Demand Proposition

William Keenan
Convergence Group

Martha Rea
PSI

Gerald Hubbard
Micro Card Technologies

Smart cards refer to a technology, not a product. As a technology, the smart card's embedded microprocessor chip, when deployed as part of an overall intelligent network or system, brings portable computing power to the individual. This technology enables the delivery of a wide variety of card-based products and services—ones that not only build on current card products but also address new business opportunities and new markets such as electronic commerce.

As chip technology can potentially support a vast array of card-delivered features and services, it is not surprising that the gathering momentum behind smart cards is a multi-industry phenomenon. The industries most actively investigating smart card business opportunities include banks, nonbank financial services, retail, telecommunications, transportation/transit authorities, healthcare/insurance, government services, travel and leisure, vending, and media/entertainment. This chapter addresses some of the components of the business proposition for smart card-based applications.

PROJECTED MARKET SIZE AND INDUSTRY SEGMENTS

In terms of card unit volume, the smart card market is projected to experience significant growth over the next decade. By 2000, some 3.1 billion smart cards will be issued (including memory chip cards and the microprocessor chip, or true "smart" cards). Exhibit 2–1 forecasts smart card unit volume by industry category.

Globally, the current smart card market is driven by the telecommunications industry and specifically, by the public pay phone application. Stand-alone, disposable, stored-value pay phone/telephone cards (which historically

EXHIBIT 2-1

Expected Significant Smart Card Growth

	World Market (Millions of Units)		
	1994	1995	2000*
Pay telephone	325	360	1,100
Banking/finance	25	27	350
Healthcare	70	75	300
Identity/access control	1	3	300
Transportation	2	2	150
Encrypted television	8	10	80
Leisure/vending/marketing applications	1	10	65
Mobile telephone (GSM)	8	18	55
Total	440	505	4,800

*Forecast

have not required use of the microprocessor chip) have accounted for roughly 70 percent or more of chip card production worldwide. Chip-based phone cards are now found in over 60 countries, with France Telecom and German Telecom controlling the application market, selling more than 200 million chip cards each year.

In the United States, chip-based pay phone cards have had little presence due to a variety of factors, including complex competition and the level of infrastructure/network sophistication. US West Communications is one notable exception. Initially launched in the Seattle market, the US West *Telecard* program is currently rolling out to five other major cities and states and Nynex has launched small pilots of optical scan payphone cards in the New York market.

In financial services, smart card volume has traditionally been dominated by the French bankcard (Cartes Bancaire), which is operated by Groupement des Cartes Bancaire on behalf of all French banks. The inclusion of a microprocessor chip on the "CB" card was successfully aimed at fraud reduction. Since 1992, domestic bank card fraud in France has been dramatically reduced (estimated at 50 percent) while purchase authorizations are performed off-line about 90 percent of the time.

As the global bank card market moves to a "hybrid" environment, in which cards have both a magnetic stripe and a chip, the smart card unit volume in the financial services area will increase exponentially.

MARKET SEGMENTS BY CARD FUNCTION AREA

Another way to view the smart card market is from the consumer perspective. When a consumer uses a smart card, what is he/she trying to accomplish? Around the world consumers are using, and will continue to use, smart cards to perform one or more of the following four functions: (1) to make payments, (2) to gain rewards, (3) to gain access to an electronic network or a physical structure, and (4) to store and manage information. (See Exhibit 2–2.)

Payments Consumers are using smart cards around the world to purchase products and services, via a prepaid (or stored value) format as well as credit and debit payment. Stored value initiatives include both dedicated, single-use programs (such as prepaid telephone or transit fare cards), and general purpose, multi-use programs. The term "electronic purse" is generally applied to multi-use of programs in which the stored value card is accepted at a variety of merchants or businesses, such as for pay phone calls, transit fares, vending machine items, restaurants, fast food stores, and sundry purchases (generally of small value) at local stores.

Some chip card payment programs do not include the stored value application. The most notable is the Cartes Bancaire program previously described. Another example is the Carta Moneta ("Money Card") program, which is controlled by one of the major banks in Italy. The Carta Moneta user can choose at the point-of-sale between two modes of payment: A "short account" in which the full balance is settled and a "long account" that gives the consumer the option to pay on an installment basis.

EXHIBIT 2–2

Smart Cards Address Four Primary Functions

■ Make payments	Card is used to make a payment—from a deposit or credit account, stored value feature, or some combination of payment options.
■ Gain rewards	Card is used to gain points or receive price concessions or services, special consideration, or privileged attention.
■ Gain access	Card is used to gain access to an electronic network, to gain entry to a physical structure, or to use equipment or machines.
■ Store and manage information	Card is used as a portable data file that stores, consolidates, and processes information.

The business rationale behind issuing smart cards for payments includes reduced fraud, increased security float, and revenue and customer relationship development.

Rewards The use of the chip to administer consumer loyalty programs is accelerating in many countries, particularly in Europe and Asia-Pacific. Some of these programs are driven by the retailer, such as Shell Oil in the United Kingdom, and Indemitsu Oil and Nissan in Japan. Other programs are driven primarily by banks and involve either a group of participating merchants or a "co-branded" bank-retailer partnership. Examples of the first include the United Overseas Bank "Smart Club" loyalty program in Singapore and the Thai Farmers Bank program in Thailand. Co-branding examples include the Compass Card in Hong Kong (Overseas Trust Bank and Hutchison Whampoa), the Takashimaya Visa Card from DBS (Development Bank of Singapore and Takashimaya department store).

While loyalty applications vary widely, a "point counting" mechanism is generally the central concept. Consumers accumulate points when purchasing items from the sponsoring retailer. These points serve as a form of value exchange which can be used to "reward" patronage with point-of-sale discounts, electronic coupons, air miles, and catalogue gifts. Other "rewards" can be individualized by using data captured from card application forms as well as by analyzing a customer's purchase behavior. For instance, loyal Takashimaya customers who make a purchase on their birthday can receive special on-the-spot rewards.

The business rationale behind loyalty or reward cards focuses on increased sales and customer satisfaction. They also provide the ability to gather key customer data useful for inventory management and marketing purposes.

Access Chip cards are also being used to permit secure access to an electronic network, or files, authorized entry to a building or other premises, or authorized use of equipment or machinery. One of the major access applications to date is the use of microprocessor chip cards in digital cellular networks. Network operators in Europe, Asia-Pacific, and South America have adopted the technical standard known as GSM (Global System for Mobile Communications). Network users have a SIM (Subscriber Identity Module) card that identifies the user to the network and contains the specifics of the subscribers' service entitlements. The SIM card concept has already been widely adopted outside the United States, and is being incorporated into some of the PCS (Personal Communications System) networks now emerging in this country.

Microprocessor smart cards are also supporting secure access for home or remote banking transactions. Corporate customers with cash management

CHAPTER 2   Components of the Business Proposition: The Consumer Demand Proposition   25

accounts are using smart cards to authorize secure transactions. Members of SWIFT (Society for Worldwide Interbank Financial Telecommunications) use smart cards to securely allow funds transfers and interbank transactions. The use of smart cards in consumer-based interactive TV initiatives is also being tried in Quebec, Canada, where the UBI (Universality, Bi-Directionality, Interactivity) consortium is testing an interactive TV system that uses a smart card as both an access device and a means of payment. Consortium members are represented by the following industry categories: cable operator, bank, post office, power/electrical utility, publishing, and lotto/games.

The use of smart cards as an access control device for buildings and equipment is found in campus settings and private/government building complexes. Japan has pioneered the concept of Intelligent Buildings, which incorporates the use of smart cards to authorize and track physical entry/exit and equipment use.

Again, the business rationale focuses on identification, authorization, authentication, and security. An added benefit to card users is convenience.

Information   Consumers are also using smart cards to store and manage information. To date, the main examples of this have occurred in the healthcare sector. Healthcare-driven smart card programs have used the chip to identify the eligibility of the insured individual and/or to maintain an accurate, up-to-date record of medical information, including emergency information, allergic reactions to drugs, and clinical data for use in emergencies. The French government pioneered the use of microprocessor chip cards for health insurance/medical information applications, and the Germans have issued over 80 million health-related smart cards in the last two years.

An example of information management outside of the healthcare industry is the Nissan Car Life program in Japan. Fundamentally a loyalty program, the Nissan Car Life Card also contains vehicle identification and service information. A convenient, up-to-date paperless file for the consumer, the card program also has marketing and administrative benefits for the car dealer.

Fundamentally, the power of the microprocessor chip centers on its ability to securely partition and process large amounts of information while enabling the secure, unaltered transfer of that information within the context of an overall intelligent system. As smart card applications develop, and memory and processing capacity increases, the use of information-based features will undoubtedly escalate.

Research conducted by the Smart Card Forum found that consumers are more interested in the information management component of cards than other applications. They want fewer cards in their wallets and more help in managing information. Businesses also see database marketing opportunities with the cards.

MULTIPLE FUNCTIONALITY

Typically, just one of the function areas—payments, rewards, access, or information—is the primary reason for a business to introduce the chip card to its customers. However, these four consumer-based chip functions are being introduced across a spectrum of industry categories and are often combined onto a "multiple application" card. The multiple applications can be controlled by the microprocessor chip itself, or by a combination of the chip and the traditional magnetic stripe.

The multiple application card has been successfully used in either closed-system or controlled environments in which the card issuer and the service provider or providers are the same legal entity or are closely associated within a specific environment. Examples would include university campus settings, town or city cards (found typically in Western European countries), shopping center programs (found in Japan), office or building complexes, and military bases and operations. In these situations, smart cards with varying combinations of payments, rewards, access (electronic/physical), and information have been used. In many cases, consumer use of the card is not discretionary. For example, a campus card that serves as student identification, access control, and payment for campus services is a necessity and not a matter of choice.

The marketing of multiple application cards in open environments in which there could be multiple issuers or multiple service providers and where consumer adoption of the card is discretionary, not mandatory, is largely uncharted territory. A range of issues including branding, issuer(s) responsibilities and liabilities, and consumer demand are in the process of active research and investigation by potential smart card stakeholders, including a special Working Group of the Smart Card Forum.

THE CONSUMER MARKET FOR SMART CARDS

WHAT DO CONSUMERS THINK ABOUT SMART CARDS?

U.S. consumers have far less experience with smart cards than European, or even Asian, consumers. But, there is an accumulating body of smart card concept research among U.S. consumers. Much of the research has focused on stored value (or prepaid) applications, but there are several studies assessing consumer reaction to different kinds of smart cards, including multiple application cards.

In one study conducted by the Smart Card Forum, consumers were exposed to an omnibus smart card concept that could be used, or thought of, in several ways: (1) As an information card, where different types of information that people often keep can be stored on the card, such as with a travel or health card; (2) a membership or identification card, where people can combine cards such as video store cards and ID cards such as supermarket courtesy or check cashing cards, into one; and (3) a payment card, where the card could include a person's credit, Automatic Teller Machine/debit or electronic purse/cash card.

U.S. consumers react favorably to the smart card concept:

- Nearly half (45 percent) of consumers indicate this concept is an excellent or good idea—with 23 percent rating it "excellent" and 22 percent "good."
- Only 15 percent of the U.S. consumer market regard the concept as poor.

Not only do consumers react favorably to the concept, they also react positively toward obtaining a smart card if it were available. In fact, only 39 percent of U.S. consumers under age 65 in the 1994 Smart Card Forum survey indicate they are not likely to obtain an available smart card. This is a low percentage for such a new, untested product concept.

CONSUMERS SEE BENEFITS TO HAVING SMART CARDS

Perceived advantages—increased portability of information and the potential convenience of carrying fewer cards, drive consumers' interest in smart cards. As illustrated in Exhibit 2–3, the benefit that ranked highest in the 1994 Smart

EXHIBIT 2-3

Portable Information and Consolidation Capabilities Are Perceived as Major Benefits

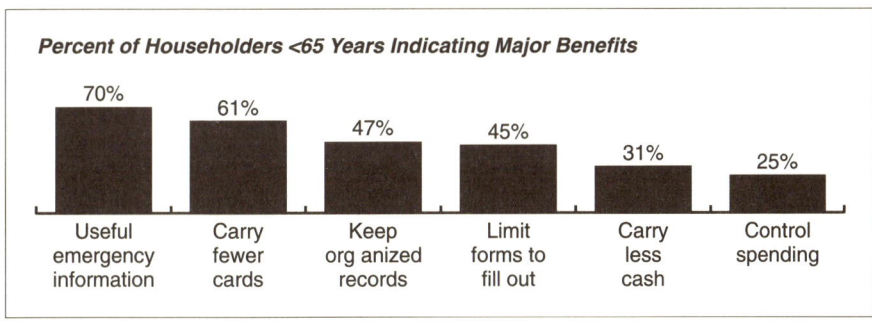

Source: Smart Card Forum, 1994

Card Forum study centers on the usefulness of the card for carrying emergency information, defined by consumers as information they needed to have available to them. The second highest ranked benefit focuses on the perceived potential for card consolidation/carrying fewer cards. Other significant benefits rated by consumers include information management, carrying less cash (if a payment card), and controlling spending for budgetary purposes.

The smart card function/feature most attractive to consumers is the ability to store and manage information. This is perceived as even more useful than financial payments—a feature that has become indispensable to the consuming public. In the consumer mindset, the card's ability to consolidate information and to make it more portable and accessible is perceived as a truly unique differentiator. Like a computer diskette, the smart card can be used by consumers to carry information that may be needed to communicate with others, share information, and make financial or nonfinancial transactions.

A visit to the physician's office is an excellent example of the perceived potential usefulness of the smart card to consumers. A consumer enters the physician's office for the first time. The consumer presents his/her smart card to the attendant or automated terminal. The card is loaded with the consumer's health insurance information and/or personal medical/emergency information. Card contents are quickly read by a terminal in the office and the patient is ready to see the physician.

CONSUMERS COMMENT ON HOW SMART CARDS CAN MAKE THEIR LIVES EASIER

Useful Emergency Information: "I could see putting some information on the card so that if I were ever in an accident the important information would be available. I'd want the medications I was allergic to, any special conditions and my insurance information so they could admit me to the hospital."

Keep Organized Records: "I get reimbursed for all my business traveling. If I could pay for everything with a card like this *and* it kept a record of everything that I could use to get reimbursed, it would make my life a lot simpler."

Limit Number of Forms to Fill Out: "I have three boys. Every time they go to the doctor I have to fill out all these forms. If I could have one card like this for each child, which I could run through each time they go to the doctor it would be great. The card would enter all our insurance information and would receive my sons' complete histories."

Carry Less Cash: "If it's as convenient as it seems…I'd put all my money on it and then just use it everywhere. I know there are toll booths where you can do something like this. I'd love it for that."

Source: Smart Card Forum

There are no forms to fill out. The doctor has quick access to accurate, up-to-date patient information.

The smart card's ability to streamline the transfer and exchange of information also extends to applications in other industries. For example: applying for, or opening, a new financial services account; applying for a supermarket courtesy shopping card; applying for a video rental card; renting a car; checking into a hotel; applying for and accessing government benefits; and many more.

A 1995 study conducted by PSI, an internationally known research firm in the financial services arena, also showed the high degree of appeal for informational features (particularly relating to health/medical and financial concerns) on a smart card. As might be expected, consumers also perceived smart cards as extremely useful in allowing them to make a purchase—whether it be credit, debit, or stored value. What's more, consumers feel that smart cards would be extremely useful in helping them electronically access information, products, and services. (See Exhibit 2–4.)

Among smart card purchase features, consumers rate the ATM/debit service as the most useful, followed by credit services and stored value/cash value cards.

EXHIBIT 2–4

Consumers Want Informational Features

	Percent of consumers who rate feature as "Extremely useful"
Any purchase feature	76%
ATM/debit	51
Credit	43
Stored value	26
Any access feature	70%
Financial access	44
Healthcare access	39
Phone card	24
Mobile phone	14
In-home entertainment	9
Any information feature	84%
Emergency medical	59
Medical info	49
Health insurance	43
Financial information	30
ID/account numbers	30
Rewards	13

Source: PSI, 1995

Understandably, consumer interest in the newly developing area of stored value/cash cards is not as high as other applications, due mostly to a low awareness and understanding of this new service. However, PSI research shows that awareness is steadily growing. In 1993, only 17 percent of U.S. consumer households were aware of stored value/cash cards. By 1995, the level of consumer awareness grew to 27 percent. In terms of consumer understanding, PSI research indicates that 21 percent of U.S. households expressed interest in a standalone stored value card for small-value purchases. This is on-par with consumer interest in the omnibus smart card concept discussed earlier and is several percentage points higher than consumer debit card ratings in 1994.

When the stored value card is explained to consumers, they see many benefits: the safety of the card versus cash; the convenience of not needing exact change; the card's potential as a budgeting tool; the increased speed of checkout; and cleanliness.

Other research by companies such as Citibank, MasterCard, VISA, Electronic Payment Systems, and Synergistics tends to find similar results on consumer interest and concerns about smart cards. This consistency is useful in building business propositions. (See Exhibit 2–5.)

CONSUMERS ALSO SEE DRAWBACKS TO HAVING SMART CARDS

Consumers are concerned that not enough merchants or service provider locations will accept the card. Without locations to use the card, the card would have little or no consumer utility. Other drawbacks of the card focus primarily

EXHIBIT 2–5

Security and Privacy Concerns Represent Highest Barrier to Multiapplication Card Acceptance

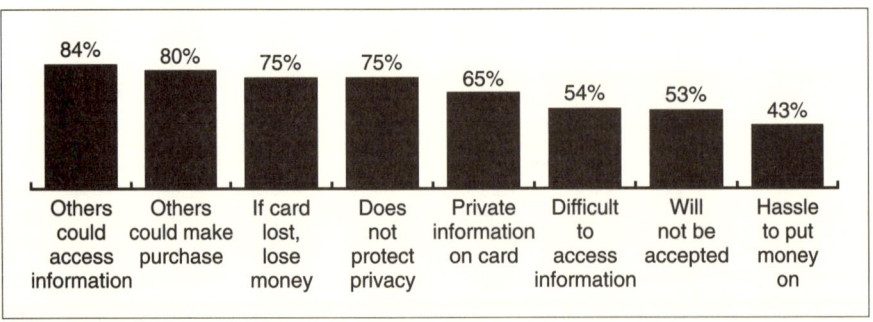

Source: Smart Card Forum, 1994

on how the card will operate and how or if value can be protected should the card be lost or stolen.

The locations that consumers would like to see stored value/cash cards accepted are naturally those where they currently conduct most of their day-to-day cash and coin transactions. Over 50 percent of consumers indicate interest in using stored value cards for the express lane at supermarkets, gas stations, convenience stores, pay phones, postage stamps, parking lots, parking meters, fast food outlets, and vending machines.

HOW CONSUMERS VIEW MULTIPLE-APPLICATION SMART CARDS

Many consumers immediately think of a smart card as a single card that will combine all of the services associated with their current cards onto one single card. They have called this card their "everything card." The "everything card" is attractive because it would be convenient and easy to carry in a wallet or pocketbook. About one in five consumer households (under 65 years of age) would use a card with all potential card services (payment, information, access, and rewards). This is similar to interest levels for stored value, or information-based, smart card concepts.

However, marketing an actual "everything card" has many pitfalls from the consumer perspective. Consumers see "the

---

OBSTACLES TO CONSUMER SMART CARD ACCEPTANCE

Others Can Access Information: "What if someone sees my number as I'm making a purchase...that means they can steal my card and then if I have information stored on the card they can access all the information as well as the money."

Does Not Protect Privacy: "I don't want everyone knowing all the things I'm buying. I don't want Big Brother watching and seeing every little thing I buy."

Will the Card be Accepted—and When? "How soon would something like this take place? I can't see it even being available for many years and then it's going to take many more years before you start to see it in places where you could use it. I can't see the guy on the corner where I get my bagel in the morning accepting a credit card. He'd have to have a little terminal."

Lost or Stolen Cards: "If you lose it no one knows how much money you had on the card, which means that they won't replace it because how are they to know that you are telling them the truth?"

How Do the Cards Operate? "How do you make sure that the way you wanted to pay is the way you do pay? How does the person at the place where you are buying your things know whether you have the money on the card to buy them? They have to get it approved somewhere."

Source: Smart Card Forum

everything card" as confusing and risky. How will they know what is on the card? What happens if they lose the card? Today, if they lose one card, they only lose one service. If they lost the "everything card," they could possibly lose all services.

Answers to these consumer concerns must be addressed in the business propositions. Privacy, security, ubiquitous acceptance, multiple application cards, customer service, and means to back-up information are not trivial problems.

If marketing a broadly conceived "everything card" is problematic, then it can be asked if there are other types of multiple-application cards that might generate higher levels of consumer interest, while minimizing potential negatives? The answer to this question is actually very intuitive. Consumers want their *current or new* cards to provide increased value through additional features or new services. They see these additional features and/or new services as an effort by the issuing organizations to make it easier and better for them to do business with that organization. (See Exhibit 2–6.)

The three primary areas in which consumers see smart cards increasing and improving the services they currently receive and/or providing new services are:

Health Services: a card with healthcare access, emergency medical, healthcare payments, and general medical information features.

Finance/Payment: a card with debit, credit, or stored-value purchase features, combined with features that support customized account access and information, and possibly rewards programs.

Mobile/Remote: a card with personalized and customized service access via mobile phones, pay phones, or other remote service terminals and carrying frequently dialed numbers.

EXHIBIT 2–6

Consumers Are Not Overwhelmingly Receptive to "The Everything Card"

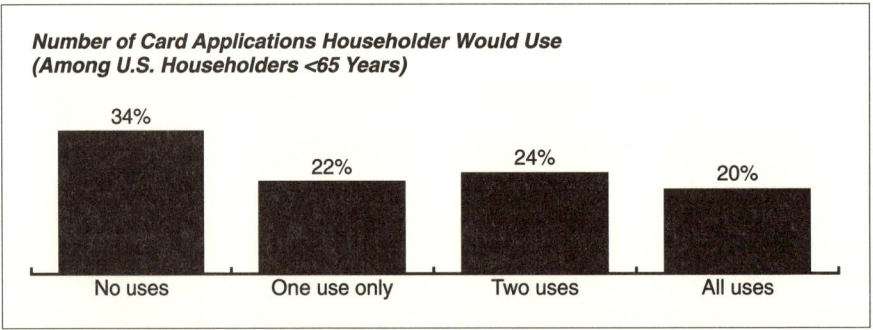

Source: Smart Card Forum, 1994

The Smart Card Forum research found consumers aggregating applications around lifestyle needs, for example, healthcare, travel, and communications. They liked the concept quite well. If they were to design the smart cards they would carry, they would design cards for these three service areas. Clearly, smart cards are not going to be designed solely from the consumer perspective. Many standalone services will be provided on smart cards and accepted by consumers because they add value to existing service offerings.

CARD LOSS AND PRIVACY CONCERNS

Currently, consumers use cards for single purposes or single functions. They realize the benefits and risks associated with carrying their existing cards, but are concerned with the additional smart card risks. To a consumer, when more information (personal and other) as well as additional financial payment capabilities are placed on these smart cards, their value increases. This increased value causes an increased concern not only about losing a card, but also about other people's ability to access its contents.

Until consumers become aware of the cards, are educated on how to use them, and develop a comfort level with their safeguards, security and privacy will continue to be a major problem. When U.S. consumers under age 65 were asked in the 1994 Smart Card Forum study what they perceived as the barriers to acceptance, at least three out of four indicated that the card does not protect privacy, and is vulnerable to other individuals' use or access to personal funds and/or information. Consumers are less concerned over whether

MORE CAN BE LESS: PUTTING TOO MUCH ON AN "EVERYTHING CARD"

Credibility: "Wait a minute, you said that we can put money, any amount we feel comfortable with, on the card. Now you're saying we could also put our credit cards on here. It's becoming very confusing and very unbelievable."

Confusion: "How do you make sure that the way you wanted to pay is the way you are actually paying: I could just see it, you pay the wrong way and then you don't have the cash you need later."

Threat: "When you go into a store and buy something you hand over cash or a credit card. With this, you'd be handing over both. You'd also be handing over all your other personal information and identifications. It didn't bother me too much to just put some cash on it and a few of my ID cards. But when you talk about combining credit cards and medical histories, it's too scary."

"If you lost this card, with everything on it, you'd be up a creek. As it is now, all this information is not going to be lost at the same time, you might lose only a piece of it."

Source: Smart Card Forum

EXHIBIT 2-7

Nearly All the Consumers Surveyed Want Refundability—
Even If It Means That the Issuer Must Track Transactions

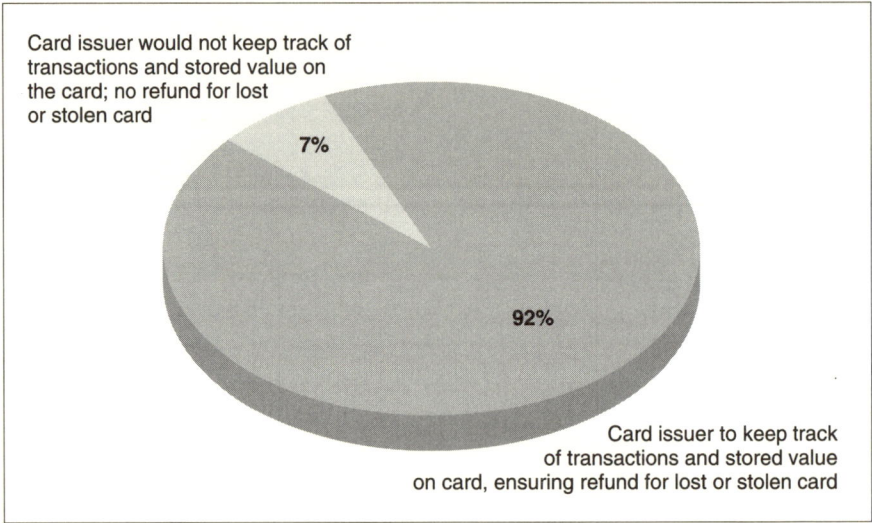

Source: PSI, 1995

or not it will be easy and convenient to use, and are willing to sacrifice some perceived personal privacy to increase the security of the card contents.

In a 1995 PSI study of U.S. consumers, 92 percent wanted refundability in the event a card is lost or stolen, the value of the card to be reinstalled, and a new card issued—even if it means sacrificing privacy so the card's issuer can track transactions (see Exhibit 2–7). Reloadable cards, especially when a PIN is used, will create applications from consumers in the United States that mirror today's credit and debit cards. Chapter Four will discuss some of the demands on issuers if consumer needs are not met.

THE SERVICE PROVIDER/ISSUER SMART CARD MARKET

Organizations interested in issuing and providing smart cards to their customers are focused on utilizing the card as:

1. A platform to deliver more and better services.
2. A management control and cost reduction vehicle.
3. A source of new and expanding revenue.

EXHIBIT 2-8

Smart Card Opportunity Areas for Issuers and Service Providers

Platform for Delivery of New/Improved Products and Services

- Deliver new products/services
- Improve product/service delivery
- Promote self-service
- Improve customer service, convenience, and access
- Acquire/retrain customers and build loyalty

Management Control/Cost Reduction

- Prevent fraud/improve transaction security
- Improve management access to information
- Control receivables/improve cash flow
- Build customer database/enhance marketing efficiency
- Improve operational efficiency
- Reduce administrative costs

Source of New Revenue

- Identify new revenue streams
- Enhance contribution of current revenue streams
- Build market share
- Increase profitability

Source: PSI, 1995

The rationale behind an organization's decision to issue or provide smart card-based services to customers depends on current business process improvements, as well as expansion into new revenue producing activities. The smart card is unique in that it can improve current service offerings and create services that were not previously possible. Current and potential providers of smart cards indicate that new developments, such as the electronic purse and improving how consumers access and utilize current services, offer opportunities of the highest market value. (See Exhibits 2–8 and 2–9.)

BARRIERS EXIST FOR POTENTIAL PROVIDERS OF SMART CARDS

The key barriers to smart card implementation are related to investment (in chip technology more so than protecting investments in current technology)

EXHIBIT 2-9

Issuers and Service Providers View Market Opportunity in Specific Smart Card Applications

Electronic Purse

- Stored value cards for small-value purchases
- Stored value cards for small- or large-value purchases
- Stored value feature added to ATM/debit cards
- Stored value feature added to credit cards

Customer Access and Convenience

- Home banking/bill payment
- Electronic shopping
- In-home entertainment and information services
- Internet and other computer networks
- Wireless and other telephony networks

Information

- Financial information
- Medical and health information
- Tracking and managing frequent buyer programs
- Tracking and managing personal financial transactions

Source: PSI, 1995

---

and infrastructure (lack of technology standards) issues. Organizations struggle with how to invest in the new card. The decision to move toward chip-based service offerings is not one-dimensional, but impacts an organization's current technology legacy systems and processes. Software, hardware, process development, employee retooling and training, marketing, customer service, as well as other related areas must be factored into the planning and investment decision process.

With these considerations, the cost of offering smart card-based services can be significant. That's why some organizations are looking for external partnerships to provide the infrastructure necessary to maximize their card-based service offers. In a 1995 PSI study of current and potential smart card service providers, three of four participants believe it is necessary to form alliances for the provision of card services. The need for alliances is principally based on infrastructure considerations, the need to share knowledge and risk, and the need to develop standards.

EXHIBIT 2-10

Banks and Telecommunications are the Priority Alliance Candidates

Industry		Priority Alliances Top Candidates/Most Mentions
Banks	+	Telecommunications
Telecom	+	Banks & nonbank financial
Education	+	Banks & telecommunications
Transport	+	Banks & government
Brokerage	+	Telecommunications & airlines/ATM networks
Government	+	Banks & retailers

Source: PSI, 1995.

The most likely alliance candidates for potential providers of smart card services are overwhelmingly organizations that can provide infrastructure—banks, financial services, and telecommunications companies. (See Exhibit 2–10.) Banks and financial services companies can provide payment processing and the settlements network as well as ATMs to load cards. The telecommunications companies can supply the network pipeline for information and payment transactions using pay phones and cellular phones as smart card readers. AT&T's investment in Mondex International is an example of the power of these infrastructure companies' visions.

Potential issuers of smart cards are far more concerned with building merchant acceptance than with cost and fee issues. Consumer concern over card loss is also a major barrier for current and potential smart card providers.

COMPONENTS OF THE BUSINESS PROPOSITION

Commerce began with value exchanges such as bartering and later migrated to product services and placement of markers. This later evolved to the exchange of coins, precious metals and today's paper currencies, checks and other payment systems. Concurrent with the evolution of currency, there were also manually intensive forms of communications and other information exchanges which included property titles, census data, tax reporting, and legal information.

Technological innovation is making electronic identification, security, and access even more complex environments in which the consumer has to utilize information and communications in making choices.

Smart card technology promises to ease the complexity overload by providing the ability to enhance service delivery and bring solutions to consumers on their own terms.

STRATEGIC BUSINESS PROPOSITION AND IMPLICATIONS

Obviously, the development of any strategic marketing plan should focus on the customer. There are many historic examples of failed product development or product entries because the marketer did not comprehend the value offered to the customer or sell the consumer on the value inherent in the product. This chapter has provided some of the critical findings on consumer interest in smart card-based applications. The fact that these findings have been replicated in almost all other research in the United States is significant.

As with any leading technology, a smart card can easily be misunderstood if the consumer has no idea what the product or service is, or in which the consumer fails to understand its delivery mechanism. The Sony Walkman is perhaps the most famous example of this. Consumers rejected the product and the value proposition in research, yet it was phenomenally successful. This underscores the marketer's responsibility to understand the dynamics of demand and provide market leadership in creating demand through education and effective marketing. Initial results from the Olympics VISA Cash Card launch indicate education is a critical factor in consumer usage as well as in acceptance.

Smart card technology can drive an organization's strategy. It can create differentiation, pre-empt substitution, and enhance an organization's bargaining position with both the consumer and supplier communities. For example, if an organization is in the business of providing cable or telephone services, a smart card can be used to differentiate parity service that is largely perceived by consumers as a commodity.

The more integrated services are bundled onto a card that delivers a strong, differentiated value proposition, the easier it will be to attract new customers and the harder it will be for them to leave the brand franchise for that of a competitor.

Smart cards and smart card applications need to be sustained with a broad set of applications executed with narrow, strategically targeted focus. Cross-functional applications, where you have three or four lines of business managing a customer relationship on a single device, can create value that is difficult for the competition to copy. For example, a telephone company may provide calling card functionality with VISA and MasterCard access and the operating system for a cellular phone—all on one card. The strategic implication is that the product technology meets a set of shareholder expectations—

financial objectives, customer satisfaction, and franchise development along several lines of business rather than just one.

Within these smart card applications is the opportunity to capitalize on customer database marketing. The microprocessor chip creates the opportunity to post process data or capture smart card information, which then becomes the incubator for institutional knowledge and information about customers who use the product. This information can be used for targeted marketing efforts and can redefine the business that organizations are in. Transactional information data and purchase activity can be passed back through processing networks such as retailers, and be downloaded for various marketing responses.

BUSINESS PROPOSITION MODEL FOR ELECTRONIC PURSE CARDS

The Prepaid Subcommittee of the Smart Card Forum's Financial Services Workgroup prepared a business case model for electronic purse smart cards that has been adopted and adapted for other industry applications. A copy of the model is available on diskette to Forum members. A few of the key variables are discussed below as a framework for putting together a model for your particular industry.

Each industry and each application has specific variables to the degree that, generally speaking, no one model can be used for smart cards. The electronic purse model is offered as a starting point.

The model documents the business impact of electronic purse cards for providers in the functional areas of Issuer, Acquirer, Reload Operator, and Network Operator. The model allows for the comparison of a typical player, based upon industry averages, with a specific player that may have a different cost structure due to such reasons as technology, scale, or organizational competency. It also allows for a four year ramp-up.

The model includes the following assumptions and other worksheet components:

Assumptions
- Card penetration
- Merchant location
- Merchant point of service
- Cardholder usage
- Electronic purse pricing
- Issuer revenue and cost

- Acquirer revenue and cost
- Reload operator revenue and cost
- Network operator revenue and cost

Other Components

- Electronic purse activity volumes
- Electronic purse activity revenues
- Acquirer profit and loss estimates
- Reload operator profit and loss estimates
- Network operator profit and loss estimates

Exhibit 2–11 is a sample of the Issuer Profit and Loss Statement with accompanying definitions. One of the values of Forum membership is the emphasis on developing realistic business models based on key components such as consumer and merchant research, cost models, industry projections, and alliance partners.

This brief introduction shows the complexity of issues addressed in developing a business proposition. The entire book is focused on information or resources that can help you develop your own models.

CONCLUSION

In conclusion, the strategic business proposition and subsequent implications of smart card technology can be as large or small as an institution's or organization's willingness to invest. The technology can be an add-on to an existing product or service, or an enabler for customers to transact across a network. Creating subsequent after markets in managing and selling transaction information can also broadly redefine how to approach a market and develop subsequent lines of business.

CHAPTER 2 Components of the Business Proposition: The Consumer Demand Proposition   41

EXHIBIT 2–11

Worksheet 12–Issuer Profit & Loss Estimates

This worksheet calculates pro forma income statements for "typical" and "specific" E-Purse card Issuers.

Resident Info, Visitor Info, and Combined Info

For the Typical Issuer, these values are calculated by dividing the corresponding values for the entire E-Purse network by the number of Issuers. For the Specific Issuer, these numbers are calculated based on input in the Issuer Revenue & Cost Assumptions worksheet. Refer to the corresponding items in the Card Penetration Assumptions and E-Purse Activity Volumes worksheets for more detailed descriptions of the individual items.

Revenues

Initial Card Sales. Price of Initial Card Charged to Cardholders multiplied by New Resident Cards Issued.

Annual Resident Card Fees. Annual Resident Card Fee per card multiplied by Average Resident Cards in Circulation.

Lost Card Replacement Fees. Lost Card Replacement Fee per card multiplied by total Lost Cards Replaced.

Visitor Card Fees. Visitor Card Fee per card multiplied by visitor Cards Issued.

Transaction Fees. Transaction Fee to Issuer multiplied by total E-Purse Transactions.

Discount Revenue. Discount to Issuer multiplied by total E-Purse Spending.

Reload Fees. Reload Fee Charged to Cardholders per reload transaction multiplied by Annual Reloads per Card multiplied by Average Resident Cards in Circulation.

Float Revenue. Interest Rate on Float multiplied by the average outstanding balance on all cards. This balance equals Average Resident Cards in Circulation multiplied by the Average Balance per Card plus Average Visitor Cards Outstanding multiplied by the Average Balance on Visitor Cards (for entire year).

Retired Card Residuals Retained. The product of the Retired Card Residuals Retained percentage, the Average Reload Value, the Average Residual on Retired Cards, and Cards Retired through Attrition.

Lost Card Residuals Retained. The product of the Lost Card Residuals Retained percentage, the Average Balance per Card, and Total Lost Cards Replaced.

Visitor Card Residuals Retained. The product of the Visitor Card Residuals Retained percentage, the Average Balance on Visitor Cards (for entire year), and Average Visitor Cards Outstanding.

Other Revenues. Other Revenues per Card multiplied by Average Cards Outstanding.

Expenses

Annual Issuance Fee. The annual cost an Issuer must pay to participate in the E-Purse network.

License Fees. License Fee per Card multiplied by the sum of New Resident Cards Issued and Visitor Cards Issued.

Card Costs. Cost per Resident Card multiplied by New Cards Activated plus Cost per Visitor Card multiplied by Visitor Cards Issued.

Distribution Costs. Distribution Cost per Resident Card multiplied by New Resident Cards Issued plus Distribution Cost per visitor Card multiplied by visitor Cards Issued.

Reload Fees to Reload Operator. The product of Reload Fee to Reload Operator per reload, Average Reloads per Card, and Average Resident Cards in Circulation.

Fraud Losses. The Fraud Losses on Charge Volume percentage multiplied by total E-Purse Spending.

Costs to Acquire New Resident Cardholders. Cost to Acquire a New Resident Cardholder multiplied by New Resident Cards Issued.

Costs to Acquire Visitor Cardholders. Cost to Acquire a Visitor Cardholder multiplied by visitor Cards Issued.

Statement Costs. Statement Cost per Resident Cardholder multiplied by Average Resident Cards in Circulation.

Other OPEX. Other OPEX per Cardholder multiplied by the sum of New Resident Cards Issued and Visitor Cards Issued.

Overhead. Equals Total Overhead per Issuer from Issuer Revenue & Cost Assumptions worksheet.

EXHIBIT 2-11 (continued)
Issuer Profit and Loss Statements

	Typical Issuer				Specific Issuer			
	Year 1	Year 2	Year 3	Year 4	Year 1	Year 2	Year 3	Year 4
Resident Information								
Active cards at beginning of year	-	36,000	90,000	180,000	-	36,000	90,000	180,000
New Cards Activated	40,000	64,000	110,000	20,000	40,000	64,000	110,000	20,000
Attrition Rate	10.0%	10.0%	10.0%	10.0%	10.0%	10.0%	10.0%	10.0%
Active cards retired through attrition	4,000	10,000	20,000	20,000	4,000	10,000	20,000	20,000
Active cards at end of year	36,000	90,000	180,000	180,000	36,000	90,000	180,000	180,000
Average active cards in circulation	18,000	63,000	135,000	180,000	18,000	63,000	135,000	180,000
Total lost cards replaced	900	3,150	6,750	9,000	900	3,150	6,750	9,000
Additional cards distributed but not activated	2,000	2,000	2,000	2,000	2,000	2,000	2,000	2,000
Visitor information								
Visitor cards issued	8,000	12,000	20,000	20,000	8,000	12,000	20,000	20,000
Average visitor cards outstanding	4,000	10,000	16,000	20,000	4,000	10,000	16,000	20,000
Average visitor cards in circulation	154	231	385	385	154	231	385	385
Combined information								
Average active cards outstanding	22,000	73,000	151,000	200,000	22,000	73,000	151,000	200,000
Average active cards in circulation	18,154	63,231	135,385	180,385	18,154	63,231	135,385	180,385
Total e-purse transactions	4,658,513	17,889,523	42,064,674	56,046,398	4,658,513	17,889,523	42,064,674	56,046,398
Total e-purse spending	$16,019,517	$66,241,468	$165,718,161	$220,800,618	$16,019,517	$66,241,468	$165,718,161	$220,800,618
Revenues								
Initial card sales	$400,000	$640,000	$1,100,000	$200,000	$400,000	$640,000	$1,100,000	$200,000

Annual resident card fees	-	-	-	-	-	-	1,800,000
Lost card replacement fees	9,000	31,500	67,500	90,000	9,000	31,500	90,000
Visitor card fees	16,000	24,000	40,000	40,000	16,000	24,000	40,000
Transaction fees	46,585	178,895	420,647	560,464	46,585	178,895	560,464
Discount revenue	80,098	331,207	828,591	1,104,003	80,098	331,207	1,104,003
Reload fees	117,000	409,500	877,500	1,170,000	117,000	409,500	1,170,000
Float revenue	23,622	94,446	231,408	307,798	23,622	94,446	307,798
Retired card residuals retained	6,109	18,132	42,371	42,371	6,109	18,132	42,371
Lost card residuals retained	13,746	57,115	143,003	190,670	13,746	57,115	190,670
Visitor card residuals retained	28,800	72,000	115,200	144,000	28,800	72,000	144,000
Other revenues	-	-	-	-	-	-	-
Total revenues	$740,959	$1,856,795	$3,866,220	$3,849,306	$920,959	$2,486,795	$5,649,306
Expenses							
Annual issuance fee	$30,000	$30,000	$30,000	$30,000	$30,000	$30,000	$30,000
License fees	12,000	19,000	32,500	10,000	12,000	19,000	10,000
Card costs	238,000	372,000	630,000	180,000	238,000	372,000	180,000
Distribution costs	60,000	94,000	160,000	70,000	60,000	94,000	70,000
Reload fees to reload operator	23,400	81,900	175,500	234,000	23,400	81,900	234,000
Fraud losses	56,068	231,845	580,014	772,802	56,068	231,845	772,802
Costs to acquire new resident cardholders	80,000	128,000	220,000	40,000	80,000	128,000	40,000
Costs to acquire visitor cardholders	24,000	36,000	60,000	60,000	24,000	36,000	60,000
Statement costs	240,000	384,000	660,000	120,000	240,000	384,000	120,000
Other OPEX	18,154	63,231	135,385	180,385	18,154	63,231	180,385
Overhead	2,000,000	2,000,000	2,000,000	2,000,000	2,000,000	2,000,000	2,000,000
Total expenses	$2,781,622	$3,439,976	$4,683,398	$3,697,187	$2,781,622	$3,439,976	$3,697,187
Net income	$(2,040,663)	$(1,583,181)	$(817,179)	$152,119	$(1,860,663)	$(953,181)	$1,952,119

CHAPTER 3

Worldwide Developments and Player Motivations

Jean McKenna
VISA International

Kenneth Ayer
VISA International

Smart cards are being used in innovative, exciting ways all over the world. They're helping people make payments more conveniently and securely, live healthier and safer lives, and communicate more effectively.

Surprisingly, North America is lagging behind in the use of these cards, a rarity in high technology. People have come to think of North America as the leading edge in technology, the place that sent men to the moon and gave birth to Silicon Valley. But in the case of smart cards, Europe leads America. This is the result of a paradox. North America has led the world in cheap, reliable telecommunications, and on-line access to databases is available at a reasonable cost. Elsewhere in the world these capabilities are more expensive, so other ways of conducting business had to be developed. Now these alternatives are opening new possibilities that go beyond what has been done in North America. In fact, a number of developing countries like China and South Africa are leap-frogging the United States with more advanced technologies. It's time to explore what those new possibilities are.

Smart cards are *how* something can be done, not *what* is done. Like personal computers in the early days, their potential is still largely unexplored. But there are several uses that are well established in other parts of the world and many others that are pointing the way to new possibilities. We will briefly survey some of these in this chapter. Our focus will be on two characteristics: either we will be talking about an application that is international in use, or one that may be local now but can be of use in many other countries. Our examples will come from several industries, because smart cards are widely useful and because groups we think of as "industries" are rapidly merging. Computers and telecommunications are frequently cited as industries whose boundaries are increasingly blurred. Entertainment and education often merge, as when students download images of Earth from space for science projects or communicate with other students in far-flung reaches of the globe. These examples are cited partly to inform the reader of what is being done, but even more to stimulate the imagination to conceive what can be done.

A smart card does two things: store data and manipulate data. What data and how they are manipulated are limited only by a consumer or business person's imagination. Just as personal computers brought computing power down to the desk top, smart cards are bringing computing power down to the individual's wallet.

Smart cards once had very limited capacity. They now have enough capacity to store all of MS DOS 1.0, the operating system that launched the personal computer revolution. A 64K card—the size of the first IBM PC—is in research and development, now. Smart cards have enough computing power to execute complex encryption algorithms in less than a second. The challenge is to understand the technology and find new and profitable ways to make it serve people better.

PLAYERS AND MOTIVATIONS

The basic players in any smart card application are the same as in any business: technology providers, service providers, and customers. The basic motivation is greater efficiency in providing services that customers want, generating a profit in the process. The service providers and customers will be the focus here, and their specific motivations vary by application and industry.

The industries and players with greatest smart card potential are:

- Financial services: banks, insurance, securities, and payment card companies.
- Telecommunications: telephone and wireless communications companies.
- Health: insurance providers, doctors and other practitioners.
- Government: internal agency use for identification of government personnel, and record keeping.
  Client customer applications—those eligible to receive government benefits, as well as ones who cater to the public, for example, the U.S. Postal Service—drivers' licenses, social security.
- Transportation: airlines, mass transit authorities, taxis, buses, and trains.
- Retailing: all types of retailers, especially high-cash, high-volume transaction retailers, loyalty and frequent buyer point scoring.

- Travel and Entertainment: hotels, ski resorts, amusement parks, sports ticketing, cable operators, loyalty and frequent traveler point scoring.
- Education: campus administration, ID, payment.
- Businesses in general: identification of employees, especially those with privileged access to information or restricted areas or who handle financial or highly secure transactions.

Note that in many cases, what we traditionally think of as industries are already alliances with many partners. MasterCard and VISA are payment systems owned and controlled by their member banks. The transportation industry uses payment system cards, cash, and checks in a partnership that agrees to accept these means of payment. Many airlines and others in the travel business co-brand payment system cards. The payment systems use telecommunications networks, which accept payment through banks. Governments regulate banks and transact much of their business through banks.

In looking for potential alliances and partners for smart card applications, it is important to realize that these will build on the existing alliances already permitting today's complex economic system to function.

PROJECTS, TRIALS, AND PILOTS

There were more than 140 chip card projects worldwide at last count. Some of these have been in use for years, others are technological or commercial trials, and still others are pilots in the first stages of rollout. The Smart Card Forum is building a database of applications to help its members identify and communicate with these pilots and trials. We have selected a few projects to illustrate some of the issues and benefits involved with smart cards. The projects are either those that require worldwide (or at least international) interoperability or that, while local or national at present, show some interesting possibilities that other areas may learn from.

CLOSED VERSUS OPEN SYSTEMS

Systems are frequently referred to as either Closed or Open. A closed system is one that is relatively simple and has only a few functional parts. A prepaid telephone card used by a telephone company that is a monopoly illustrates a closed system. The telephone company issues the cards, owns the telephones, operates the network and has full control over almost the entire system. All it needs are cardholders to use the cards.

An open system is one with more players and more complexity. Master-Card and VISA illustrate relatively open systems. The systems operated by these card associations contain multiple players at every level. Thousands of different banks issue cards from many manufacturers to hundreds of millions of people who use these cards at millions of merchant locations, who, in turn, deposit to their account at their own banks.

This system is much more open than the simple telephone system. The merchants generally know little or nothing about the cardholder. The banks involved may not have any direct relationship with each other. The system uses a variety of technologies, and it is open to anyone who meets the system's and the banks' rules.

Most systems usually fall somewhere in between. Telephone systems may not be monopolies and usually have to deal with other telephone systems for international calls. Many systems have far fewer members than all the people, banks, and merchants in the world who participate in either MasterCard or VISA. The distinction is best thought of as a continuum; systems are relatively closed or relatively open.

A closed system makes the technological challenge much more manageable, but potentially limits the number and kinds of players. More open systems may require equipment from many vendors, from many different parts of the world. Open systems represent a challenge for vendors and system operators alike, demanding shared specifications and standards to which all parties conform.

Then there is interoperability across different system operators. Like globe-spanning telecommunications systems, built and managed by many different organizations, smart card operators must not only agree on technical standards, but make appropriate business arrangements to pay for the goods and/or services that pass among them.

Thirdly, there is interoperability across applications. This means that a smart card having several applications (e.g., a payment application, a loyalty program, and some form of identification) must have an operating system that accommodates each. It also demands careful consideration of how much information partners can and should share, and of how to protect one partner from access by the other, as dictated by privacy and security.

INTERNATIONAL STANDARDS AND SPECIFICATIONS

Shared standards and specifications are essential to interoperability. (The terms "standard" and "specification" are sometimes synonymous and sometimes differentiated. We will use them interchangeably.) International applications require worldwide agreement on standards so that cards and terminals from various providers will work properly together. There are several international standards and specifications agreed upon by the various industries implementing smart cards. These are voluntary, generally enforced not by government edict but by the fact that conformity is in everyone's interest. An overview of standards and specifications follows to facilitate reference. Additional discussion of the specific ISO standards can be found in Chapter 15.

International Organization for Standardization

The International Organization for Standardization (ISO) is the most important international standard-setting body for a variety of technologies, mechanical and electrical as well as for smart cards. These standards set minimums, but they include many options and leave some issues unaddressed. *The result is that conformance to ISO standards alone does not necessarily ensure interoperability—nor does it ensure that cards and terminals built to the specifications will work together properly.* ISO may also leave certain needs unfulfilled, so that they have to be supplemented by industry specifications.

Telecommunications—Global System for Mobile Communications (GSM) Specifications

GSM is a specification for cellular telephone systems, primarily offering international compatibility. A GSM subscriber can make or receive calls in any of the 70 countries currently participating. The specifications tie a telephone number to a smart card, called a Subscriber Identification Module (SIM) or User Identity Module (UIM), rather than to a telephone handset. The SIM is inserted into a telephone to activate it. Whether or not the telephone is in a subscriber's home city or country, the system will seek out the SIM and route a call to its handset. That means a subscriber does not have to leave a forwarding telephone number or even know what city he or she will be in at any particular time. The SIM also encrypts the conversation so that no one can casually listen in to it.

More than 100 companies in the 70 participating countries currently offer GSM services to over 10 million customers, with the number growing daily. In the United States six regional telephone companies plan to offer GSM service, while other companies are advocating different technologies. Many of the Personal Communication System providers who bid for markets in 1995 in the United States plan to use GSM specifications.

FINANCIAL SERVICES SPECIFICATIONS

EMV Specifications: Credit and Debit Cards
The ISO standards provide several options, with the net result that cards and terminals from two different systems can be ISO compliant but still not work together properly. The options have to be reduced somewhat, but not eliminated, to achieve interoperability.

CHAPTER 3 Worldwide Developments and Player Motivations

At the end of 1993, the three major bank card associations, Europay, MasterCard and VISA, decided to develop a specification for the use of smart cards by their member financial institutions. The usual ISO process that creates an international standard is often slow, depending as it does on achieving a consensus of all parties. To get this specification completed quickly, just the three organizations were involved. Once the specification was completed, others could adopt it if they chose to do so. The motivation was primarily to be able to offer bank customers new services. Increased security could be an additional benefit.

The specification is called the *Integrated Circuit Card Specifications for Payment Systems,* though it is usually called the "EMV specification" (for Europay, MasterCard, and VISA.). It is available on VISA's (http://www.visa.com) and MasterCard's (http://www.mastercard.com) home pages as well as through the Smart Card Forum. The 1996 release is organized into three separate books: one each for the cards, the terminals, and the applications. The only application at the moment is credit/debit.

The EMV specification is international and worldwide. Financial institutions currently offer their card holders worldwide acceptability, which needs to be maintained. Merchants do not want to have one terminal for VISA cards, another for MasterCards, a third for cards issued by Europay, and so forth. The same terminal must accept all payment system cards. That requires more cooperation, because smart cards are so much more complex than magnetic stripe cards.

Once smart cards are used, additional services can be provided on the same card because it can carry several different applications. The applications can be isolated from each other and individually protected because the card's data processing capability can differentiate between applications and even provide each with its own password.

Europay, MasterCard, and VISA are currently having cards and terminals built and tested for interoperability. Cards will continue to be issued by each payment system individually and will continue to carry their respective brands. Terminals, however, will have to accept any of the cards and process their transactions properly, in accordance with the rules of each individual payment system. "Terminals" can mean anything from simple point of sale devices to complex and highly integrated electronic cash registers, automated teller machines (ATMs), automated fuel dispensers (gasoline pumps), and other card accepting devices.

Thousands of VISA credit/debit cards built to the new specification are already in use, with millions more to follow over the next several years. Europay and MasterCard are also completing their implementations and will be issuing cards over the next several years. The banks that own these payment systems will be the final arbiters of where and when they decide to issue smart cards. The total market for payment system cards currently exceeds 600 million and is growing. This has the potential for being one of the largest, as well as the most open and complex, smart card application.

American Express and other financial service providers are likely to make their applications EMV compatible, or at the least or adopt the specification for credit and debit.

INTERESTING POSSIBILITIES

Throughout this book the reader will learn about many of the emerging uses for smart cards. Many of these have been in place for a number of years and others are in the early stages of implementation. Two of the industries increasingly focused on developing smart card applications are financial services and healthcare. These efforts are currently national in scope, but efforts are under way to either make them international or to launch similar national projects in other countries. A brief description of some of these projects and applications follows.

French Bank Cards Smart cards have been in use in the French banking system for a number of years. All bankcards in France have a chip imbedded in them. They also have magnetic stripes, so they can be used in other countries. When a French cardholder makes a purchase, the transaction is processed at the point of service using the chip and not the magnetic stripe. The cardholder enters a personal identification number (PIN) that is verified by the card and the majority of transactions are completed off-line, thus reducing the cost of on-line authorizations. Smart cards were introduced to reduce fraud by implementing secure off-line PIN validation. The cost of making a telephone call for every transaction, an alternative used elsewhere, was much higher than the expense of changing to chip cards. The fraud reduction has been very successful and there are now more than 24 million French bank cards in circulation. This is the largest financial services smart card implementation in the world.

Stored Value Cards There are many local and some national stored value card systems in use. Over 30 countries worldwide have stored value card or electronic purse systems. The majority of these stored value systems are telephone cards. The cards are loaded with value and then used in specially equipped pay telephones to make calls. Most telephone cards carry value in the form of units which are variously defined by the different telephone companies. These are units of telephone time, not currency, so they can't be used as a general purpose stored value card.

CHAPTER 3 Worldwide Developments and Player Motivations

In recent years there has been a growing use of stored value cards outside of the telecommunications industry, often in local or national applications. Stored value cards are being distributed by many types of organizations including financial institutions.

Currently the cost of processing transactions is too high to use conventional bank cards for low value (generally less than U.S. $10) transactions. Stored value cards place monetary value directly on the card, rather than accessing an account the way most bank cards do. A stored value card is like cash in that any person having one is assumed to be its legitimate owner and can use it without question. They can even be used in vending machines.

Stored value cards offer convenience to the user. They work quickly and securely, deducting the appropriate amount without requiring that the customer have the right coins. This is a considerable advantage for parking meters, photocopy machines or coin operated laundries. Many buses and other mass transit agencies require exact change, which stored value cards can provide.

Stored value cards can be implemented with a variety of technologies, including conventional magnetic stripe cards. Many mass transit railways use some form of these, perhaps disposable cardboard tickets with magnetic stripes. Many libraries offer stored value cards to operate photocopy machines, and there are numerous other examples.

The stored value card's advantage to the merchant includes giving faster, better, and more secure service. Stored value cards can deduct the right amount in less than a second, much faster than any clerk can make change. Librarians can devote their time to serving patrons in more useful ways than making change for the photocopy machine. Cash handling can represent up to 5 percent of the cost of doing retail business. Coins are bulky, heavy, have to be counted and packaged, tend to get lost in transit, and are generally a nuisance.

Thieves sometimes break into coin boxes, especially where they are unattended. The damage to the equipment is often greater than the money loss—as much as $1,000 per device in the case of some pay telephones. Customers are inconvenienced by not being able to use the equipment until it's repaired or replaced and meanwhile the owner of the device loses revenue. Stored value cards can eliminate this problem because it takes sophisticated electronic equipment, not force, to collect the value stored in the machine.

Banks and other financial institutions want to issue stored value cards because they open new markets. Currently banks are involved in monetary transfers through credit cards, debit cards, and checks, but are not involved with cash to the same degree. Handling cash is a major expense for banks, who have to count deposits and withdrawals.

Major stored value card projects with world wide ambitions include VISA Cash, MasterCard Cash, Europay Clip, Proton Cards, and Mondex, described below. American Express currently has a stored value card, but has not made their global rollout plans public.

VISA Cash VISA Cash began a headquarters pilot in April of 1995. Australia began its VISA Cash pilot in November 1995. During the summer Olympics of 1996, VISA Cash was accepted at the Olympic venues and at surrounding merchants, with First Union, Wachovia, and NationsBank all participating as issuers. After the Olympics the banks intended to continue offering VISA Cash to their customers.

The VISA Cash system has both disposable and reloadable cards. The disposable cards are discarded once the value on them has been used up. They are anonymous and can be used by tourists, children, and others without a local bank account. Like all stored value cards, they have the value on the card itself, so no costly authorization calls are needed.

The reloadable cards can have additional value placed on them by the cardholder. Though the cards are still anonymous when purchases are made, loading the card usually means placing value on the card from a bank account, which of course is not anonymous. The reloadable cards are EMV "compatible", which means they can be combined with credit or debit applications on the same card. They are not EMV "compliant", which would mean that the data elements and commands used by them are not in the EMV specifications. As commands such as "LOAD" are not in EMV, stored value cards need additional specifications.

In addition to the Olympics in Atlanta, Australia, Canada, Argentina, Hong Kong with the bank of China and Standard Chartered Bank, the UK, and Colombia also have VISA Cash systems in operation. As these cards are denominated in national currencies, they can not be used internationally. A card with Australian dollars will not be accepted in an American terminal, nor will one with U.S. dollars be accepted in Canada. Additional features will address this situation.

MasterCard Cash MasterCard International chose Canberra, Australia, as its initial showcase for the MasterCash smart card. The cash function is designed for transactions of $10 or less. Because the service is closely tied to bank accounts, the cards are positioned as "relationship cards," and the chips coexist with magnetic stripes.

After preparatory work dating back almost a year, MasterCard launched the trial in March 1996 with Australia and New Zealand Banking Group, Commonwealth Bank of Australia, and Westpac Banking Corp. They set out to sign 10,000 consumers and 250 retailers. Market research indicated 55 percent of consumers would definitely or probably take MasterCard Cash cards if offered, and 60 percent said they would change banks to get the service. MasterCard and the banks will be evaluating results into 1997 and incorporating new features, such as cross-border/multicurrency capability.

With the Australian project under way, MasterCard turned its attention—with Visa—to the first large-scale interoperability test of the card-association-sponsored smart cards. It will take place in New York City's Upper West Side neighborhood starting in early 1997. The participating banks—Chase Manhattan and Citibank—plan to issue 50,000 cards for use at 500 merchant locations. It will be a critical test of the EMV specification, in that all terminals will be accepting both brands of cash cards.

Mondex Since 1990, National Westminster Bank of London spent more than $100 million on research and development of Mondex, one of the most aggressively promoted of the smart card concepts. Mondex emerged from the laboratory in July 1995 with a trial in Swindon, a city of 190,000 people about 70 miles west of London, which was selected because of its manageable size and typical demographics.

Natwest and Midland Bank, its partner in Mondex UK, signed 600 merchants and 10,000 cardholders, or about one-fifth of their combined retail customer base in Swindon. Within a year, the system had become a fixture in the local payment system, accepted in pay phones, parking lots, news kiosks, and merchant outlets ranging from cinemas to supermarkets, though it still accounted for a small fraction of total sales. Surveys showed that 66 percent of the cardholders had come to prefer Mondex to cash. Average card loads were the equivalent of $35 to $45, and the majority of transactions were under $7.50.

The Swindon trial was only an early step in Natwest's grand plan. Mondex UK was one of a global network of franchises designed to create a "global alternative to cash," built on the multi-currency chip card and an associated "electronic wallet" tied in with banking accounts. The system accommodates "wallet to wallet" transfers of value, a true functional equivalent to the passing of cash. This is considered controversial, raising questions about monetary control and central auditability of transations.

In July 1996, Natwest Group relinquished control of its invention by incorporating a global association, Mondex International. It listed 17 charter owners: Natwest and Midland in the UK; Hongkong & Shanghai Banking Corp., with rights to much of Asia; Wells Fargo Bank and AT&T Universal Card Services in the United States; Royal Bank of Canada and Canadian Imperial Bank of Canada; and 10 Australian and New Zealand institutions, including those involved concurrently with MasterCard and Visa experiments in the region.

Each of the Mondex regions will run its own pilots, modifying the system to local needs, customs, and regulations. In the United States, Wells Fargo ran a test in and around its headquarters in San Francisco in preparation for a broader rollout by the Mondex USA organization. While there had been some concern about Mondex's independence from the EMV effort, the company has conducted demonstrations of its compatibility with the bank card groups' specifications.

Proton The Proton program in Belgium was one of the pioneering stored value card systems sponsored by banks. The organization responsible for launching Proton was Banksys, a payment service company owned by the Belgian retail banks and expanding from its automated teller machine and debit card base. Having proven its electronic purse technology and recognizing demand in other countries, Banksys has successfully sold its EMV- compatible system in at least three other countries—the Netherlands, Brazil, and Australia.

Banksys announced Proton in 1993 and began a pilot in February 1995 in two university towns. As of May 1996, just before Proton's official rollouts in Belgium's larger cities began, the company reported more than 30,000 cards had been issued and loaded, and more than 300 loading devices were in place. The average amount put onto the cards was $43. Average transactions were running $8 in retail stores and $1.20 in vending machines and telephones. Bansksys planned to merge purse and debit card capabilities in January 1997.

Proton technology was incorporated in 1995 in the Netherlands' Chipknip program, Brazilian Proton program, and Australia's Quicklink. Sweden and Switzerland also had Proton-based technology in preparation.

Clip Europay International, MasterCard's European marketing partner, announced its electronic purse entry, Clip, in June 1996. Taking time to develop the product after others had come on the market, Europay claimed to have incorporated the best available features and functionality, including the multicurrency capability that should be especially attractive within Europe, and compatibility with the very latest version of EMV. Europay had initial commitments from banking groups in Italy and the Czech Republic to adopt Clip, and others were expected to follow.

Europay explicitly—and at least as vocally as MasterCard and Visa—opposed the "unauditable" aspects of Mondex and vowed to comply with all central bank directives about control of money creation. Europay also has been vocal about its cost-benefit calculations, saying that a conversion to smart cards would save its members almost $3 billion over seven years. The figure is based on reduced demand for on-line communications, fraud reductions, and general transaction processing efficiencies. The total does not include revenues from any "value-added" services such as shopper-loyalty programs.

Healthcare Smart cards may be the ideal medium for storing medical record information and are being issued in many countries for health care programs. The security features of smart cards make them especially appropriate for this use. In many countries medical records have to be signed by the attending physician and the signature must be verifiable by outside third parties (insurance companies, legal authorities, etc.). Prescriptions also require a doctor's signature and that signature, too, must be verifiable. Smart cards can contain data encryption procedures that, among other uses, can include an electronic signature acceptable for these purposes.

The security features can also authenticate that the person offering the card is the one authorized to use it. These can range from PIN and password protection to various biometric features. These features can also increase the security of medical records and limit access to those authorized to obtain a specific piece of information.

In Japan, smart cards are being used by patients who require periodic renal dialysis treatments. Previously, a patient had to go to the center holding his or her records, which severely limited travel. With the requisite information on a card, a patient can make use of facilities throughout Japan. For the first time, a patient can take a vacation or business trip that involves more than a few days absence from the clinic vicinity.

In the summer of 1992 the German Social Security Authority and the Sickness Fund Doctors Association announced that they would issue a smart card health insurance card to every German citizen. Medical costs were soaring and administrative costs were high. The system will require close to 80 million cards, renewed every three years, and around 150 terminals.

France has been working toward developing its own health insurance card using a smart card. The objective is to issue a single health care card to 45 million people, replacing the 800 million claim forms produced yearly. The system would be rolled out over a number of years. Patients will carry cards with their identification and eligibility information and a record of services rendered and fees earned.

Signaling further possibilities, Schlumberger in France has added a smart card reader to Apple Newton notebooks. The modified Newtons become the ultimate in portable computers for doctors, who can insert patients' smart cards for updates on their medical records. In the future, payment applications can be added.

In the United States, a few programs have been launched in Florida and Oklahoma. The U.S. government is considering smart card technology if agreement on a national healthcard is reached. This is discussed in greater detail in Chapter 10.

CONCLUSION

Smart cards are being used now in the GSM telecommunications application. In the financial industry, the standardization groundwork has been laid for worldwide interoperability of credit and debit cards, and manufacturers are now building the cards and terminals that will implement the specifications. The first implementations have begun and more are expected over the next several years. All the major payment associations are experimenting with stored value cards, learning how to give customers and merchants greater convenience and creating a new revenue stream. The health care industry is using smart cards for insurance identification and medical record keeping in ways that promise greater efficiency and lower costs. Some of these, like GSM and the EMV cards, inherently require international interoperability. Others are more local, but demonstrate the benefits smart cards can bring and show others how to use them profitably.

The rest of this book contains many other examples of how smart cards bring exciting new possibilities to consumers and businesses. These are just the beginning. Just as personal computers were first used for relatively simple tasks and are now opening whole new worlds of communications and expanding our mental horizons, the future of smart cards is limited only by the creativity and imagination of the people who will be the industry's leaders.

CHAPTER 4

Shifting Boundaries

William J. Barr
Bellcore

Catherine A. Allen
The Santa Fe Group

John Burke
Foley, Hoag & Eliot

The widespread use of computers in the last couple of decades has begun the transition from materials-based commerce (e.g., paper and physical delivery) to electronic commerce. The pace of change, however, has been excruciatingly slow. As we head toward the twenty-first century, however, the pace of change has suddenly reached a fevered pitch as corporations try to understand what the new world of electronic commerce will look like once they get past the niche market stage, and adjust organizational structures and priorities to prepare to address this emerging marketplace.

Shifting boundaries is the theme of this chapter—technology is often the driver and the results are rapid change, ambiguity, adaptive behaviors, and chaos. It is one of the most exciting and most terrifying times in business. Billions are at stake in markets where choices are unclear.

The smart card industry is participating in this environment in the same way as other information technology industries. As we have seen in the first three chapters, smart cards have been finding useful application niches in many areas around the world. We foresee a future environment in which smart card technology is a key element of electronic commerce. The transition to this future from our current environment of partial electronic commerce will be quite chaotic for some. While not random, the changes will be particularly disordered for companies steeped in the processes and traditions of materials-based commerce.

A CHANGE IN TIME

One of the most difficult changes for organizations to deal with has been the apparent acceleration of time. A new terminology describes this occurrence.

A "Web Year"—the time it takes to make a year's worth of change in the environment of the World Wide Web—is generally understood to be somewhere in the neighborhood of two to six months or less. Thus, the proverbial "5 Year Plan" performed annually in January is now completely obsolete by Halloween. Our old buddy, time, upon whom we could rely as a constant and unchanging yardstick, has gone hyper on us. It is no longer possible to gradually build a new capability within a corporation to meet some new market opportunity. The pace of change will not allow it. By the time a new capability, generated along old business models, is ready to go, the market environment has significantly changed.

A CHANGE IN BEDFELLOWS

Because of the change in the speed of market movement, many corporations will change their strategies for capturing market share. Increasingly, companies are looking to find partners to acquire the necessary capability to bring new products and services to market quickly. Another approach to corporate growth is to expand product scope into adjacent markets. Again, partnerships play an important part in this growth. Only this time, the partners are not the ones in the traditional value chains but, rather, break the old molds to expand into new markets. An example here is the alliance between Bellcore, a software and professional services technology company, and Adler Boschetto and Peebles (ABP), a Madison Avenue advertising company. This alliance was formed to bring ABP's clients the ability to create leading edge World Wide Web sites by combining ABP's creative talents with Bellcore's technology capabilities. Each company retains its core capabilities but a new value chain has been created, allowing each to participate in a broader market.

As it examines the expanding world of smart cards, this book will look at the trends in each of the major industries currently addressed in the Smart Card Forum Working Groups. An industry by industry analysis, however, misses an important fact of life: industry boundaries are changing. Exhibit 4–1 depicts some of the movements taking place.

These boundaries are changing for many reasons. A dominating factor is the introduction of an electronic infrastructure to reduce barriers that might otherwise inhibit partnerships and product line expansions into new areas of products and services. Thus, we argue that electronic commerce accelerates the changes to traditional industry boundaries for everyone.

Information Services Like it or not, most industries are moving toward having information services become a critical component of their product and service offering. This is true whether a company has a consumer-oriented

CHAPTER 4   Shifting Boundaries   59

E X H I B I T   4–1

Shifting Industry Boundaries

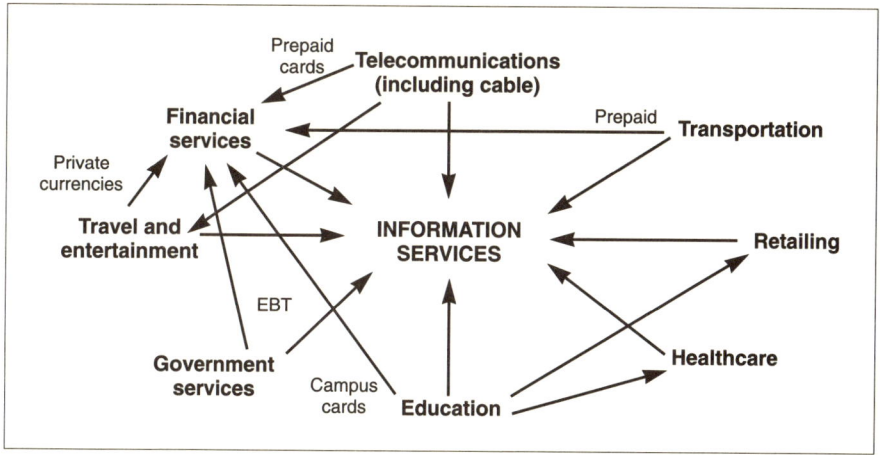

marketplace or a business-to-business marketplace. Thus, we see all of our industry groups moving towards the information services industry.

Financial Services   Exhibit 4–1 contains various implications for a number of different industry groups, but financial services is unique in that it can be seen as a relatively near-term target for many other groups. There are two reasons for this: Maturity of the financial services industry as an information service provider and the low barriers other industries face when entering the payments and transaction processing businesses. As Colin Crook, the Senior Technology Officer at Citicorp, likes to say: "Money is the purest form of information."

Maturity   The financial services industry has been automating and moving toward information services at a very rapid rate. Trillions of dollars are moved over electronic networks every day without a piece of paper being handled. Customers are now able to transact most of their financial transactions remotely, if they choose to do so. This provides an opportunity for non-banks to extend their brand and offer financial services. This is particularly useful for companies with strong brand recognition and a good customer interface. Witness the success story of the AT&T Universal, GM, and Shell credit cards.

Low Barriers to Entry   Unlike brick and mortar banking, information technology provides relatively low barriers to entry. In this environment we can see a new entrant, like Charles Schwab, move quickly by using information technology to establish a significant market position. Other industries are launching closed payments systems in their market. While expansion into open systems is not a foregone conclusion for these companies, the option certainly exists. Examples of companies positioned to move nationally or globally include US West with its prepaid, smart card-based, phone card in the telecommunications industry and Club Med's test of replacing their legendary bead-based monetary system with one that uses smart cards. Other possibilities are less far along. Airline companies, considering using smart cards for electronic ticketing and frequent flyer programs, are also considering closed system stored value applications, for example, to buy drinks or rent headphones in flight. This again is a step towards the financial services industry.

A good portion of this book looks at the applications of smart card technology on an industry by industry basis. One of the impacts of organizing the material in this fashion is the impression that smart cards will be used, issued, and carried along that type of structure. Again, nothing could be further from the truth. Rather, a main attraction of the smart card to consumers is the potential to consolidate the number of cards they have to carry around. As discussed previously, Smart Card Forum market research indicates that the true attraction of smart cards for the consumer is not as a purse to carry electronic money (the stored value application) but as a purse to carry around all the various pieces of information that currently take up one dedicated card apiece. Once the card as an information carrier is in place, the viability of stored value as an additional application is much more attractive.

COMMUNITIES OF INTEREST

The electronic infrastructure is currently an extremely complex environment. While many classify it by using popular phrases like "Information Superhighway," and "Electronic Village," with entirely positive connotations, we prefer to think of it as an "Electronic Casbah." This is a place in which, at least for visitors, the rules are at best confusing and at worst nonexistent. It costs an outsider a great deal of energy to figure out how to engage in effective commerce in such a nonintuitive environment. Modern corporations, as well as consumers, often can spare neither the time nor the energy to figure these things out. Consequently, there is a strong move toward creating electronic communities of interest within which the participants can set the rules and the culture to meet the needs of the community.

These electronic villages attract companies and customers with similar cultural and environmental biases. They create rules that are comfortable and meet their needs. They create marketing environments in which cross-selling is natural and convenient. They create electronic environments in which partnerships are easy and natural. The low barriers to entry and exit, discussed earlier, mean that other factors determine the participation in business deals.

There is a wide range of types of communities of interest and other sorts of electronic villages. Fundamentally, there are no differences (at least as yet) in motivations or behaviors in the electronic domain from the physical domain. It's just easier and faster to do things because moving bits is easier, faster, and cheaper than moving large collections of atoms.

HIDING COMPLEXITY AND ENDING CONFUSION

Consumers confronted with this environmental chaos are looking for ways to make sense of the whole thing. What is a telephone company doing providing credit card services? Why is a bank selling me a screen-based telephone? A community of interest provides a branded mechanism for hiding this complexity to the consumer. A community of interest will provide a single point of contact for the services desired by all community participants. This will begin to end the confusion and hide the complexity of the environment from the individual. It is the community that will provide the rules, services, and culture to satisfy its members.

From a business perspective, the community of interest is about partnerships. Such a community constitutes an electronic "Chamber of Commerce," but goes even further. The success of the community depends on the good will and behavior of each member. Providing clear and simple services requires each community member to abide by community rules and partner with each other. This is not to say that competition will not exist in the village—clearly it will—but the rules for competition will be clear, as it must be to ensure the survival of the community. Just as barriers to entry are lower for companies entering new businesses, there are very few exit barriers preventing *customers* from leaving and joining a new community. Indeed, we can expect that many customers will belong to several communities at once.

The Smart Card Forum is an example of a "community of interest" that has been responsible for launching the smart card industry in North America.

A COMMUNITY OF INTEREST IN MY POCKET

A smart card is a very intriguing piece of technology. It already has as much power and memory as early personal computers. Smart cards will continue to ride the technology curves providing increasing power and capability at decreasing cost. As this happens, a target will emerge for business: to become the provider of the multifunction and multiapplication smart card that carries all of the information about a consumer's participation in a community of interest. This card will be able to do everything the consumer needs it to do: make phone calls, pay bills, speed up the visit to the doctor's office, upgrade an airline seat to first class, or get the reduced price on potato chips at the supermarket.

Just as the electronic infrastructure supported by the Internet and its interconnected networks is creating a community of interest on-line, the smart card industry is evolving toward the same end point. Exhibits 4–2A and B depict two lines of evolution that are being followed toward creating the multifunction community of interest in my pocket.

Partnering among niche providers At this writing, the smart card marketplace is primarily a single function niche market—though some of the niches are quite large. Each participant is looking at how smart card technology can improve its business environment. Already, we can see that these participants are motivated to partner with each other to provide increased capability on a single card, turning the card into an opportunity for access to a larger market. As depicted in Exhibit 4–2A, this combining of niche players into broader product offerings is one way to get to the larger goal.

E X H I B I T   4–2A

Partnering to Achieve Multiapplication Goals

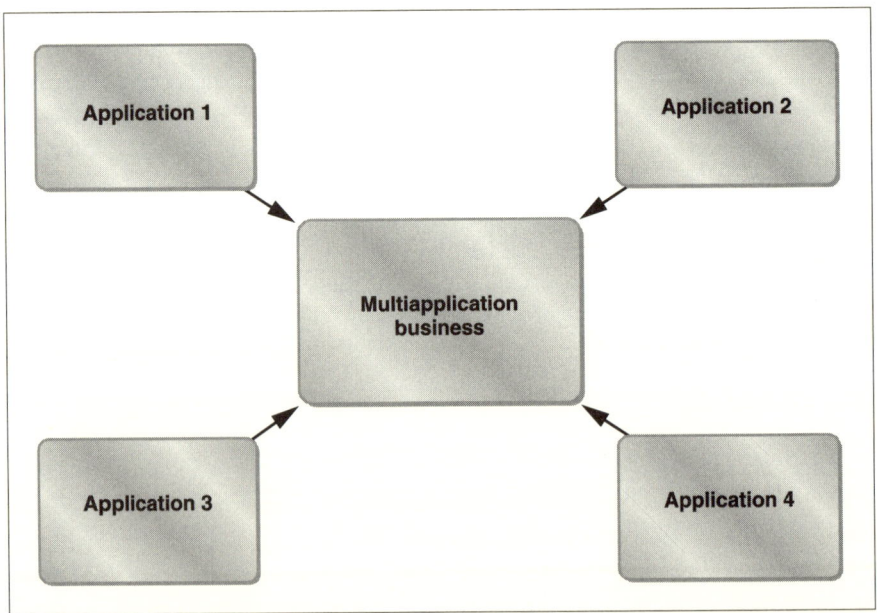

EXHIBIT 4-2B

Growing Niche Market for Multiapplication Cards

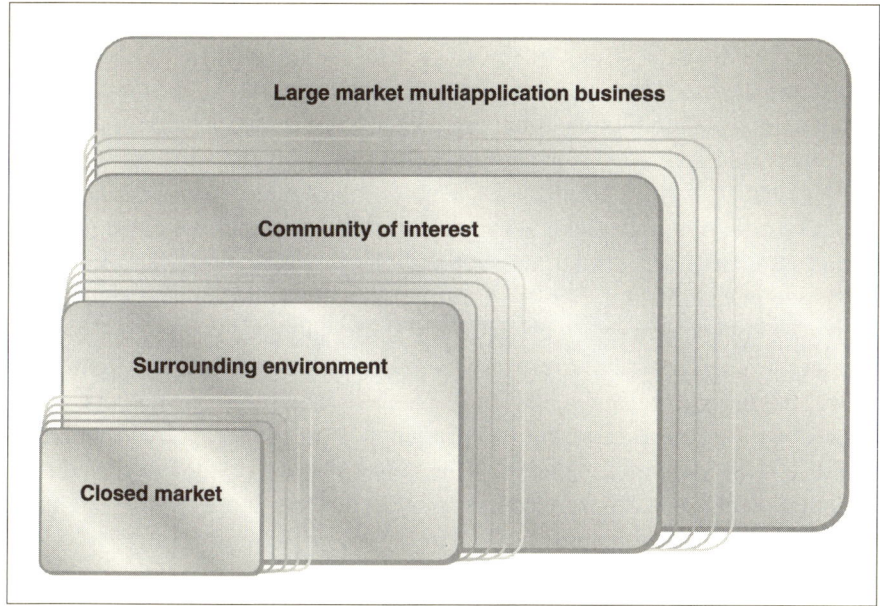

Expanding markets The second way to achieve a multifunction service in a wide market, as depicted by Exhibit 4-2B, is to start small and grow. This is what is happening at several university campuses. The university environment, for economic, security, and other reasons, has put together all the necessary partners and other business relationships to provide multifunction cards that provide vital services such as meal plans, dormitory security, online access to digital libraries, college grill purchases, college bookstore services, laundry machine operations, and other services critical to college students. However, once in place and successful, this initially closed system finds the marketplace demanding that it open. The pizza place adjacent to the university competes directly with the college grill and demands that the stored value card that buys students a burger at the grill also be capable of buying pizza across the street. Students and faculty demand that their card also work on buses and trains operated under municipal authority. And so on. This ripple effect is most effective in "college towns," those relatively small communities dominated by a college or university. Similar ripple effects will also work for other communities of interest.

What does this mean to the shifting boundaries of the various industries we will look at? For one thing, there is a tremendous opportunity for a single company to brand the card that will make the consumer's life easier and thus manage the consumer's relationships. The consumer's mind has room to remember only a limited number of relationships, certainly less than ten. Thus, the opportunity to provide the relationship management service is very attractive.

Can you be the relationship manager? Since all of the relationships we are talking about are rooted in information services, and all industries are becoming information service intensive, the opportunity essentially exists for anyone to manage the consumer's relationships. This is particularly true for companies with strong brand identification and a consumer image associated with "trust" and "reliability." However, this opportunity will not come easily. A number of new information services will be required to manage a consumer's relationships. Most important among these is a backup service that can accurately restore the contents of a consumer's smart card. This is not difficult for static information such as identification numbers. However, dynamic information such as frequent flyer miles requires inter-relationships with essentially everyone the consumer has relationships with—a daunting proposition. The companies who can sort this challenge out and bring a high trust product to market will be in a strong position.

MULTIPLE APPLICATION CARDS

Value Added Propositions The business case for smart cards in North America depends largely on shared infrastructure costs and value added application propositions. The rest of the world has justified smart cards on the basis of cost or fraud reduction, but they too are seeing the value of multiple applications on a single card.

The Smart Card Forum initially based its existence on the vision of multiple industry players with multiple services working together to enable interoperability on cards as well as systems. Similar industry groups are emerging in Europe, Asia, and South America to focus on multiple application cards.

As mentioned previously, Smart Card Forum research found strong consumer interest in multiple application cards. Fifty percent of respondents thought they were a good-to-excellent idea. Exhibit 4–3 indicates that interest.

Multiple application cards were desired in vertical applications such as government services, calling cards, travel cards, and healthcare. Exhibit 4–4 shows some of those desired applications.

The questions raised in the industry on who issues the card, holds the liability, services the customer and dictates the branding are much easier to address when one player controls the card. The challenges come with open system multiple application cards that include multiple issuers, multiple

CHAPTER 4 Shifting Boundaries

EXHIBIT 4-3

Consumers Are Favorable toward Multiple Application Cards

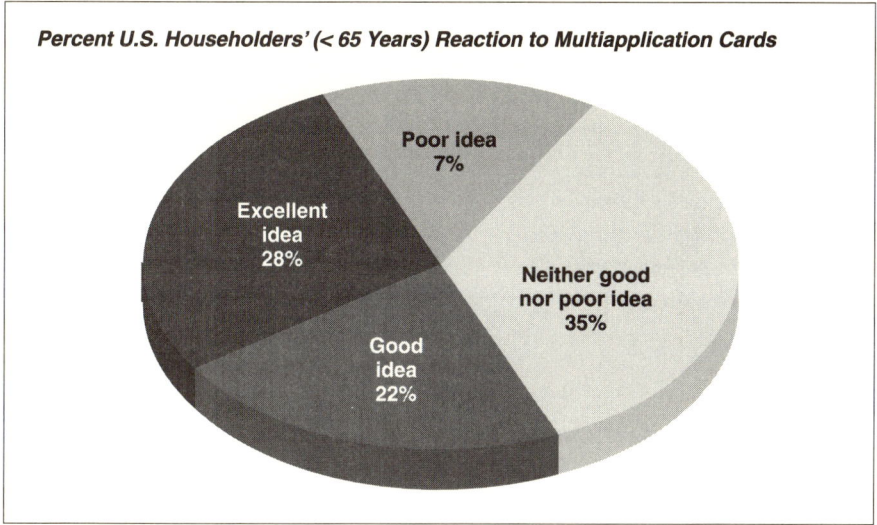

Percent U.S. Householders' (< 65 Years) Reaction to Multiapplication Cards

- Poor idea 7%
- Excellent idea 28%
- Neither good nor poor idea 35%
- Good idea 22%

Source: Smart Card Forum, 1994

EXHIBIT 4-4

Multiple Application Cards Are Desired as Vertically Integrated

Calling Card
- Phone numbers
- Prepay
- Directory services
- Wireless communication
- Internet access
- Registration

CIGNA
- Eligibility verification
- Medical profile
- Co-payment
- Emergency records
- Benefits description

Delta Airlines
- Crown Room verification
- Frequent flyer i.d.
- Ticket/boarding pass
- Redemption
- Travelers checks
- Car keys

Driver's license
- Social Security
- Benefits
- Library card

EXHIBIT 4-5

Smart Card Trials in the United States

- Education/campus cards
- Banking/electronic purse cards
- Access card for delivery systems, e.g., screen phones
- EBT/healthcare cards
- Transportation/electronic purse cards
- Travel/rewards cards
- Purchasing cards
- GSM/telecommunications cards
- Interactive television cards

acceptors, and multiple functions. Exhibit 4–5 shows current smart card trials in the U.S. that are already underway.

Let's move beyond general categories and look at some specific areas:

- The Governor's office in Utah has led a project, now being implemented in Salt Lake City, that pools public and private sector partners in introducing a statewide card with payment, loyalty, and membership information. It may eventually include driver's license and Electronic Benefits Transfer (EBT).
- NationsBank, Wachovia, First Union, VISA, MARTA, Bell South, and others worked together to provide a stored value card system (VISA Cash) for the Atlanta Olympics, but are also planning for longer term, multifunction card deployment.
- Ohio is implementing an EBT smart card that will eventually serve as a consolidated welfare program card and driver's license.
- Operators of Personal Communications Systems (PCS) in the U.S. will implement the Global System for Mobile Communications (GSM) telecommunications cards that will include electronic purse applications.
- The Department of Defense is rolling out the MARC card to 12 million military personnel—a multi-purpose, personal data card that is likely to have payments applications on it.

The technology to create and implement multiple application or multifunction cards certainly exists. The issues are operational. They include:

- Who owns the cards and applications?
- Who issues the cards, owns or updates customer information and owns application keys?
- Who performs application certification and authenticity?

- Who pays for infrastructure development?
- Who controls real estate on the card and the chip?
- Who is liable for lost, stolen, or malfunctioning cards?
- Who gets the various revenue streams?
- Who owns the branding?

There are no set answers to these questions, at least not yet. The Smart Card Forum created a "strawman" for multiple application cards that is used in Working Group discussions. Existing alliances have addressed these questions on a case-by-case basis.

BRANDING AND OWNERSHIP

Credit card issuers understand the importance of "share of wallet" and "share of mind." That's why millions of dollars are spent by issuers as well as VISA, MasterCard, American Express, and Discover, to brand their names and logos. Consolidating multiple cards and services to one piece of plastic could have long-term impact on brand recognition for those who lose access to the face of the card. One has only to look at the back of an ATM or debit card to appreciate the issue.

Co-branding and affinity cards have become facts of life to credit card issuers but branding remains a serious concern. Visa and MasterCard, in anticipation of this issue for stored value cards, passed regulations last year prohibiting co-branding on the same card, either with each other or with American Express.

Consumers, on the other hand, are interested in reducing the number of cards in their wallet and want to be able to choose which applications (and brands) they want on a card. Microsoft's initial approach to smart cards with the Medici project focused on cards that consumers could load themselves. JAVA on a chip will make this a reality. The ability to download "applets" of smart card applications on a geographic basis could make standards discussions moot.

Ownership of the card becomes a critical start-up factor because smart card costs depend on the size of the chip's memory, which in turn impacts ability to have multiple functions. The owner of the card must budget for multiple applications, then "lease out" excess capacity. Consumers might choose (and pay for) increased functionality and memory if they desire fewer cards, but they will still run into resistance from applications providers who want their brands exclusively on their own issued cards.

In the end, customers will resolve this issue when choices are available—business-issued cards with multiple applications such as a Citibank VISA multiple application card or customer acquired cards that allow downloading of multiple services via their ATM or PC. This model is more likely to be promoted by the Microsofts, Intels, or IBMs of the world.

APPLICATION AND INFORMATION MANAGEMENT

Until chip memory sizes increase to support more mature operating systems, card applications will be embedded in firmware. Proper development and certification of applications as well as card initialization, become key. Codes must be installed in a secure environment. Management of cryptographic processes and keys becomes a challenge in customer downloaded applications.

Issuance and maintenance of information contained on the card becomes a similar problem. The ISO 7816-4 standard provides for partition and control of application data files, but this becomes more difficult in the consumer-driven option.

INFORMATION DEVELOPMENT

A wide variety of card acceptance devices, accepting businesses, and a supporting processing infrastructure is necessary for successful deployment of multiple application smart cards. The infrastructure may be application-specific such as telecommunications or transportation. The business case for multiple application cards must be proven for different types of services—making it a more complex task than for a single application. The problem (or opportunity), however, is that cost justification for developing the acceptance, issuance, and settlement infrastructure should be made on the basis of an open, interoperable system and shared across the various applications.

The financial services industry learned its lessons with credit cards and ATM networks. Industry players profit from collaborating in developing infrastructure and common rules as has happened in credit cards. Smart cards, however, create new business opportunities across a wide range of industries that impacts a far larger infrastructure including payphones, kiosks, PCs, wireless devices, television set top boxes and point-of-sale terminals, to name a few. Coordination and interoperability will remain a challenge, but no one player has the capability to make it happen. Alliances and partnerships become the *de facto* infrastructure.

REVENUE SHARING

Ownership of the customer relationship, the infrastructure and the applications influences the revenue collection and sharing options. Allocating revenues from the float or funds pool in a consumer driven model is relatively easy and straight-forward based on contractual negotiations after selection of applications. In the issuer or business driven model, the negotiation involves partnering with other organizations which influence processing requirements and costs.

LIABILITY

The potential liability for lost, stolen or malfunctioning cards will eventually come back to the issuers, if U.S. consumer protection laws and regulations like Regulation E guidelines, as drawn for financial services companies, are any gauge of what's to come. It is likely that PINs and other security or identification components will be needed with smart cards to reduce potential fraud risks as well as most customer demands.

Another approach to liability may be insurance pools to protect individuals as well as issuers—the equivalent of FDIC insurance for stored value.

The business and operational issues we have just addressed are identifiable and even resolvable. The emerging legal and regulatory issues are not only some of the most challenging but are also the most difficult to resolve without industry collaboration. The Smart Card Forum's Legal and Public Policy Committee has taken leadership positions on many of these issues.

LEGAL, REGULATORY, AND PRIVACY ISSUES

The creativity generated by the effort to develop the most successful smart card applications breaks new legal and regulatory ground and provides a new vehicle for the never-ending public debate over privacy and consumer protection. The best indicator that smart cards have arrived as a significant business tool is the number of lawyers and government regulators interested in smart cards and studying the legal, regulatory, and policy issues presented by the technology's implementation. While that may not be comforting to the business executives determining which applications have the best prospect for revenue generation, the business case for every smart card application, particularly multiapplication cards, must address legalities and the presence of lawyers.

The philosopher/satirist Voltaire lamented, "I was never ruined but twice: once when I lost a lawsuit, and once when I won one." Perhaps if Voltaire had been a bit less philosophical and more attentive to the interplay of economic and legal issues, he could have avoided those lawsuits. The purpose of this segment is to address some of the principal legal, regulatory, and public policy issues which business executives must consider in assessing the economics of bringing a smart card application to market.

THE FEDERAL RESERVE BOARD AND REGULATION E

The ultimate advantage of a multiapplication smart card may be the ability of an issuer to "consolidate a consumer's relationships" on a single card. That is an exciting prospect. However, combining on a single card functions and businesses which have never before been so intertwined creates difficult legal and regulatory issues, in large part because many of those functions and businesses—banking, telecommunications, and healthcare—are already regulated in some fashion. In a sense, the issuer of a multiapplication card is much like a landlord who leases space and must ensure that the various proposed tenant uses are permitted by applicable zoning ordinances and similar regulations. If a smart card "landlord" or "tenant" anticipates a financial use, a key element of many multiapplication cards, particular attention must be paid to Regulation E.

Regulation E was promulgated by the Federal Reserve Board as the implementing regulation for the Electronic Fund Transfer Act of 1978. It is designed to protect consumers and defines the rights and obligations of consumers and "financial institutions" with respect to electronic transactions affecting consumer accounts. The term "financial institution" has been given a very expansive definition by the legislation and the Federal Reserve Board. As a result, many smart card issuers which are not traditional banks or lending institutions will be covered by Regulation E.

Regulation E is important because it:

- Provides rules for the manner in which certain "access devices," such as debit cards, may be solicited and issued.
- Establishes the conditions and terms of disclosure for providing those devices.
- Requires documentation in the form of transaction receipts and periodic account statements.
- Sets forth limitations on consumer liability (at present $50).
- Details how consumer disputes will be resolved.

The Federal Reserve Board has determined that stored value cards are subject to Regulation E and has recently issued proposed amendments to "Reg E" explaining how it believes the regulation should apply to stored value cards. However, the Board has chosen not to apply Regulation E to all stored value cards or stored value card systems. Exhibit 4–6 is a summary of how Regulation E, in its proposed form, would apply to stored value cards.

Significantly, Regulation E would exclude from coverage any stored value card which has a maximum stored value of $100. For cards exceeding that amount, there would be regulatory distinctions based on the type of stored

EXHIBIT 4-6

Summary of Regulation E Proposed Stored Value Card Requirements as of Summer 1996

A. System Types	B. Prohibits Unsolicited Issuance	C. Initial Disclosures	D. Change in Terms Notice	E. Receipts	F. Periodic Statements	G. Liability Limits	H. Error Resolution Procedures	I. Annual Error Resolution Notices
1. Stored value account not greater than $100	No	No	No	No	No	No	No	No
2. Off-line unaccountable stored value systems	No	No	No	No	No	No	No	No
3. Off-line accountable stored value systems	No	Yes	No	No	No	No	No	No
4. On-line stored value systems	Yes	Yes	No	Yes	No*	Yes	Yes	No

* Balance and transaction history provided upon request.

value delivery system used. An off-line unaccountable system (no immediate electronic authorization and no tracking of individual transactions) would be totally excluded from coverage. An off-line accountable system (no immediate electronic authorization but tracks individual transactions) would be subject only to the initial disclosure requirements of Regulation E.

However, the Board has proposed more rigorous requirements for on-line systems (immediate electronic authorization and tracking individual transactions). Those systems would be excused from some Regulation E restrictions, but would remain subject to the transaction receipt and consumer liability limit mandates. The rationale for this distinction between systems appears to be that the additional requirements should not be unduly burdensome for on-line systems, because their ability to comply with the receipt requirement is already built in, and the tracking mechanism allows faster cancellation for a lost or stolen device. That appears to reflect a misunderstanding of the technology. For example, not all stored value on-line systems are set up to provide transaction receipts. In addition, the imposition of greater costs and liability risks for on-line systems may result in a movement by issuers to less secure off-line systems. That may not be beneficial to consumers. These and other issues were raised by the Smart Card Forum with the Federal Reserve Board during the comment period which ended in August, 1996. Clearly, the evolution of Regulation E should be followed closely by businesses developing smart card applications with financial components.

OTHER FEDERAL AGENCIES

Other federal agencies are currently reviewing the legal and public policy issues presented by the financial aspects of smart card technology.

The Federal Deposit Insurance Corporation (FDIC) has established an internal New Banking Technologies Task Force which is studying developing technologies, such as stored value card programs, on-line (PC) banking, and electronic checking. One of the significant issues yet to be resolved is whether the value represented on a stored value card is a "deposit" for purposes of federal deposit insurance coverage.

The Office of the Comptroller of the Currency (OCC) has formed an Electronic Money Working Group to analyze the impact of what it calls "E-money" on banking regulation and financial stability. According to Comptroller of the Currency Eugene Ludwig, the purpose of this Working Group is to "assure confidence in a payment system that offers security and guarantees privacy" and to generate a "thorough, thoughtful debate on how best to create a truly competitive, high-tech, safe, and sound financial services industry and economy." Among the specific issues being addressed are:

- Who should be permitted to issue electronic cash?
- If nonbanks are permitted to issue electronic cash products, what supervision is appropriate?
- Will the involvement of nonbanks create a competitive inequality for the banking industry?
- Must electronic cash transactions be auditable for law enforcement purposes?

Mr. Ludwig has expressed concern that many of the current laws and regulations are based on geography while emerging technologies make geography irrelevant. In this environment, "many institutions face multiple federal and state regulatory bodies—a hydra-headed monster that requires legions of lawyers and compliance officers to combat effectively."

The reference to "legions of lawyers" does raise the question presented by Calvin Trillin: "If law school is so hard to get through . . . how come there are so many lawyers?" Part of the answer is that, frankly, it isn't that hard and there is no mysticism to the practice of law. Business people should not cede the field to the lawyers. As untasteful as it may seem, they must stay involved in the legal and regulatory issues, understand them, and appropriately direct their lawyers.

PRIVACY AND CONSUMER PROTECTION

One of the concerns raised by the OCC is how to address consumer privacy and protection. The OCC is not the only federal agency asking that question. Over the past year, the Federal Trade Commission (FTC) has developed an increasingly active interest in commercial transactions which use new age technologies. The FTC's Division of Credit Practices is exploring the consumer privacy issues rising from the provision of financial and other services involving computer and smart card type technologies. So far, those efforts have been limited to information gathering and informal discussions and it is not clear where these will lead. The FTC's public statements to date are that it is seeking ways to encourage voluntary consumer protection policies by the industries using these technologies and that it does not want its commitment to consumer protection to stifle future technology innovations. However, this is an important agency to watch.

While Regulation E and other issues, such as escheat (discussed later), may ultimately have a greater impact on smart cards and the level of economic return on smart card applications, no issue receives as much visibility as privacy. Privacy is extremely complex and it cuts across a number of disciplines including philosophy, psychology, the law, and public relations. In a philosophical sense, privacy is a tool which allows us to define ourselves in some fashion. It is a blend of autonomy and dignity; it is the right to be left alone. To some business people, privacy is simply a consumer preference; that is, another choice that a consumer in this highly commercialized society can make—a choice that can be bargained away to the highest commercial bidder in return for some perceived benefit (like a credit card).

The media love the "privacy issue" and consumer surveys consistently reflect the fact that privacy is a major consumer concern. A cynic might point out that the concern American consumers have over losing their privacy is more highly developed than is their awareness that there is actually little privacy left to lose. Whether or not this consumer concern is justified, it exists, and it must be addressed.

The less consumers understand a particular technology, the greater their level of concern. The new technologies of the Information Age are often confusing or misunderstood. To consumers, these technologies allow for the creation of data images—virtual selves—which must go out and compete in a brutal, invisible marketplace in which decisions are made, at multiple megabytes per second, that will determine a consumer's destiny, grant or deny that consumer access to benefits, privileges, or property rights or cause a reputation to suffer or survive intact. Perhaps the issue is not privacy so much as it is the loss of control and a resulting loss of trust. Consumers are not necessarily reluctant to share personal information for legitimate purposes. What they resent and fear is losing control over that information once it is provided. Lack of full disclosure as to how the information will be used also creates concern. Privacy in the economic world is about tradeoffs. Understanding what benefits are being received in exchange for the requested loss of privacy will lead to greater consumer acceptance.

Smart cards are actually consumer empowerment tools. They provide consumers with a high degree of data base control. The consumer carries the information with him or her on a microprocessor chip and, to an unprecedented extent, decides what information goes on the card and who receives access to it. The consumer can play a large role in custom tailoring his or her relationship with the issuer and the merchant or other third party.

However, smart cards also have the potential to pull a great many transactions from the anonymous world of cash into the carefully mapped world of transaction records and audit trails. Those facts create legal and consumer acceptance issues, such as:

- Who "owns" the personal data stored on the cards and who is responsible for its security and accuracy?
- What transaction records exist?

- Who will have access to the documentary trail of such areas as purchases, telephone toll records, and transportation records, which could translate readily into a diary of a person's movements? Direct marketers? Family members? Employers? Private detectives? Benefits officers? Historians? Social scientists? Bank personnel? Law enforcement investigators and their computers?

It is not possible to go to one source to answer these and similar questions. U.S. privacy law does not unfold in a comprehensive, organized regulatory structure. Instead, it has developed over time, in response to perceived abuses or deficiencies, sector-by-sector, bestowing strong protection on some varieties of personal information, such as attorney-client communications, and virtually none elsewhere, such as supermarket transaction records, telephone toll records, or travel information.

The variety of privacy legislation can be seen in Exhibit 4–7, which is a *non-inclusive* list of types of information protected by selected federal privacy statutes. At the state level, in addition to legislation covering many of these same areas (sometimes mirroring the federal approach, at other times with a different and often more protective spin), there are efforts to protect additional categories of personal information, including personal information in the employment relationship, information in the hands of insurers, library records, medical records (e.g., HIV/AIDS info), prescription drug purchase transaction records, rape victim identification records, and Medicaid records.

EXHIBIT 4–7

Examples of Information Protected by Federal Statutes Alone:

- Credit records (Fair Credit Reporting Act)
- Tax return and tax filing information (Internal Revenue Code)
- Banking and financial records (Electronic Funds Transfer Act)
- Information communicated electronically (Electronic Communications Privacy Act)
- Labor-related records such as union membership (National Labor Relations Act)
- Benefits-related records (Computer Security Act; Privacy Act)
- Video rental or sale records (Video Privacy Protection Act (Bork Bill))
- Cable television subscriber records (Cable Communications Privacy Act)
- Family and educational records (Family Educational Rights and Privacy Act)
- Certain types of medical records (though these are primarily addressed at the state level)
- Social security numbers and information

Smart card activities and the consumer relationships issuers develop will have to adapt to this patchwork structure, but it is beyond our scope, here, to provide them with an in-depth guide. However, the issue of privacy in the smart card context does not have to be a liability. It can be a marketing opportunity for those issuers willing to educate consumers and address their concerns: to enter into a "contract with consumers."

CONTRACT WITH CONSUMERS

To meet the privacy issue head on, the card issuer should start with the premise that the consumer is the owner of the personal information being requested and clearly describe what information is needed—and why. Specifically, the contract should:

- Define the consumer's rights to, and responsibility for maintenance or updating of, personal information stored on a smart card.
- Make full disclosure not only of the purposes for which the personal information will be used but also of the circumstances under which it, or information generated as a result of a smart card transaction, will be disclosed to business affiliates or third parties.
- Stipulate the privacy protection measures that will be followed by the issuer, its business affiliates and third parties with respect to that information.
- If the particular application requires compliance with state or federal laws (Reg E, Fair Credit Reporting Act, State Privacy Acts, etc.), identify those laws and confirm a commitment to compliance.
- Specify how long the information will be retained, as well as when and how it will be disposed of.
- Provide the consumer with the right of access to the information and a process for correcting errors.
- Reference or attach the issuer's corporate privacy protection policy.

In summary, while privacy issues can be complex, the basic consumer issues of control and trust can be met by providing consumers the knowledge they need to understand the tradeoffs for using smart card products to their advantage.

ESCHEAT

Escheat is not something one does with respect to income tax returns. It is, at first glance, much more esoteric. Escheat is a feudal law concept succinctly described as "a reversion of property to the state in consequence of a want of any individual competent to inherit." Why is this concept a concern to businesses contemplating smart card applications?

The answer lies in the fact that every state has adopted some version of the escheat concept, most states adopting a version of what is known as the Uniform Unclaimed Property Act. Banks are very familiar with these statutes because compliance is required for abandoned consumer accounts. However, these statutes do not apply just to banks nor do they apply simply to accounts at financial institutions.

Under the statutes, states may claim "abandoned property" which is generally defined as property which has been "dormant" for a statutorily prescribed period of years (5 years for most property; 15 years for traveler's checks). The concept of property is defined broadly enough to include many, if not all, stored value products. As an example:

Customer pays retailer $100 for a closed system, stored value card, uses the card once ($10 purchase) and does not use the card again for the dormancy period. For unclaimed property purposes, the retailer is a "holder" and the customer is the "owner" of a $90 performance obligation. The retailer/holder must comply with the reporting, notice, and delivery requirements of the state statute.

Reporting requirements vary by state, but in general the holder must report the name and last known address of the apparent owner of each item of property over a particular value (no specified amount in New York, $25 for the Uniform Act and California, $50 for Texas and Delaware, and $100 for Massachusetts). For items under the specified amount, the holder can report the value in aggregate.

At the time the report is filed, or up to six months thereafter depending upon the state, the holder is required to deliver the property [the $90 obligation in the example] to the state, as "custodian" for the owner, at which time the holder is freed from further liability. The Uniform Act and other state statutes, however, require the holder to maintain available records for such property for up to 10 years after it has been reported.

Which state has jurisdiction? If the address of the owner is known: the state of the owner. *Texas v. New Jersey*, 379 U.S. 674 (1965). If the address of owner is not known: the *state of incorporation* of the holder. *Delaware v. New York*, 113 S.Ct. 1550 (1993).

"Anti-cheating" provisions are designed to preclude creative efforts to avoid these statutes. For example, a contract between the owner and the holder that specifies that any unused value reverts to the holder upon failure to use or at an expiration date is generally void.

As might be expected, there are no reported cases involving the application of the unclaimed property statutes to smart cards. However, compliance with the unclaimed property statutes is highly recommended because of the severe penalties for failure to properly report unclaimed property as abandoned.

CONCLUSION

There are a number of other legal and regulatory issues which may have to be addressed depending on the nature of the smart card application. For example, is the issuer of a stored value card going to be treated as a "bank" for federal or state purposes? Will there be export control restrictions with respect to smart cards because of the encryption used with applications? And, finally, how will general commercial law principles which have evolved in connection with "old-fashioned" payment systems apply to new payment vehicles like smart cards. The purpose here, however, is not to address all issues but to highlight those which are most significant and current. It is clear that the technology of smart cards is adaptable. Whether consumers, regulators, and lawyers are remains to be seen.

Shifting boundaries, as discussed in this chapter, apply not only to what businesses and industries we play in and who the players are, but also to how the playing field is created. The legal/regulatory issues briefly discussed will be critically important factors in how the field looks and the game is played. Smart card technology is an enabler to organizations seeking competitive advantage. The strategies, products, and services emerging now for smart cards are an example of how business will be conducted in the 21st century: Through joint development and deployment, alliances, and adaptable/flexible organizations that bring continual streams of new innovations to market.

CHAPTER 5

Leveraging New Business Opportunities and Differentiating Your Products and Services

William Keenan
Convergence Group

Martha Rea
PSI

Gerald Hubbard
Micro Card Technologies

Bringing a new product like smart card-based applications to market is like walking up the down escalator. If you stand still you are going to go backwards. There are many critical success factors and interdependencies that will either make or break the introduction of smart cards. Considerations include timing, product features, pricing, cost structure, adaptability, and resources. However, the most important requirements are customer demand and filling wants and needs, providing real value and benefits to customers. An organization's success will largely be determined by the competitive environment, marketing effectiveness, substitution alternatives, and the bargaining position of both the suppliers and buyers of a product. Marketing and communications are the keys to managing the realm of perceptions. What customers perceive about a product becomes the reality. The challenge with smart cards is not only introducing a new technology but new applications such as electronic purse or stored value or loyalty programs. This chapter emphasizes the tools and strategies that can favorably position smart cards in the consumer's mind.

TRADITIONAL VERSUS INTELLIGENT MARKETING

Segmentation, in its simplest form, is the notion of identifying and marketing to homogenous consumer groups with similar likes and dislikes and demonstrating a greater propensity to buy a company's product than other consumer segments do. By contrast, product positioning communicates the material or psychological benefits of a product against a competing frame of reference. The objective would be to occupy or own a position in a consumer's mind. The customer is the starting point for developing a profitable position.

The first step is to analyze the relevant applications markets for smart cards. This includes profiling competitors, their respective product lines and projected financial performance. This is difficult to do right now because of the emergence of new players and applications for smart cards.

The second step is to develop a comprehensive insight into the appropriate market segments. This may include qualitative research, such as focus groups for various concepts and product configurations, which are then presented to small groups of representative buyers for their evaluation and feedback. Qualitative research provides directional insight for narrowing product focus and aiding in product development. The next step would be to conduct statistically significant, projective quantitative research. Various techniques can be used to identify and weigh unique product features and attributes in terms of consumer appeal, the most notable of which is conjoint analysis (a research technique that measures the influence of unique features and combinations of features of a consumer's propensity to buy and continue using a product).

The problem with researching customer acceptance of new technologies and applications is the proliferation of unknowns. Most smart card issuers are doing concept testing and organizations like the Smart Card Forum are doing quantitative research: But it's in the pilots where real learning takes place.

Concurrent with the research and product development processes, field market trials can be conducted and provide excellent indicators for new product initiatives. Dry testing (a technique for doing a market trial in a controlled environment in which such things as advertising concepts and packaging design are tested, but not the actual product) is another technique that many companies use to deploy technology in a lab environment prior to market release. All of these forms of research are useful in getting market feedback which then can be built into the product design to enhance market receptivity and quality. In the United States, issuers have been cautious to position their efforts as pilots or operational trials rather than rollouts, because of the challenges and opportunities smart cards present.

Developing an offering that creates or fulfills consumer demand is as much presentation as substance. There are many examples of similar or equal products that have differentiated themselves based on presentation or positioning. One example is Coke and Pepsi. Pepsi has identified itself as the youthful brand for the Pepsi generation while Coke has established its market leadership position as the "real thing." The taste difference between the two products is narrow but the imagery clearly addresses separate market segments. The same could hold true for smart cards. VISA Cash is positioned as a disposable stored value card for small value transactions. American Express is taking a position closer to the travelers check business with customer relationships as key.

Breaking down the components of a market entry strategy into its marketing and media mixes can be helpful in managing the process. The classic marketing mix can be broken down into the four Ps: Product, Promotion, Price, and Physical Distribution. The traditional media mix can be broken down into general advertising, direct marketing, telemarketing, and interactive media. Each of these ingredients requires a dedicated strategy and commensurate resources.

As an example, a product strategy may include developing a smart card product with three applications. It may be used as a credit card, a calling card, and for frequent flyer management. The one device provides three applications. This may lead, assuming research supports it, to a positioning around simplicity and convenience—three cards in one. From this assessment, a pricing strategy must emerge that captures the full economic value of the product, recovering costs, and achieving profit objectives within demand parameters established by the consumer. It also requires coordination between application providers for product positioning, customer service and distribution. What happens if the credit card application is canceled by the issuers or customer? Are the other two applications on-going or is the card recalled?

A promotional strategy may include providing the card to existing credit card holders with the option to activate other applications on the chip at the customer's choice, reinforced by aggressive promotion by the supplier. Distribution strategies may include direct marketing or general advertising supported by inbound telemarketing. Each element of the marketing mix is unique to given circumstances, organizational design, and marketing objectives. The media mix is an important dynamic which needs to be managed along several dimensions, especially identifying the appropriate channels and understanding how to communicate. The success of the marketing and media mix can be determined by calculating return on investment by channel as well as net present value against stated image awareness and product sales.

We discussed the diverse aspects of branding and service for multiple application cards in previous chapters. It becomes even more complicated if marketing strategies are not in sync.

TRADITIONAL MARKETING

Traditional vertical marketing presumes that the product drives the business decision (value proposition). A product focus presumes an organizational design around manufacturing and subsequently finding markets that will consume plant capacity. A value proposition or product is designed to meet consumer wants and needs. The model presumes consumers have three fundamental needs: Functional, psychological, and self-redeeming qualities. Functional needs include safety and security while psychological needs include ego gratification and ultimately self-actualization such as food, clothing, shelter, freedom from harm, when all other needs are satisfied. This model illustrates the importance of emotion when consumers make purchase decisions. The difference between a need and want can be illustrated by the following example. People need water but many may want a branded bottled water. From this example, the need is for water but the want is for a name brand beverage. When a value proposition is successfully communicated to a consumer and meets a set of needs, a purchase decision is weighed and made. Often a consumer purchase is the result of friction. This friction may be the conflict between problems and appropriate solutions or between needs and the appropriate need-satisfying benefits affiliated with the product.

With smart cards, the need may be for convenience in payments or managing information. The want may be a technology-driven new card with interesting graphics that make it a collectible. The cards bought for the Atlanta Olympics are an example. Many were bought, but few were used.

The objective in any marketing campaign or new product development initiative is to understand these dynamics, appropriately position the product and build sufficient image and awareness to circumvent any natural filtering the consumer may employ. Getting the message heard in an environment exposed to a lot of noise and clutter is the name of the game.

INTELLIGENT MARKETING

Traditional marketing models have evolved over time by rearranging elements of the media and marketing mix. Breaking the marketing process down into its key component parts has provided a means for customer focus in an otherwise product-oriented environment. Until recently there was little capability for mass customization. Recent technological advances permit many organizations to develop relationships with one customer at a time. As just-in-time inventory helped redefine the cost structure and market responsiveness for the retailing industry, just-in-time manufacturing will be the next milestone for customer-driven organizations. As successful vertical marketing is propelled by growing use of plant capacity, intelligent marketing is driven by the need to gain share of the consumer's mind.

Intelligent marketing is a customer versus product focused strategy. It is a multi-dimensional approach to fulfilling consumer needs and communicating product values. Intelligent marketing correlates the marketing and media mixes. Moreover, unlike traditional marketing, an intelligent marketing process emphasizes the interdependencies and interrelationships between each of the four Ps. Rather than viewing product, promotion, price, and physical distribution in isolation, it manages strategies that may fall along one or all of those

EXHIBIT 5–1

Intelligent Marketing Elements

Marketing Mix	
Media Mix	
■ Direct mail	■ General advertising
■ Telemarketing	■ Interactive marketing
4 Ps	
■ Product	■ Price
■ Promotion	■ Physical distribution
4 Cs	
■ Consumers' wants and needs	■ Communication
■ Cost to satisfy wants and needs	■ Convenience to buy

dimensions. It views the various elements as an interdependent set of strategic initiatives that comprise a complete set of customer interactions.

In addition to the four Ps, it is important to include the four Cs in your marketing strategy. The four Cs comprise the consumer's wants and needs, the cost to satisfy the wants and needs, communication, and convenience to buy. The emphasis of the four Cs is on the customer. With the evolution of technology and a company's ability as an organization to source information and track consumer behavior transaction by transaction, it is now more possible than ever to be market focused. Unlike the vertical marketing model, intelligent marketing presumes every organization is in the business of satisfying consumer needs and wants, and fulfilling or creating demand for products that can be manufactured profitably to meet underserved or unserved markets. The objective for any campaign is to create awareness, interest, desire and a call to action or to purchase the product. Intelligent marketing elements are shown in Exhibit 5–1.

Stored value cards are well suited for multidimensional real-time marketing. Stored value cards represent one of the few products with inherent value that can be consumed while providing a medium which can reinforce value and serve as a channel for communicating end benefits. Unlike a bar of soap, which is consumed and must be repurchased periodically, a stored value card is a self-replenishing device. Various currencies and files of information can be loaded on to the card and replenished electronically as they are used.

Communications to customers may be stored electronically and communicated through the rewrite function of the appropriate network. As consumers use the card, the chip can direct that various messages be printed on receipts to remind a customer of the inherent value remaining in the card or to alert them of upcoming promotions. Few products offer the interactive potential of smart cards.

The graphics on the fronts and backs of smart cards can create a customized, personalized appeal to customers just as information in the chip can. Opportunities for branding and advertising make the card a communication vehicle as well as the product itself.

CREATING ADVANTAGE

In creating advantage, there are five tools for sustaining a competitive position. They include life cycle management, SWOT (Strengths, Weaknesses, Opportunities, Threats) analysis, an expansion of Michael Porter's Five Forces Analysis, activity chain/service blueprinting, and organizational focus. The starting point for creating competitive advantage is to recognize that every value proposition and product has a specified life period. Understanding where an organization and product ideas are within the life cycle is an essential starting point. Smart card issuers are looking for ways to differentiate themselves, especially when some of the applications, such as credit, debit, and even stored value, will become commodities.

Life Cycle Management An average smart card life cycle can be represented within a bell-shaped curve starting with an introductory phase, followed by a competitive phase, a retentive phase, decline, and ultimately repositioning. A typical life cycle matrix may capture several dimensions along the life cycle continuum. A simple curve may include age and income. Capturing a high share of the youth market with a smart card-based credit or electronic purse product may demonstrate low current earnings potential but high lifetime values. Typical credit and electronic purse transactions within the youth market result in high transaction, low dollar value activity. Intensity is high but profits are low. This may be offset through a cradle-to-grave strategy. The presumption is that the first card in a wallet may offer the highest brand loyalty. If you manage the product appropriately along the product life cycle, you can step up the appropriate product ladder through upgrades and other features and enhancements as income and key life events change. The smart card itself can be the enabler for capturing information that can be used to secure competitive advantage.

EXHIBIT 5-2

Smart Card Life Cycle Matrix

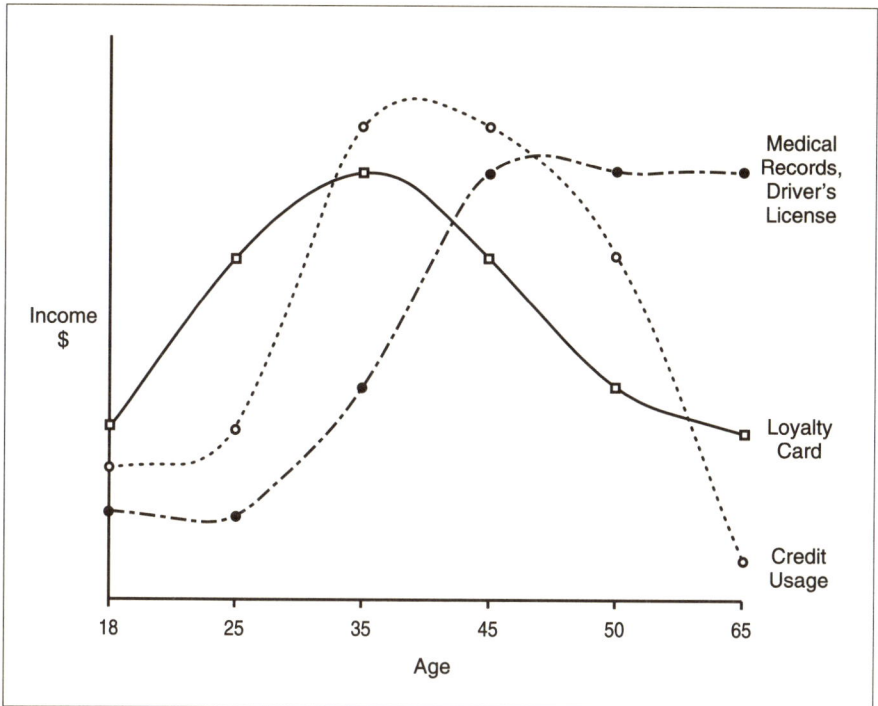

As life events change—a customer is married, enlists in the military, or has children—this information can be captured from the card and used as a means for communicating valuable information that can result in new market opportunities.

The life cycle matrix is an example of capturing a number of value propositions within one device. This capability provides unique competitive advantage. There are few products that can simply capture and communicate need-satisfying attributes across several lines of business. Most products are lined along vertical markets where credit is served and delivered by credit institutions. Telephony products such as calling cards are provided by telecommunications companies, and frequent buyer or couponing is provided by various retailing establishments. All of these capabilities can be automated and economically provided on a single device, which is difficult for competitors to duplicate, thereby raising the switching cost and increasing franchise loyalty to your brand.

Anticipating and meeting the needs and wants of your customers along the product life cycle is another way to build and sustain competitive advantage. Offering to fulfill underserved or unserved needs in advance of the competition enhances brand loyalty and diminishes the need to divert resources to win back customers.

SWOT Analysis A SWOT analysis is an important supplement to the life cycle consideration. SWOT is largely a self-assessment of the organization and product prior to launch. SWOT analysis is also used periodically to identify current market position or subsequent shifts. Against a backdrop of the competitive environment, it is essential that your organization identify core competencies or strengths as well as weaknesses relative to the competition. Against this backdrop, opportunities and threats need to be identified and evaluated.

Five Forces Analysis A useful tool in defining where your organization and product stand against the competition is a variant on Michael Porter's Five Forces Analysis. The forces include rivalry, substitution, buyer power, supplier power, and threat of new entrants. Additional considerations include technology and information. Combined, these elements form the foundation for a knowledge-based organization.

To perform a Forces Analysis, it is important to measure the intensity of the rivalry or competition within the category in which you decide to compete, and also the number of substitutes or alternatives to your product available to the consumer. The other important elements are buyer and supplier power. If suppliers have a capacity that exceeds demand and there are several supplier options with little, if any, artificial protection through patents, then the buyer has a superior power position. This can affect how the product is brought to market and the manufacturer's underlying profitability.

The barriers to entry will help determine your product's defensive position or potential for future threats and margin squeeze based on attracting new competition. Technological and information forces relative to non-smart card applications will likely determine the functional superiority of the product over other options. Each application of the smart card has its own set of industry considerations, such as stored value competing with cash and debit. Smart card technology competes with magnetic stripe and optical technologies. Each must be plotted out to consider impact on product launch.

Activity Chain Analysis With the SWOT and Five Forces Analyses we now have identified the constraining and driving influences for likely or probable success within the life cycle matrix. The activity analysis is a tool to break down the product and business into finer elements in order to identify opportunities to reach profit goals. The starting point is to identify hard sell markets. The smart card is one of the few products that can load applications that cut across various categories of business. For example, you can put frequent shopper, credit card and electronic cash functionality all on one device. There are different business fundamentals for each of these product attributes. All three horizontal markets are competing for the largest share of the revenue. Feature profitability will be determined by the relative power position of the supplier and buyer. If it is decided to integrate horizontally through strategic alliances as opposed to acquiring capabilities, it may be prudent to build core capabilities around service delivery and marketing and to generate revenues by assessing a tax or licensing fee on all of the feature providers. Acquired horizontal integration may also prove to be an effective strategy but with varying profitability.

Breaking out each of the horizontal markets into respective vertical markets is the second step in identifying the complete competitive landscape. In addition, it provides opportunities for increasing the services provided and capturing additional share from new markets. Exhibit 5–3 illustrates the break-out process.

EXHIBIT 5–3

Illustration of Multiapplication Card

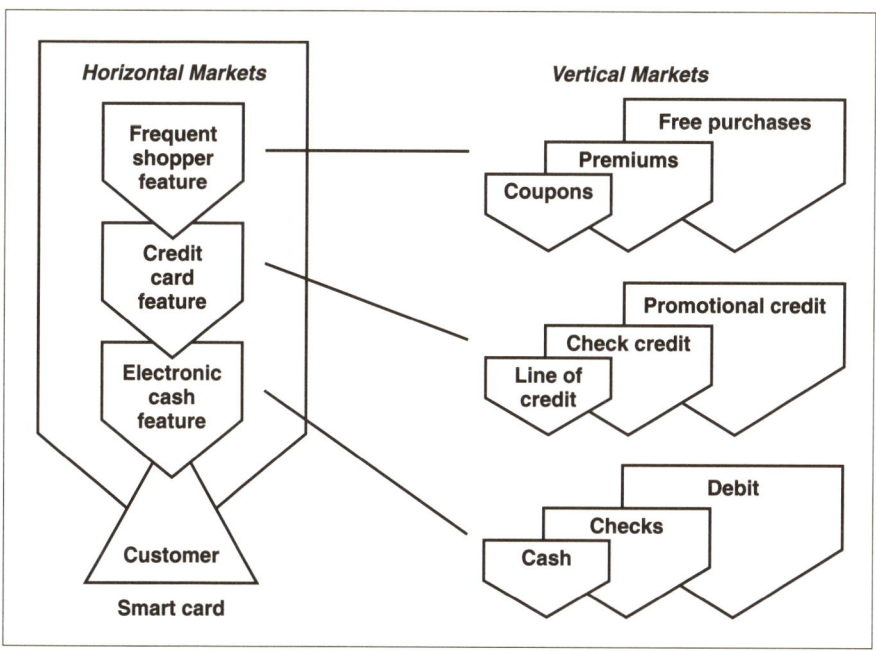

The frequent shopper feature exemplifies the relationship between the horizontal and vertical markets. The frequent shopper feature is unique when compared to the credit card or electronic cash functions. However, within the frequent shopper feature there is direct competition in the category from coupons, premiums, and free purchases. In order to compete within the vertical markets, an organization may want to consider adding these various functionalities to its card. The primary opportunity with smart card technology in loyalty programs is in cross-market functionality, in which building a brand and capturing critical consumer transaction data can enhance issuer marketing capability.

Organizational Focus All of these dynamics are important in building and sustaining competitive advantage. However, it is essential to have a focused strategy when integrating these tools. It is important to build a core competency around one strategy value discipline while meeting industry standards and the other attributes on which you wish to compete.

The central ingredient or core competency to focus on within an organization may vary with vision, mission, organizational values, and core competencies. They are unique to each organization and are influenced by shareholder or stakeholder expectations. The important thing is to have clarity in vision, insight, and executional excellence. With a central theme or organizational focus, a company can build on that platform to add unique value that is difficult to substitute in the market.

Pricing (Value)/Cost The marketing mix is an organization's attempt to create value in the market place. Pricing is an element of the four Ps but differs in that it is the first to capture some value in the form of profit. Effective pricing cannot compensate for poor execution in the other elements of the marketing or media mix, nor is it the exclusive reason for the purchasing decision. Other elements include creative, target market, and the overall offer. Ineffective pricing, however, can prevent many of those other attributes from resulting in profitability. An organization must integrate its value-creating activities within its pricing decisions.

The Japanese provide an excellent model for effective strategic pricing. Their starting point is the price which the market is willing to pay for their products while providing them the ability to earn a profit. Value-based pricing must begin before investments are made. The target price must be based on the estimate of value, not cost. Risk-based pricing is prevalent in the consumer financial services industry. However, it is just one component of cost and even a lower factor in determining value for high-risk consumer segments. Other relevant ingredients may include credit line size, relationship to the number of other accounts within the household, and payment terms.

The objective is to make the pricing decision first, predicated on extensive consumer research, and price elasticity analysis, then manage costs within the established targets to achieve profitability. The objective of value-based pricing is to capture more value, then price a product accordingly, not necessarily by making more sales. Thus the marketing challenge is to raise the customer's willingness to pay the price that reflects the product's value.

With smart cards a company can now combine calling cards with credit cards, drivers' license, and medical information to develop a direct consumer relationship that is interactive and can be monitored or modified over time.

Based on a customer's unique requirements, an organization can create models, transaction-by-transaction, and develop unique pricing schemes that meet very unique expectations. The pricing decision embodies weighing attributes and analyzing tradeoffs. Greater value is assessed with more intensity of use. Smart card technology is positioned to redefine the economics of service and product delivery. This can be illustrated with stored value cards. The telephony industry has profitably deployed smart card technology to reduce coin-handling costs within their paid phone services groups. The high margins of calling card transactions coupled with the reduction of coin-handling costs justify the investment in smart phones as well as smart cards. Building on that smart card platform to add additional features such as electronic cash, credit cards, driver's license information, medical records or frequent shopper features can be viewed as incremental costs and be priced accordingly, resulting in higher profitability.

CONCLUSION

Smart cards are an enabling technology. Their potential is yet to be tapped. Innovative experiments and creative minds will make the promise a reality. Strategic marketing will make it happen!

CHAPTER 6

Smart Cards And Electronic Commerce

William J. Barr
Bellcore

Frederick J. Honold, Jr.
AT&T Solutions

The previous five chapters have focused on smart cards as applications and payment enablers. The real potential of the technology, however, lies in how smart cards will evolve as part of a larger electronic commerce business opportunity. This chapter discusses electronic commerce in detail and provides a glimpse of how the future might look for smart cards.

A MODEL OF ELECTRONIC COMMERCE

Definition Basic commerce can be defined as the exchange of goods and services for value between buyer and seller in the marketplace. Those exchanges are accomplished via the performance of a series of interactions. This process begins with an exchange of information punctuated by an order for a good or service. When an agreement is reached, the relationship is consummated by the exchange of cash value for the good or service. This is followed by customer service. All of these interactions—by smart and growth-oriented sellers—are carefully monitored in search of more profit and new growth opportunities.

Electronic Commerce is the performance of these interactions through electronic means. Customers are reached anywhere, anytime, via the tools of information technology. For the consumer, doing business becomes convenient and easy, no matter where the interaction takes place—from the home, office, in public places, or while mobile between these arenas. The tools for conducting commerce electronically include portable computers, software to organize data into information, data networks for transport, and electronic payments mechanisms and directories. Smart cards, we believe, will play a significant role in facilitating electronic commerce in the future. Rather than viewing electronic commerce as something completely new, we find it helpful to identify the past practices of commerce and understand how they change in the new electronic infrastructure.

Size of the Opportunity Commerce in the United States today is a large market experiencing rapid change. In 1995, 360 billion payments were made from consumers to business with a total value of $2.4 trillion. Of these payments, 94 percent were material based—cash, coin, and checks, and 68 percent were for a value of less than $2.00. Electronic payments—credit cards, debit cards, and EFT—represent less than 10 percent of all payments, but are growing at 17 percent annually versus 1 percent for paper based. These payments occur in primarily two environments:

1. Point of Sale: 87 billion payments occur at the point of sale.
2. Point of Billing: 13 billion payments take place in the home at point of billing.

The rapid growth of personal computers and Internet technologies is expected to accelerate electronic commerce activities over the Internet as well. Current estimates of electronic commerce over the Internet range from $50 billion to $250 billion by the year 2000.

TECHNOLOGY BRINGS ABOUT DISINTERMEDIATION

Major changes in commerce have always been driven by technology. Technological change brings about infrastructure changeout. An important principle to keep in mind is that one implication of an infrastructure changeout, such as we are undergoing today, is the disintermediation of significant and established players in the old infrastructure. This means established positions as intermediaries between buyers and sellers are being eliminated. For example, banks have carefully positioned themselves as the vehicles for financial transactions to consumers and businesses. In the new electronic infrastructure, many of the old functions of intermediator will

---

A NEW ORDER OF THINGS

"... There is nothing more difficult to carry out, nor more doubtful of success, ... than to initiate a new order of things. For the reformer has enemies in all those who profit by the old order, and only lukewarm defenders in all those who would profit by the new order, this lukewarmness arising ... partly from the incredulity of mankind, who do not truly believe in anything new until they have had actual experience of it."

From Niccolo Machiavelli (1469–1527) in *The Prince* (1513)

no longer be needed and many others will be significantly changed. The replacement intermediaries are likely to be software services rather than brick and mortar institutions, providing a market entry opportunity for companies such as Microsoft and Intuit.

CONSUMER TO BUSINESS: A PERSPECTIVE ON THE FOUR PHASES OF ELECTRONIC COMMERCE

Commerce can be broadly divided into nine different processes, which, in turn, can be grouped into four major phases. These four phases are Decision, Order, Delivery/Service and Management. We will examine each of these four phases separately, along with their nine specific processes numbered as they occur. As a user moves from the information acquisition phase through negotiation and payments, all of the issues noted in this chapter will come into play. Smart cards will have a role in all four phases, which will be explained as we address each area. Keep in mind this model is dynamic, rather than static as the buyer and sellers interact. The four phases with their nine processes are portrayed in Exhibit 6–1.

To demonstrate what electronic commerce could become, we will describe what we think that totally automated world could look like. We use the example of purchasing a four-wheel drive vehicle in the year 2010, when all the elements are hypothetically in place and commerce is functioning as an end-to-end electronic system.

EXHIBIT 6–1

Four Phases of Interaction by Process between Buyer and Seller

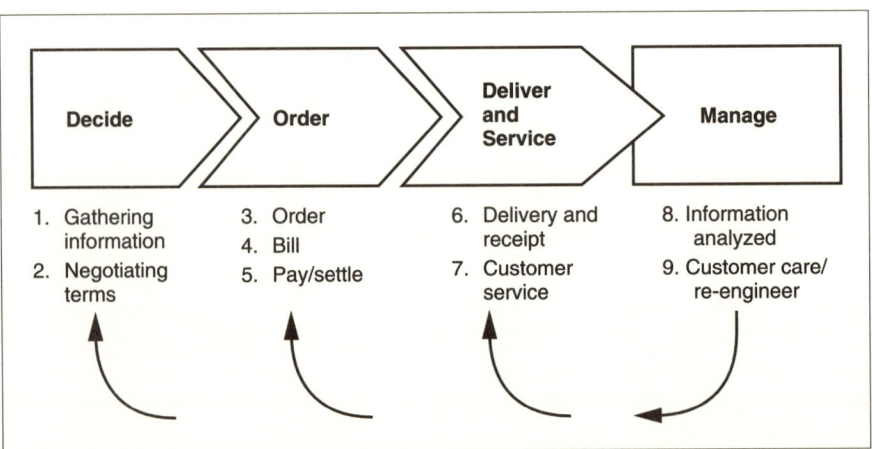

PHASE I: THE DECISION PROCESS—POWER SHIFTS TO THE CONSUMER

Before any order is placed, the consumer seeks to understand the availability, features, and pricing of certain products on the market; the suppliers of these products float controlled information in the direction of interested consumers.

1. Gather Facts and Opinions and Analysis
2. Negotiate Terms and Conditions of Purchase

2010 I insert my smart card into my laptop reader, and use it as my intelligent master ignition key to power-up my laptop for a purchase; destination, the final frontier of cyberspace. Mission, to purchase the new model year edition of the four-wheel drive convenience vehicle called the "Silver Bullet." I enter the Internet and request several items of information at once:

From the manufacturer I receive the specifications on the new Bullet, and the location of convenient manufacturer showrooms for a test drive. From the industry on-line magazine, I access articles on the Bullet and similar vehicles. From the consumer rating service, I obtain all the relevant statistics on the performance and reliability of the Bullet. From three buying services, I download a spreadsheet noting by model type and optional features the wholesale price versus the common retail price and optional financing plans.

Within 20 minutes, all of the requested information, opinions, and analysis have appeared on my screen for review. The information confirms my initial decision. Following a very enjoyable test drive (some fun parts will remain outside the world of electronic commerce), I decide to purchase the Bullet. I select my preference for the Limited Edition, the options, and float a request for bid to the selected buying services. I request an answer in three hours. Within this timeframe I have two bids, select the best option, and decide to place an order. What is significant is that I have completed the first phase of electronic commerce and have not left my office . . . except for the test drive. The smart card was my access key for information.

Issues in 2010 for Phase I

Information Distribution The distribution of information can be driven by either suppliers or consumers. In a paper-based information infrastructure, suppliers dominate the information network. To remain competitive, commercial entities must find ways of presenting their information to the consumers. Simply being passive and putting your information in directories or catalogues in libraries results in being invisible—a fatal condition for a supplier. To assure visibility, we have mass mailings, newspaper and magazine advertising, billboards and other techniques designed to place our commercial information in front of the most desirable audience. The critical aspect is the need for physical transportation of the information.

In the information infrastructure circa 2010, however, the tables are turned. Information networks like the Internet present information without the need to transport anything more than electrical signals—bits. This puts the power and the initiative in the hands of the consumer, potentially redressing the balance between consumer and supplier. Now, the consumer can rapidly search the entire universe of available information without having to leave a computer terminal. This creates an environment in which the consumer can initiate an action to ensure that the right information is available at the right time.

If there are charges for accessing information, such as a Consumer Report on an auto, the transaction can be paid from the credit or stored value applications on the smart card. Stored value allows for anonymous transactions of small value and will be used for this type of information gathering.

Negotiation The electronic infrastructure also shifts some of the power from the supplier to the consumer during the negotiation phase. In the physical world, inertia puts a great deal of power in the hands of the supplier. If a supplier has a consumer physically present in a store, or even in a telephone conversation, the supplier has a considerable advantage in negotiation, because the supplier is the only presence in the information stream available to the consumer. Further, the physical energy required to reject a supplier proposal and seek information from a new supplier is relatively large. In 2010, using an electronic information infrastructure, negotiating with several suppliers at the same time can be made relatively easy. Finally, the notion of electronic agents which could be cheaply dispatched to seek out information from, and even negotiate with, a large number of suppliers simultaneously is an additional tool strengthening the hand of consumers.

PHASE II: THE ORDER PROCESS—POWER SHIFTS TO THE SUPPLIER

With terms and conditions negotiated, a decision is made to purchase. This activates a whole new series of events with the chosen supplier. Traditionally much paper exchanges hands in this phase—the buyer/supplier agree on the order specifications, a bill is rendered, and subsequent payment is made or arranged to settle the account.

    3. Order
    4. Billing
    5. Payment & Settlement

2010 For the order function of my Bullet, I remain at my multimedia personal computer. To order, I confirm the standard vehicle, the options, and all terms and conditions. I may want to pick-up my vehicle on a trip. I may request that the vehicle be delivered to my driveway at 12 noon the following Saturday. While I as a consumer am putting the order in motion, the buying service is arranging for billing, based on the terms and conditions electronically negotiated. As part of the process, I provide the buying service with the approval to conduct a credit check, and access to certify an escrow account established for the purpose of a 20 percent down payment immediately. Further authorization is provided for the buying service to electronically confirm the five-year auto loan arranged with my consumer credit union. In this exchange, my smart card plays an integral part. It provides authentication that I am indeed the buyer, and with the appropriate PIN and/or biometrics (e.g., digital signature, finger print, etc.), and authorizes the buying service to access my appropriate financial institutions for payments. In turn, the buying service downloads an electronic authentication key to my smart card. I will use this key to confirm to the dealer and/or deliverer of the car that I am indeed the true and rightful purchaser.

If the value is smaller, such as $10,000 or less, the choice of using the credit application on the smart card also provides the buyer with greater options.

Issues in 2010 for Phase II

While suppliers may have given up some advantage using an information infrastructure for information distribution and negotiations, they gain some advantage in the payment process. The consumer also may potentially benefit by acquiring an opportunity to exercise more choice.

The three primary payment mechanisms in use today—credit cards, checks and cash—will still be recognizable in the world of electronic commerce, but they may change somewhat. Smart cards will provide the necessary authentication, authorization and even payment services to facilitate commerce.

Credit Card Payments The credit card industry in the United States is primarily an electronic payments infrastructure. However, one major problem in today's system is that fraud, a significant portion of which is due to counterfeit cards, is growing rapidly. While credit card fraud growth has flattened recently, it is still significant. Industry figures indicate that the total global credit card fraud exceeds $1.5-2 billion, while the total U.S. fraud exceeds $750 million and over 20 percent of the total fraud is traceable to counterfeit cards. Lost or stolen cards account for 40 percent of fraudulent use. The introduction of smart cards by credit card issuers will significantly improve the accuracy of card authentication and thus reduce fraud by providing an irrefutable mechanism for proper user identification. The use of the smart card to purchase the Silver Bullet, complemented by on-board biometrics, identifies and validates the authenticity of the buyer and the purchase to all parties involved. Such authentication is critical in the electronic transfer of funds, especially when large amounts are involved and the incentive for fraud increases.

Checks In today's marketplace, checks are a convenient instrument to provide payment instructions to a consumer's bank. As the electronic information infrastructure takes hold, these tools will likely evolve into electronic checks. The Financial Services Technology Consortium has advanced an electronic checking approach that mimics the existing paper check environment, even reusing part of the existing check clearing infrastructure. Digital signatures replace signatures on paper with a pen. Smart Cards or PCMCIA (Personal Computer Memory Card Interface Association) Cards replace the paper check book. E-mail replaces the trucks and airplanes used to transport the paper checks. The primary difference the consumer will see is a reduction in check clearing time from three days to one. (Note that this reduction in clearing time is happening without electronic checks as banks seek to reduce the costs of handling paper checks.) The significant change for the supplier is reduced fraud and risk of checks "bouncing" as on-line account validation will be done at the same low cost as on-line credit card validation.

Value In the paper world of currency, and in smaller metal-based denominations, we think of the "coin of the realm" as the vehicle for transmitting value. Cash and coins are primarily used in what is popularly becoming known as micropayments, payments under $10. In the United States, of the 360 billion annual consumer transactions, some 15 percent are made with checks and credit cards and some 300 billion are in the form of cash and coins. Typically in the world of manual commerce, the financial instrument of cash and coin does have one significant disadvantage—both parties must be in the same place at the same time. Electronic stored value for micropayments will remove this disadvantage. Also, the significant characteristic of this form of payment, "anonymity," will be preserved in the world of electronic value, at least to some degree. ("Absolute anonymity" is relatively rare. The personal exchange of paper cash gives the recipient an opportunity to view the giver and thus determine something relative to trust.)

PHASE III: THE DELIVERY/SERVICE PROCESS—POWER TO CONSUMER AND SUPPLIER

Coordinated with the phases of the order process and based upon the terms and conditions of the decision process, the product is delivered and maintained once in the hands of the consumer.

6. Delivery and Receipt
7. Customer Service

2010 At 12 noon, on schedule, the delivery service drives my new Bullet into the driveway. As the consumer, I finally leave my computer, walk to my front driveway, and meet the delivery service personnel. I present my smart card, the delivery service associate inserts the smart card into a handheld wireless point of sale register. The smart card has my authorization key from the buying service which I confirm with a predesignated PIN. Authorization is confirmed, giving me the right to take possession of my new Silver Bullet; a paper receipt is handed to me for my files, but the electronic receipt with all details has already been transferred to my smart card. This exchange, vehicle for electronic key, also triggers payment and settlement initiation. I have the Bullet. The buying service receives the money in full for the Bullet from my credit union via electronic funds transfer. My credit union has the right to electronically extract a regular payment from my account over the next 60 months.

As the subsequent three months pass by, I can converse with the customer service agent via my computer on any questions, and can schedule my first maintenance check at 1,000 miles. Eight A.M. on a Monday morning is confirmed. Upon pick-up of my Bullet, I use one of my many credit card numbers embedded in the smart card for payment. At the point of sale exchange, the customer service agent has all the relevant details of my first maintenance check downloaded to my smart card for future reference. The Japanese and Swedes are already testing this concept in research and development efforts on cars.

Issues in 2010 for Phase III

In this scenario, the consumer clearly feels that he is being marketed to as a "Segment of One." This is so. The smart supplier has surrounded the buyer with all the convenience and amenities necessary to gently coax the buyer to the ultimate purchase, and the buyer has enjoyed the experience. The buyer feels that the freedom of choice and the ability to garner the best deal is a win-win situation. From the seller's perspective, the technology, properly used, bonds the customer to the seller with a bundle of branded offers.

PHASE IV: THE MANAGEMENT PROCESS—POWER TO THE SUPPLIER

In this final phase, the supplier can gain an undisputed edge. If the supplier has methodically gathered the right information with the intent of tailoring his business closer to his selected segment, he moves into an increasingly powerful position. When done properly so that his customer is totally satisfied, the supplier has a customer for life.

8. Information Gathered and Analyzed
9. Customer Care/Business Process Re-Engineering

2010 It is in Phase IV of the Management Process that the supplier can gain significant advantage in the next cycle of dealing with current customers and prepare for better offers to current and future customers. During the first three phases (Decision, Order, Deliver/Service), the smart suppliers are focused on accomplishing two tasks. The first task is carefully gathering planned data on their interactions with customers. The second focus is being open to new opportunities of which they were unaware. In the final management phase, these gathered and analyzed data are then creatively utilized to provide better customer care and to re-engineer select business processes as appropriate. For the supplier, this is a point of critical competitive advantage in the world of electronic commerce. Customer intimacy can be achieved at significantly lower cost than in a materials-based environment. Here, indeed, is an opportunity to do something "cheaper, faster, and better," all at the same time!

Smart cards can contain data on customers such as transactions and maintenance records that aid in this process.

Issues 2010 for Phase IV

This final phase of putting information to work is what the Information Age is all about. The smart supplier, utilizing the horsepower of strategic planning capability, begins to take the lead in the competitive business race. To separate from the pack of existing suppliers, the smart supplier selects specific information to tailor the business as closely as possible to each customer. By the year 2010, the plethora of information will be overwhelming. Therefore, the issue will be around how to rapidly select the best information relevant to one's business and customer base. The challenge, once the information is gathered, is how to put the information to work. In 2010, the metric may be a redefined ROI, where the "I" stands for "Investment in Information". In such an environment, a premium should be placed on an ability to plan and quickly apply new information to the changes required in your business.

THE STAKEHOLDERS: PARTICIPANTS' VIEWPOINTS OF ELECTRONIC COMMERCE

In the following sections we will examine the world of electronic commerce, taking the perspective of the two participants. We will examine the perspective and requirements for success of the consumer or user and the supplier.

THE CONSUMER MODEL

The consumer in the world of electronic commerce and smart cards sees a significantly different world than the world of materials-based commerce. The *virtual marketplace* available over the electronic infrastructure can provide instant and direct access to a wide variety of information services. Exhibit 6–2 illustrates this view.

The key to the success of electronic commerce when seen through the eyes of the consumer are two dominant issues: Simplicity and Ubiquity.

SIMPLICITY

A key element for success in the eyes of the consumer is simplicity, defined as ease of use. The world of electronic commerce contains immense technical complexity behind the scenes. Yet, for the market to move beyond the early

EXHIBIT 6–2

The Consumer Model of Electronic Commerce

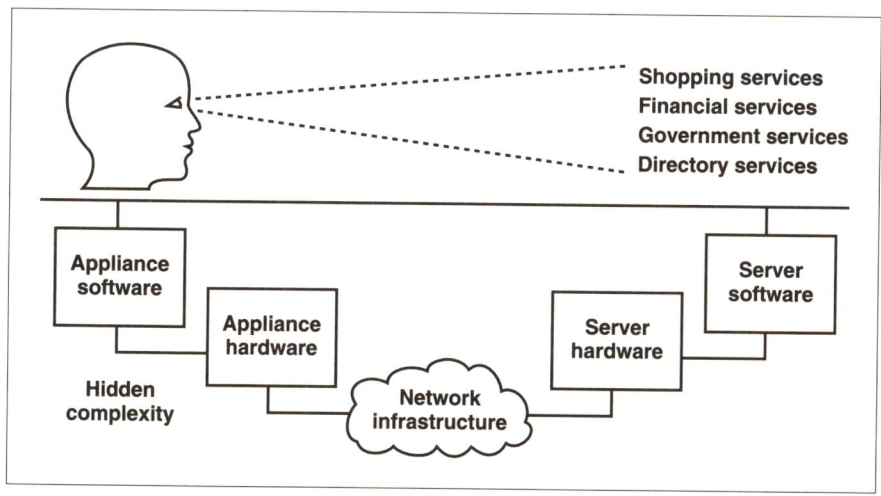

adopters and fast followers who are part of the world of electronic commerce and smart cards in 1996, the complexity of the technology must be effectively hidden from the consumer.

Simplicity begins with the information appliance, the device that the consumer interfaces with directly. The notion of "booting-up" a computer in order to accomplish a straightforward task introduces an element of complexity that will inhibit the success of electronic commerce. The use of an ATM card in an ATM machine is simple and it therefore becomes a matter of common habit. Smart cards must interface with readers similarly.

As an important benchmark of simplicity, consider our most widely used existing information infrastructure—the telephone network. Telephones are intuitive to most people. If a consumer walks up to a telephone in a strange office, there is not much doubt about how to make that particular information appliance perform the task the consumer wishes to perform. Typically, the most complex question from a business office is "Do I have to dial 8 or 9 to get out?"

Clearly, we will be asking new information appliances to perform much more complex activity than we expect of the plain old telephone. However, intuitive operation and simple, consistent interface technology are needed to attain widespread consumer acceptance of information appliances. This is true whether the appliance is a descendent of the personal computer like the smart card or a descendent of the telephone, such as a screen telephone.

Simplicity is not only needed in the user interface. It is also critical that the complexity of the support technologies be hidden from the consumer. In the 1970's, in the early days of the technical field of distributed computing, we called the worldwide telephone network the world's largest distributed computer system. The complexity of that distributed computer system was completely hidden from the user. The simplicity with which the telephone network works does not minimize the complexity of the underlying technology. The same sort of simplicity will drive the success of the emerging electronic infrastructure and smart cards. Keep the model of the telephone network in mind when trying to understand the important issues to be worked.

To spawn simplicity, the key issues being worked include:

- **Addressing.** Consistent, simple, worldwide addressing must exist. The World Wide Web is a start. The web format of "www.something.com" is intuitive if somewhat limiting. Addressing schemes that more closely appeal to a numerologist's intuition, such as CompuServe e-mail addresses, are likely to slow the acceptance of electronic commerce rather than advance it.

- **Directories.** To facilitate interaction, we need directories. The purpose of a directory is to enable someone to find someone or something. There are some new notions in directories that are created by the technology for electronic commerce that are not available in a materials-based infrastructure.

Chief among these are interactive *search engines*—computer systems that accept English language phrases and attempt to find information sources relevant to the query. Search engines are the automated version of the telephone's information operator. Like the telephone operator, search engines must prove simple to operate and reliable in obtaining a quick answer every time. Search engines will continue to evolve and combine with other technologies to provide effective directory mechanisms. Smart cards that have multiple applications will need the same kind of search capability.

- **Problem Resolution.** The enormous complexity of the emerging electronic infrastructure is no excuse for poor problem resolution capabilities. Early programming languages in computer science had error messages such as "Bailing out somewhere near line 16." Such messages were not particularly helpful to the programmer trying to make something work. Early error messages on the Internet have proven to be similarly unhelpful. We can expect that these capabilities will continue to evolve until the infrastructure is capable of actually being helpful to a user in completing a task. And they must be simple. For smart cards this means one stop customer service and quick service turn-arounds.

UBIQUITY

A second key for success in the eyes of the consumer is ubiquity; being able to utilize the electronic information infrastructure anytime and anyplace. Again, consider the model of the successful existing electronic information infrastructure, the telephone network. Telephones are essentially everywhere. Phones are in homes, offices, and public locations like airports. Now, they are even on airplanes. The emergence of global satellite-based networks, such as Motorola's Iridium Network, will result in reasonably economical telephone service even to remote places.

To use the smart card, consumers want ubiquitous access at the merchants where they shop, not just national chains. Deployment and usage of smart cards will depend on such a ubiquitous infrastructure.

In mass markets—by definition—consumers expect ubiquity. We are a mobile people who like to be able to do what we want when we want to do it. Information appliances will emerge that will provide the ubiquity that the consumer expects. The Personal Digital Assistant (PDA) was largely driven by this notion of ubiquity. In the case of the PDA, the notion is that your information appliance should be small enough to carry with you at all times so you never have to worry about finding an information appliance with which you are comfortable.

A second solution to ubiquity has emerged, again similar to the approach followed by the wireline telephone network. Network computing devices can be created at a cost sufficiently modest that they can be deployed as ubiquitously as pay telephones. That is, an airline traveler could expect to see a wall of them in the airport, available to be used at the touch of a button. In order to achieve cost targets, such appliances would be relatively simple, with the intelligence to drive the appliance resident in the network.

The problem with this model goes back to our earlier need for simplicity. Consumers have become used to having either a universal standard interface to their information appliance (the telephone) or a personalized interface to their appliance (the PC). Increasingly, the market seems to be saying that the ability to personalize the human interface is an attractive aspect of information technology. How then to provide a simple way to personalize the interface in a public appliance? We believe that a critical link which will provide for simple and ubiquitous interface across all customer interface devices is the smart card.

SMART CARD-BASED PERSONAL SERVICES

As stated previously, the success of the consumer mass market requires simplicity coupled with ubiquity. For electronic commerce to succeed, consumers will want access whenever convenient to them. They will want device independence. This independence can be provided through the smart card, which can personalize the device the consumer utilizes at the particular point of interactivity. In a smart card-based model, a consumer stores complex personal information—"my profile"—in a server data base located in the electronic information infrastructure (more simply, "the network"). Information about where in the infrastructure my profile is stored along with access codes and the like, is loaded on a smart card and carried in a pocket. Personalization can now be accomplished by walking up to a network computer and inserting the smart card into a reader on the appliance. The appliance only needs to be smart enough to take the information off the smart card and launch the appropriate query into the infrastructure. The infrastructure server can then take over and create the look and feel the consumer wishes on the appliance.

THE SUPPLIER MODEL

There are a variety of ways to model a supplier's perspective on electronic commerce. Recognizing that, in the world of electronic commerce, suppliers primarily supply *information*, Exhibit 6–3 provides a model that focuses on two aspects of information: the amount of information, and the security needs of the information.

Issues for Suppliers: Each of the four identified areas in our model has a series of issues that illustrate business needs in electronic commerce. Of particular

EXHIBIT 6-3

The Supplier Model of Electronic Commerce

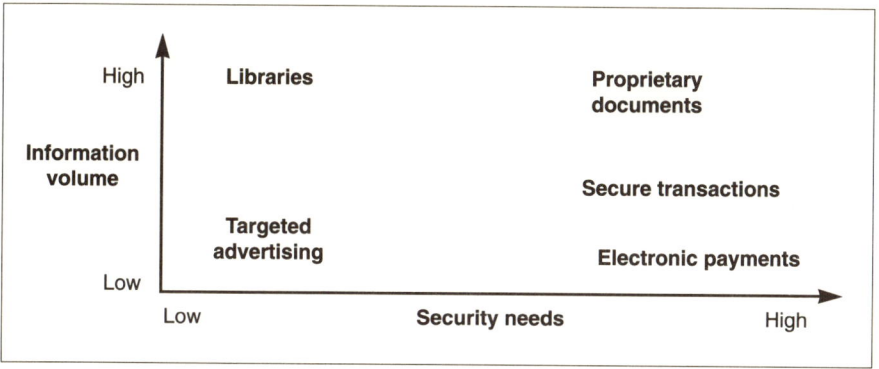

interest to this book are issues that can be resolved, in part, through the use of smart card technology or systems that include card technology.

We will discuss the extremes of this model, including a discussion on libraries, proprietary documents, targeted advertising and electronic payments and secure transactions.

PUBLIC LIBRARIES (LOTS OF INFORMATION, RELATIVELY LOW SECURITY)

A library is a place where information is frequently "free." The Internet is an example of an electronic environment where information is assumed to be free. Not all libraries need to be free, however. The security needs of a library increase as the desire to protect its intellectual property increases. For example, the business school in a university may wish to provide subscription access to its proprietary library of business cases or the collected works of a famous author. In this instance the smart card becomes the smart library card. For more proprietary publications, a PIN or biometric ID can be used.

Issues around Libraries

- **Public Libraries.** In the physical world, public libraries protect the intellectual property of authors by 1) maintaining a limited number of copies of a given work and 2) requiring physical presence to access a work. Both of these dimensions disappear in the electronic world. Either Public Libraries as we know them will change character in the electronic world or the model of remuneration of authors will change (or authors will starve). Most likely, we will see "Public Libraries" evolve into Private Libraries.

- **Private Libraries.** New models will be developed for access and billing to private libraries. A major issue is authentication of users, accurately determining who to charge for access. A reverse issue is authentication of the supplier: How can a user be assured that he or she is accessing the real information source and not information supplied by an impostor? A variety of business approaches are being employed by suppliers including subscription models and metered usage (pay as you go). Metered usage allows some degree of anonymity assuming a relatively anonymous payment mechanism such as e-cash or stored value cards.
- **Archives of Publications.** Major publications can offer low cost access to their archives with powerful search mechanisms. Detailed knowledge of the interests of individual subscribers allows highly personal service through the use of detailed user profiles. However, publishers must be careful, as user perceptions of privacy of their profiles can cause backlash if not used sensitively. An additional issue is likely to emerge around the rights of advertisers. Electronic techniques allow the insertion of contemporary advertisements in archival information. This brings up the issues of whether a user sees the original advertisement or a modern replacement? Future agreements with advertisers will need to include provisos covering the life of such ads.
- **Transaction Warehouses.** A particularly interesting form of private library is the warehouse of transaction information that is collected by transaction processors (e.g. credit card associations or telephone companies). One legitimate business use of this information is fraud analysis. The degree to which the information in these warehouses can be mined for other purposes without violating privacy rules will continue to be a source of private and public debate.

PROPRIETARY DOCUMENT (LOTS OF INFORMATION, HIGH SECURITY)

Proprietary information can take a variety of forms. The electronic infrastructure and the existence of ubiquitous telecommunications networks allows corporations to establish virtual boundaries rather than being confined by the physical boundaries forced by a paper-based infrastructure. Access to information over these networks, however, brings with it a variety of issues.

Issues around Proprietary Information

- **The Virtual Corporation.** Much has been written about the virtual corporation or virtual organization. Of interest here is access to the proprietary information that constitutes the intellectual property of the virtual corporation. Implementation of the virtual corporation depends on making this intellectual property conveniently accessible to all authorized members of the corporation while keeping the information absolutely secure from prying competitors. Thus, strong authentication is the first issue to emerge here. As companies merge and divest, issues of information format standards and formatting take on great importance. The very dynamic organization structures present an administrative challenge as does the high degree of mobility of the work force.

- **Document Delivery.** Reliable delivery of proprietary documents over open public networks raises a number of important and difficult issues. We are talking about the lifeblood of a corporation and its revenue stream. Traditionally, this topic is sufficiently important that corporations have built secure private networks for this purpose. This is expensive, however, and a public information infrastructure must support this capability. A useful application to keep in mind as an extreme is the reliable delivery of computer software over the Internet. Not only must no piece of the document get lost (a common meaning of "reliable") but no extra information can be added along the way (e.g., insertion of a computer virus). There is also the important issue of making sure that the information being transmitted and received is indeed the information intended by the author and is not being transmitted by an impostor.

- **Mobile Work Force.** The fact that the work force is mobile creates additional issues in accessing proprietary information. There is little expectation that a single standard information appliance will emerge as the metaphor for the telephone in today's voice-based information network. Thus, information suppliers must be able to deal with a variety of information appliances. Further, the environments become asymmetrical. That is, many of the information appliances will have low capability for complicated computations (e.g. a screen phone).

- **Multimedia Contracts.** Many of the documents that support the legal structure of the corporation will find new forms in the coming world of electronic commerce. For example, traditional contracts may be replaced or supplemented by multimedia contracts, electronic documents containing images or even full motion video clips of the signatories. Ensuring that these documents are accessible and unalterable provides new challenges for digital signature technology.

TARGETED ADVERTISING (LOW INFORMATION QUANTITY, LOW SECURITY)

The world of electronic commerce allows suppliers to become increasingly specific about targeting specific advertising. As mentioned previously, a supplier may know enough about a specific customer to tailor advertisements to an individual. However targeted, these advertisements are likely to still be subject to relatively low and inexpensive security needs.

Issues around Targeting Information

One of the great opportunities in electronic commerce is increased specialization, both of supplier expertise and in targeting consumers. As suppliers make increasing use of this capability, however, privacy issues begin to emerge. People have demonstrated a willingness to trade privacy for value. It is reasonable to expect this trend to continue in the electronic world. The following examples look at some ways in which information can be targeted to provide value to users and at issues that might arise around that use of information.

- **Passive Electronic Advertising.** Initial advertising on the World Wide Web followed a model very close to advertising in the paper and broadcast media. That is, a piece of space was leased to an advertiser and everyone who visited the Web page saw the same advertisement. The issue here, of course, is qualifying the visitor. With this shotgun approach, it is very difficult to know whether an advertisement is reaching the target audience.

- **Active Electronic Advertising.** Electronic advertisements can be increasingly targeted by utilizing knowledge about a visitor to select the advertisements he or she will be shown. For example, a user who uses a search engine to find information about cars might be shown advertisements for automobiles or related products. Similarly, a user who is known to be in a high income bracket might be shown advertisements for expensive cars. Given that a supplier knows who the user is, (in order to solve the authentication issues discussed above) there is no real limit to the amount of information a supplier *could* know about the interests of the user and the uses to which that information could be put. At some point, however, such detailed targeting begins to get intrusive and users/customers will reject the supplier.

- **Personalized Information Services.** As mentioned earlier, many people will willingly trade privacy for value. For example, I might be willing to trade the details of my normal commuting times and routes for a service that would reliably advise me in a timely way of traffic problems and provide alternative route suggestions. The role of *intelligent agents* in seeking out such personalized information is another way of accomplishing the same sort of task. However, it remains to be seen how much information an agent may need to give up to acquire specific information.

- **Electronic Coupons.** Standardized approaches to measuring the effectiveness of electronic advertising have not been resolved. One approach to measuring the success of specific approaches to electronic advertising is the electronic coupon approach advocated by Smart TV, as described in Chapter 13. In this approach, an individual seeing an electronic advertisement would be able to take a simple action to cause an electronic coupon to be downloaded onto a smart card. The initial application of this approach is to television advertising. However, the availability of smart card reader/writers on personal computers and other information appliances makes this approach attractive for other media as well. Such an approach allows the supplier to collect feedback on the success of specific advertisements as well as, privacy issues permitting, information on the specific coupons a specific user redeems.

ELECTRONIC PAYMENTS AND SECURE TRANSACTIONS (LOW INFORMATION QUANTITY, VERY HIGH SECURITY)

The most crucial example of the need for secure transactions in the area of electronic payments is the transmission of electronic demand payment instruments or "e-cash" as well as the use of credit, debit, or stored value cards. Any form of electronic payment must be subject to strict encryption and validation techniques to avoid potential duplication or counterfeiting.

Issues around Secure Transactions and Electronic Payments

Four issues have emerged in this domain which illustrate the environment of concern. These will be discussed separately.

- **Standard Secure Environments.** Microsoft's success in establishing its technology as the industry standard has prompted a number of replication attempts in other portions of the industry. Environments for secure transactions appear to be one of these segments. Many companies have been working to establish proprietary solutions to the problem of creating a secure environment for electronic transactions. Some are looking to provide open interfaces that can mediate across proprietary solutions. While it is not necessary to have only one approach to secure transactions, having at most a small number is very desirable.

- **Appropriately Secure Technology.** Absolutely unbreakable security is extremely difficult if not impossible to obtain. More important, it can be very expensive to try. A sensible approach here is to apply appropriate security, that is, security appropriate to the value of the asset being protected. Thus, security measures might be stricter for the protection from duplication of electronic legal tender then for an electronic check in which duplicates can be identified on-line before value changes hands. One rule of thumb is that security technology can be considered appropriate if it costs ten times more to break the security than the value that is received as a result of the break. This environment is continually changing and a factor of ten on the cost curve may take no more than a year to achieve, so flexible security environments in which it is easy to change the degree of security are also important.

- **Anonymity.** A significant issue in electronic payments is the degree of anonymity supported by the mechanism. Some electronic payment instruments attempt to imitate cash, like the so called "e-cash" or stored value systems. It is important to recognize that even paper cash is not totally anonymous; physical proximity is generally required to exchange paper cash. It is theoretically possible, however, to achieve total anonymity of the customer with an electronic payment instrument. That may or may not be desirable from a public policy perspective. In many environments, a complete trail of stakeholders is a positive feature (e.g., an electronic check).

It is not very meaningful to try to capture a list of electronic payments systems in a non-electronic medium such as this book. The book is simply too stable and the electronic payments environment is too volatile. An appropriate medium, such as the World Wide Web is better for that. The FSTC Electronic Commerce Project documentation on their Web site at *http://www.fstc.org* contains a survey of existing electronic payments projects.

RECENT OBSERVATIONS

An analysis of the issues raised above indicates that the dominant concerns lie in areas of privacy and security. The key technologies of electronic privacy and security are cryptology, encryption, cryptographic protocols and the like. These disciplines, based in advanced mathematics, are the key technologies of the emerging information infrastructure.

Mobility Complicates the Situation

A common view of information technology is that software is at its heart. However, in today's technology, software is not very mobile—even with the emergence of JAVA and JAVA-like languages, the best way we know to have software move around is in a piece of hardware. This is where it becomes clear that smart cards are likely to be a significant component of the information infrastructure. People are mobile. A successful, ubiquitous information infrastructure must be as convenient to use as today's information infrastructure, the telephone network. A mobile individual must be able to walk up to an information appliance on a street corner, or in an airport, and be able to adapt that appliance to the information access and exchange mechanism desired by the individual. Smart cards are capable of being:

- Electronic Key Rings. Card memory can hold the electronic keys to information files owned by, or concerning, an individual in such a way that the individual retains control over access to the files.

- Encryption Devices. The cards are capable of encrypting information sent to or received by the information appliance without relying on the capabilities of an unknown, and therefore untrustworthy, appliance.
- Authentication token. The card can be an authentication token. Where strong authentication (more than possession of the card and a possibly breakable PIN) is required, biometrics can be used involving an interaction between the person, an application on the card, and an application in the network.
- Personalization device. The card can be used to trigger an exchange with a network-based server to provide customized services such as creating the correct look and feel on an information appliance.

CONCLUSION

In this chapter on smart cards and electronic commerce, we have portrayed the generic four phases of commerce and the component phases which will be transformed into an end-to-end electronic system. As a way of driving home what the ultimate state of electronic commerce could look like, we utilized the illustration of purchasing a four-wheel drive vehicle in the year 2010. The purpose of the illustration is to show you what electronic commerce could look like when all the electronic elements are in place, functioning as an electronic system. We hope that portraying the transition from the manual world to the electronic world will prove useful as you think through the implications of electronic commerce for your business.

We also provided perspectives on electronic commerce from the two major stakeholders: Businesses and consumers. We believe that understanding both viewpoints will clarify the roles that smart cards will play in electronic commerce.

PART TWO

Applications

OVERVIEW

During the past two years, a variety of industry players have launched smart card-based applications. So many different pilots have begun that no one industry dominates the card market. Stored value, loyalty, and security applications are introduced by financial services, education, telecommunication, healthcare, and retail organizations, for example.

Part Two addresses the various industry perspectives, motivations, applications, technological, and legal/regulatory issues in detail. We encourage you to read all industry chapters, because as boundaries between industries shift, smart card applications will look more alike wherever they are implemented.

Another reason for reading about the various approaches is the fact these players are likely to be your partners in regional alliances when you bring your smart card applications to market. Understanding their needs and perspectives makes for better partnering for multiple application cards.

A third reason for understanding multiple industry perspectives is that this is where real innovation comes from—the "out-of-box" thinking and fresh approaches nontraditional players take when entering a new industry, product, or service area. Banks should not be talking only to other banks. Telephone companies should not just think linearly about opportunities. Cross-industry, cross-discipline approaches lead to real innovative thinking.

The magic of the Smart Card Forum has been just that—a forum for private and public sector executives with different disciplines and industry experiences working together to launch an innovative technology and industry. Open your horizons, learn from others, read on.

CHAPTER 7

Financial Services

Ron Braco
Chase Manhattan

The financial services industry is undergoing unprecedented change. These changes are the products of a variety of important elements that, when viewed collectively, create either incredible opportunities or enormous threats to ultimate survival. While financial institutions have been transforming themselves constantly, nothing will compare to the future.

Three factors—deregulation, consumer demand, and technology—will accelerate the pace and magnitude of change in the financial industry. We'll take a brief look at why.

1. Deregulation As barriers to service offerings fall and boundaries to presence, both physical and virtual, are eliminated, a vast consolidation will occur. The survivors will possess substantial capital and resources and be capable of marketing a wide spectrum of services, anywhere. Deregulation will also mean that new competitors, both non-traditional and perhaps entirely new players in the financial services industry, will emerge as formidable and hungry competitors.

Exhibit 7–1 illustrates how some of these boundaries are shifting.

2. Consumer Demand Today's financial services' customers demand far more than ever from a financial institution. They seek convenience, product choice, and broad, complete packaged offerings. Consumers demand value from the product offering, both in price and in quality of service, and they will switch institutions if they don't get the service they want. Full relationships are the key to profitability in financial institutions, yet new technology will offer more alternative capabilities and more convenient ways to

CHAPTER 7 Financial Services

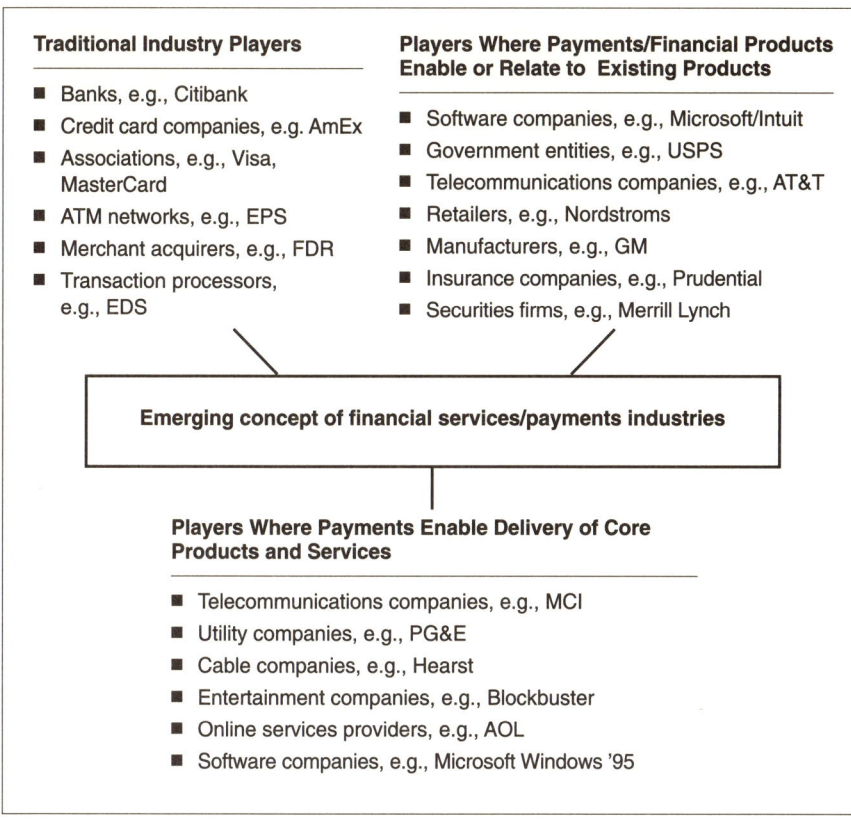

EXHIBIT 7-1

Shifting Competitive Environment in Financial Services

Source: The Santa Fe Group

acquire them. Loyalty will not be maintained simply by the inconvenience of going to new providers.

Exhibit 7–2 (following page) illustrates some of the drivers of technological developments affecting banking and related to changing consumer demands.

3. Technology No single factor has changed, or will change, this industry more than the rapid changes in and emerging use of technology. Driven by advances in microcomputers, enhanced telecommunications, object-oriented software, and human-centric breakthroughs such as voice technology and navigational tools, products can be created, developed and deployed in

EXHIBIT 7-2

Consumer Demand for 24-Hour Access to Goods and Services from Home is Driving Technological Developments

On-Line P.C.	Interactive Telephone
■ 24-hour access to banking details allows complete financial management ■ Ability to pay bills and transfer finances from home	■ 24-hour purchasing of goods from home ■ Infrastructure already in place ■ Smart phones offer secure payment
Internet	**Interactive Television**
■ 24-hour access to a global network of computers ■ Ability to purchase goods and information from global market ■ Opportunity to pay in a single currency (e.g., Digicash/Cybercash)	■ 24-hour purchasing of goods and services from home ■ Ability to browse through goods

Source: Edgar, Dunn & Co.

unprecedentedly short timeframes. Product replications and enhancement will rapidly change the competitive landscape.

For the financial services industry, the ability to create innovative value added services in a rapid timeframe is critical, not only to success, but perhaps to survival. The challenge is to develop new revenue sources—leveraging infrastructure that speeds time to market and reduces expenses—while continuing to offer services that thoroughly delight the consumer. Given the fragile condition of the financial services industry, choosing the correct strategic path to meet this challenge successfully will require a deep knowledge of the consumer and the implication of companies fostering offerings. Innovations that enhance value to customers and sustain competitive advantage will survive and thrive.

SMART CARDS AS A TECHNOLOGY ENABLER

Smart cards represent a key technology enabler for financial institutions. Few technologies offer as many avenues of opportunity for financial institutions, and the customers they serve. Because information management represents a very major element of the financial industry value chain, smart cards have the potential to become the cornerstone for a wide array of new service and product offerings.

Three characteristics—processing power, portability, and interactive properties—of the microprocessor chip demonstrate its importance to the financial industry.

1. Processing Power Smart cards offer limitless ability to store and process large amounts of data. Chip manufacturers are striving to manufacture a computer chip that remains small in size, yet achieves quantum leaps in storage and processing capability. Today's smart cards can easily store several pages of data in 1k to 8k of memory, and perform a variety of routine calculations. It is anticipated that this capability will increase several magnitudes, allowing storage of hundreds of pages of data and calculation of complex formulas without much variance from today's costs. A 64k chip card is in research and development at this time.

These shifts in technical growth will create myriad new products and services, allowing a financial service provider to offer a customer a full and complete summary of their relationships and calculations with enhanced financial management. For example, account numbers and latest transactions and balances can be stored on a card, along with information needed to apply for mortgage or home equity loans.

2. Portability Smart cards allow consumers the ultimate convenience—personal portability. Substantial quantities of financial data will be resident in credit card format with the ability to permit access to intelligent devices such as home or office personal computers, automated teller machines, both public and private phones, and handheld personal assist devices. The card will have the capacity to store various unique operating systems to allow communication with a broad set of devices, unique security providing ubiquitous access, and personal data specific to the card holder.

In the future, smart cards will hold biometric, voice, and video information that can further enhance a customized relationship with the consumer.

Portability clearly addresses one of the most fundamental elements of value to the consumer, *convenience*, anytime, anywhere. Small, yet powerful, smart cards, easily transported and with many points of interaction, suggest a winning proposition for the customer.

3. Interactive Properties Unlike magnetic stripe technology or memory cards that maintain pre-loaded data, smart cards are truly microprocessor-oriented, and compute information as well as store it. They can be updated to reflect changes to existing card data caused by an interaction or enhanced to create new product or service offerings. Financial service providers will seek to capitalize on this technology in a variety of ways, from security management to the introduction of new services such as loyalty programs, to access to new devices. Chip updating will be accomplished through devices like home phones with smart card readers, personal computers, and issuer-owned kiosks or automated teller machines. Limitations to these enhancements will be a function of the chip memory and computer processing capability.

STAKEHOLDERS

Smart cards offer incredible potential for the financial services industry. Clearly there are ample profit opportunities for a number of parties in the value chain. These are represented by enhanced consumer convenience, revenue and fees, and cost reduction. Yes, smart cards will require substantial change in existing infrastructure: new cards, new acceptance devices, unique processing requirements, new software, marketing expenses and the risk of new technology. Yet, the cards appear to be a value-added proposition for all concerned parties. These stakeholders include card issuers, consumers, merchants, device providers, and third-party intermediaries, each group with its own perspective.

1. Card Issuers Card issuers, primarily financial institutions, may absorb the greatest risks in the introduction of smart cards. Issuers must develop the value proposition, purchase and issue the cards, and ensure that a full infrastructure exists to accept their product offerings. It is the card issuer who also anticipates a substantial share of the benefits that card programs create.

For the issuer, key benefits will be derived from cardholder merchants who accept smart cards, as well as from potential processing and licensing fees resulting from programs dependent on smart card technologies.

2. Financial Consumers Today's financial consumers regard convenience as essential to choosing a provider for their financial services needs. Smart cards introduce an entirely new level of convenience for the consumer. Consumers will find true convenience in three key areas: payment, access, and information.

Payment product will be designed through the introduction of stored value, debit, and credit applications. Consumers will no longer be concerned about cash and coin. Access can be achieved from a variety of electronic delivery points including the home, bank automated teller machines, merchant terminals and even public kiosks. The creation of stored value, consisting of electronic data representing value transferred from a consumer's funding account, will offer easier and safer use of funds to make purchases, and add the convenience of easy access.

The information access capabilities of the card can incorporate secured access for personal computers, public networks, and other electronic delivery devices, allowing secured retrieval and processing of data. Data can be added, deleted, or computed within the operating system of the chip, with instruction provided by the owner. Once again, these are highly convenient options in a world of vast and changing information needs.

3. Merchants Merchants have continually sought new forms of technology to enhance their profitability, and in this context, smart cards have the potential to provide substantial benefit. Stored value applications, for instance, offer reduced coin and cash handling, which then cuts expensive merchant costs in processing physical items and lowers internal loss from fraud or employee "shrinkage."

Plastic payment products have also traditionally increased customer sales. Finally, stored value chip-based products can be enhanced to include co-branded opportunities leading to merchant loyalty programs such as frequent buyer initiatives and electronic couponing. These value programs are intended to offer consumers more and better reasons to continue their relationship on a frequent basis with their valued merchants. They also provide retailers with a way to capture information on the customer and their transaction.

4. Device Providers Widespread acceptance of smart cards will also create an entirely new industry of material providers. Direct revenue opportunities will exist for the manufacturers of smart cards and terminal devices. Smart card growth can be expected from several sources. Financial institutions will migrate debit and credit card programs to smart cards as programs become more clearly defined and acceptance by consumers begins to emerge. Cards co-branded by merchants and financial providers will also appear, stirring even more cards into the market mix.

As cards are issued, terminal vendors will be actively developing a variety of products to facilitate acceptance. Devices will be required in a variety of shapes, sizes, and product functionality. Consumers will seek formal and portable balance and transfer devices to function as electronic wallets, or personal computer peripherals to load card data. Merchants will seek stand-alone devices, integrated products, or a combination to accommodate their workplace environment.

Broadly accepted standards are key to the manufacture of these vital raw materials for the smart card industry. The risk of introducing products prior to generally accepted design criteria could be risky and cost prohibitive. Development that follows anticipated specifications—and allows upgrading as specifications are enhanced—will surely result in greater profitability potential, faster time to market, and less overall risk.

5. Third-Party Intermediaries Third party intermediaries will also play a critical role in the advancement of smart card applications for the financial services industry. As providers with processing resources or powerful marketing capabilities, third parties can be important allies. As smart card programs progress, the need to ensure critical mass can only be achieved through the cooperation of large issuers in creating similar processing schemes and common baseline services. Associations like MasterCard and VISA, ATM network providers like Banksys, and large issuers like American Express are generally considered likely third-party providers who will offer technology, processing, and the marketing components of smart card products. Other third party providers will offer key support functions that can include data management, transaction processing, merchant enrollment, and card management. Providing these functions will generate revenue opportunities for these intermediaries and enhance marketing organization's brand.

STRATEGIC CONSIDERATIONS

Smart cards appear to offer financial providers many benefits to enhance customer value and offer potential for unique differentiation. There are many opportunities and also many challenges in implementing the technology. Smart card applications will incorporate a broad array of offerings to the consumer. The card will store, maintain, and compute vital data elements which will require sophisticated security and protection. From a security perspective, issuers must balance the cost and risk of security enhancements. Card security must consider such factors as securing transactions, detecting security breaches and recovering from them, and most important, maintaining customer confidence.

The greatest security threats for smart cards issued for use by financial service providers involve false authentication at the terminal, counterfeiting, data alteration, repay of claimed transactions, and fraudulent acceptance devices. Countermeasures designed to thwart these threats can be designed, utilizing a variety of techniques that can be incorporated on the card.

These techniques must consider the overall cost of implementation, whether that results from the need for more memory or processing capability on the chip, or from elaborate detection schemes designed within the issuers' internal systems. Without question, smart cards have the capacity to add sophisticated security enhancements that can address vulnerabilities. As a payment product or information storage vehicle, no technology to date can replicate the chip.

Smart card costs continue to exceed those of typical payment and information cards that use magnetic or optical stripe technologies. The amount of memory and computing power required by issuers will strongly influence the cost of the card and the required volume of cards dictates the unit cost of cards. From an issuer's perspective, there are several key considerations for issuance: card expiration, amount of functionality, and future enhancements. Each of these factors will affect the cost of cards, both during initial issuance and as new services are added. With common standards currently under development, introduction of smart card programs must be viewed carefully because future standard developments will alter chip requirements to facilitate interoperability. The importance of interoperability should also be considered in the context of card acceptance. Devices to accept smart cards must be designed from common specifications to be deployed in large quantities, thus creating the market for cardholders. Card obsolescence will occur if standards requirements or new product offerings require greater chip processing capacity than offered.

VALUE TO THE FINANCIAL INDUSTRY: STORED VALUE CARDS

The financial industry is challenged by the need to create new products and services to differentiate itself from its competitors. These products and services must provide enduring and real value to customers, thus encouraging deep and long-lasting relationships. Smart cards, with their power and portability, certainly meet that objective.

It is anticipated that stored value products will likely become one of the earliest applications to be introduced by the financial industry. Clearly, stored value is an evolutionary payment product that plays an important element in the "pay now, pay later, pay before" cycle of plastic cards. Credit cards have long fulfilled the "pay later" concept, debit cards are quickly emerging as a "pay now" offering and stored value as an alternative to cash will soon become the "pay before" service. Stored value will become the foundation for the issuer and act as the basis for future enhancements. Financial institutions are familiar with payment products and will easily understand the issues of stored value. Consumers will recognize stored value simplicity and understand that the product requires very little investment. Merchants will welcome smooth cash handling, security benefits and a low payment product cost. With stored value introductions expected, other related functionalities can be developed to include loyalty programs, allowing consumers to benefit from visiting a merchant on a frequent basis through discounts on products and services.

The creation of new access products will also be facilitated by the security resident on the card and utilization of its portability features. With the use of a smart card, access to a consumer's full data bank of financial services may be in reach from anywhere. Updating specific streams of data will be accomplished from a variety of devices that the consumer will access. The financial industry issuers will also be able to develop behavioral habits to better customize a consumer's financial life, and incorporate these behaviors through features that can personalize information specific to an individual. This customized capability might include predicting withdrawal amounts, account preferences and specific data requests upon entry to an on-line data bank.

A smart card's ultimate advantage to a financial services issuer is the ability to consolidate consumer relationships. The issuer gains a distinct competitive edge by providing a vehicle that stores and processes key elements of a customer's financial information.

The financial industry can increase revenue by enhancing and deepening customer relationships, as well as by acquiring new business from the powerful new sets of products and services offered. While issuers will seek various methods for product profitability, several specific areas are clear.

Stored value can potentially generate revenue from the cardholder, in the form of transaction fees or monthly maintenance fees, and from the merchant, in the form of transaction fees or daily settlement charges. It is also likely that consumers will determine their willingness to pay fees on the basis of perceived value from the card. If loyalty programs and electronic couponing programs succeed, consumers will recognize value outweighing the modest fees that might be assessed, thus increasing card use and creating a robust market place. Card issuers may also determine that the chip has excess capacity and will make that excess memory available to other providers who may wish to offer a series of related products, such as travel or merchandising. These services could be "rented" on the card with the issuer receiving the financial benefit.

Smart cards also represent opportunities to lower delivery costs and reduce paper handling in the financial industry. The cost of cash handling at ATMs could be reduced if stored value becomes widely accepted.

BUSINESS MOTIVATION

It is clear that the power of smart cards can create real benefits for the financial services industry. However, as with most new technologies, there are challenges and values that must be reconciled before the deployment of full scale programs. It is extremely important to understand the business issues before launching a smart card program.

Strategically, the financial services industry must take a leadership role. As an industry whose history is deep in the payment business, financial services providers must recognize that smart card technology can enable the non-financial industry to create payment products capable of infringing on the very businesses financial services providers have controlled since the formation of banking. A defensive position may not be sufficient to ward off powerful entities with strong technological experience and substantial financial resources, such as Microsoft, Intuit, and AT&T. The financial industry will need to aggressively pursue solutions that are competitive, innovative, and present value to its customers. Stored value products, independently offered frequent purchase arrangements, access vehicles, and other information products will be deployed by non-financial services providers if the issuer business is left unattended.

Financial services providers can succeed by recognizing that competitive entrants can move into this market. There are real opportunities for success and early market interests may recognize real value. The key to success appears to lie in the creation of a multi-application offering, incorporating a related series of products and services that interact with each other to offer the customer enhanced value.

It may initially be impractical to launch a multiple application card. However, a longer-term plan can establish a building block of products to be improved over time. This can be done, without replacing the card, through download upgrading, similar to the enhancements available for many of the on-line service products on personal computers. Since card replacement is expensive, creating processes to increase utility on unused portions of a chip will be important in maintaining expense management. This will also help accelerate time-to-market for services valuable in differentiating the issuer from competition.

BUILDING THE BUSINESS CASE

A business case to support the launch of a smart card program for the financial services industry must reflect strategic considerations as well as the analytical assessment of financials. The technology's embryonic stage, and its current acceptance level, make it extremely difficult to develop straight forward economic rationale. There are, however, elements that can be explored to reasonably address the business model.

Stored value provides a good business case example and a logical starting point. As established earlier, stored value refers to products that can replace cash and coin for lower cost transactions, offering consumers and merchants real benefit. As a strategic value proposition, it is conceivable that the issuers can extract fee revenue from the consumer and merchant, while merchants and consumers receive value from convenience, security, and cash handling simplicity. Thus the strategic business case might be derived from the attractiveness to all parties in the process. The benefits of a stored value product include:

- *Reduced risk of fraud, theft, or credit loss* as cash is exchanged for electronic value and stored in advance from a legitimate funding account relationship
- *Secured access* offered through enhancements in the chip allowing card authorization and positive identification for loading of value
- *Lower processing costs* resulting from minimal on-line data authorization and/or transmission; access and processing time for conducting transactions can also be substantially reduced
- *Enhanced Cash Handling* through reduction in cash and coin, simplifying merchant settlement, and reducing deposit handling costs and fees
- *Added revenue potential* through maximizing chip card "real estate" for co-branding or joint marketing arrangements
- *Multiple Applications* evolving from payment products to complementary services such as loyalty programs and electronic couponing

Reviewing the business case for stored value from a financial perspective incorporates a complex list of cost and revenue dynamics that must be modeled in the absence of historical reference. Business case elements include expense and revenue for stakeholders in the stored value business, primarily the issuers, the acquirers, and the processing operators. The issuer is responsible for the distribution of cards. The acquirer establishes the relationship with merchants and enables the acceptance of cards, facilitating the settlement process. The processor designs and maintains the transaction flow, acting as clearing agent and data manager while maintaining overall integrity of the stored value process. The business model is intended to identify the resources and expenses for each partner and highlights the financial effect that cardholders, pricing, and card activity have on the stakeholders.

Cardholder activity is an extremely important element of the business model. The number of cards issued, the frequency of new card issuance, and the value of the transaction must be considered.

Because smart cards are typically more expensive than traditional payment cards, re-issuance frequency and replacement cost of lost or stolen cards are critical. Issuers must also estimate how often consumers will add value to their cards.

Issuer's revenue can stem from a number of areas and will vary from issuer to issuer, depending on anticipated profitability and the competition. In general, issuers will benefit from one or more of the following:

- Cardholder fees
- Load fees
- Float revenue
- Co-branding/licensing of chip "real-estate"
- Potential merchant fees

Expenses will generally be a function of:

- Card costs
- Processing fees
- Network expenses
- Marketing

Acquirers and processors will charge merchants and issuers fees for their services. These fees will vary according to volume, relationship, and complexity of service.

Financial institutions can participate as issuers, acquirers, and processors. Clearly they will act primarily as issuers, and then optionally choose to participate in the other operations. Creating a business model for financial institutions will require unique development as elements of the various programs will vary widely.

In whatever fashion the business model is developed, numerous assumptions will be required to complete its evaluation. In the absence of historical information, market research is critical to the model. An investment in market research reflecting specific smart card aspirations will lend credibility to any smart card business model. Market research that reflects consumer and merchant behavior regarding acceptance, usage, perceived value, and drawbacks offers important data for building pricing and marketing approaches, acceptance levels, and merchant penetration. All of these are key elements in creating a business model.

IMPLEMENTATION

Smart card program implementation timing will vary depending on the use of either a closed or open system. Closed systems—operating with a single issuer or for specific environments such as universities or corporate entities—require much less attention to universal standards or open systems specifications. Closed programs are realistic starting points, but need to be configured cautiously in the context of future migration to more "open" systems.

Open systems, relying on established standards and rules, allow many entrants with common acceptance points. They are longer term and tend to reflect a higher degree of complexity. Few, if any, card schemes can be considered open today, although major initiatives are underway to create common operating specifications. Financial institution issuers and merchant terminal developers will use these specifications to accelerate the move to open systems and to increase the desire to implement programs. MasterCard, Visa, Mondex, and Banksys are currently developing open systems.

While none of these programs can operate with each other, some effort is being made to create common specifications for noncompetitive functions, thus facilitating interoperability and open systems.

Selecting the appropriate provider is a function of many factors. For a "closed" system program there are multiple card manufacturers who have developed robust operating systems with specific functionalities. These providers offer an excellent means of rapidly introducing a card program and assisting in the overall integration of hardware, systems, and operating procedures.

Open systems involving multiple issuers and merchants require further strategic consideration to ensure interoperability of card acceptance devices, settlement procedures and operating workflow.

Program design requires specific attention to the type of initial applications planned and to possible future applications as well. Choosing the processing capability of a smart card chip will have major implications for the cost and future migration of additional applications. In general, limiting the product to a few baseline functions may best optimize cost and product offering during the early stages of smart card introduction.

To be successful, pilot programs must reflect a realistic view of the anticipated rollout. Functions and services that will be offered in a full rollout need to be reflected in a pilot to establish the rollout's true impact, operating issues, devices, and financial implications. Pilots must allow consumers and merchants time to adapt to these technological and behavioral changes.

Numerous smart card pilots are underway around the world, primarily testing stored value concepts. Exhibit 7–3 shows a sampling of countries with stored value projects.

In March, 1996, MasterCard launched a multiple application payment card in Canberra, Australia with several large financial institutions. VISA opened a major smart card program for the 1996 Summer Olympics in Atlanta, Georgia. Mondex has launched a pilot in 1995 in Swinden, England, with Nat West, U.K., and Midland Bank. Many other "closed" smart card programs,

EXHIBIT 7-3

Worldwide Electronic Purse Projects

United States	France	Hong Kong
Canada	Germany	China
	Portugal	Japan
	Spain	Taiwan
	UK	Korea
	Italy	Singapore
	Ireland	Thailand
Mexico	Denmark	Indonesia
Brazil	Finland	Australia
Colombia	Belgium	
Argentina	Switzerland	
Chile	Austria	
Peru	Netherlands	
	South Africa	

Additional column: Estonia, Russia, Poland, Bulgaria, Latvia, Lebanon, Czechoslovakia

Source: The Santa Fe Group

particularly related to campus environment and corporate facilities, are also being implemented. With this high level of pilot activity, substantial information and data will be captured, resulting in a refinement of concepts and ultimate rollout to broad bases of merchants and consumers.

SUCCESSFUL DEPLOYMENT CHALLENGES

The financial services industry's success in the deployment of smart cards will rely heavily on market acceptance of the value that can be extracted from the cards' powerful characteristics. The ability to store and compute data in a portable chip will create new value for customers and merchants. Developing a marketing approach highlighting the true value that cardholders will gain is essential in gaining market acceptance, and until market acceptance becomes obvious, merchants will be unwilling to accept the new payment form. Therefore, it is extremely important to address the critical mass issue from several perspectives:

- Standard card operating specifications allowing interoperability among issuers and thus reducing merchant reluctance to install a terminal device must be established.
- A critical mass of cardholders motivated by value propositions that enhance convenience and access to financial services products will be required.

- Establishing a business case model for the key stakeholders, reflecting strategic and economic benefit, will be essential.
- Creating innovative marketing and testing initiatives ensuring product awareness and knowledge cannot be overlooked.

The creation of smart card programs driven by financial institutions will also result in substantial scrutiny from regulatory groups, government agencies, and general parties. The power of a smart card to store and maintain quantities of personal data may raise serious issues of privacy and security and affect the overall flow of money. Debate has begun at various levels of government and will continue as a clearer understanding of smart card technology emerges. More in-depth scrutiny can be expected as specific smart card schemes are constructed and closely evaluated to determine their impact on these issues.

LOOKING AHEAD

A few predictions impacting the financial services industry include:

- Use of JAVA on the chip to download appropriate "stored value applets" in each city or country visited
- Growth of interest in purchasing petty cash cards for businesses that want to facilitate transaction and information tracking
- Digital cash companies such as Cybercash and Digicash will use smart cards for portability and access
- Nonbanks will drive electronic purse applications as readily as banks and financial services companies
- Multiple third party providers will emerge to compete with the traditional card associations

CONCLUSION

The introduction of smart cards offers financial institutions a unique opportunity to create innovative products and services for their consumers. Although at an early stage, the potential power of this technology appears limitless in its ability to offer a vast array of applications designed for payment alternatives, secured access, and data management.

Financial institutions will clearly need to overcome the initial investments required to enter this business, and must work closely with those responsible for establishing standards. They will need to develop a strategic vision for the smart card and construct initiatives that add functionalities. Considering the competitive challenges facing financial institutions and consumers' demand for convenience, smart cards can play an important role in introducing innovative, differentiated products.

Smart cards will likely play an important role for the future of payment products in the financial industry. Smart cards will surface as issuers, consumers, and merchants recognize the potential benefits of products and services that can be derived from cards incorporating an intelligent chip. It is likely that smart cards will appear initially as payment products addressing lower value purchases and quickly migrate to other applications that will store and retrieve data, enhancing the consumer experience for purchase, payment, and information management.

CHAPTER 8

Telecommunications and Information Services

Ken Lutz
Bellcore

The telecommunications industry is the largest user of smart cards in the world today. Most of the cards in use are prepaid smart cards for public pay phones, and there is a growing application for digital cellular telephones. The opportunities for other applications and uses are enormous, partly because of the unprecedented changes taking place in the telecommunications industry. As the industry transforms into an information business, smart cards will play an essential role.

Ten years ago, the telecommunications industry was focused on telephony, although telephone companies had spoken of the *information age* since the late 1970s. Today, there are no boundaries necessarily separating telephony from other information services. Alliances are being created among telecommunications companies, cable TV operators, entertainment producers in both television and the movies, networks, publishers, and computer companies. Aside from the cultural differences that have caused some of these alliances to break up, it is clear that the future will bring all types of communications to each of us over common pathways. A single communications path could carry voice for traditional telecommunications, one-way video for television and movies, two-way video for video conferencing, and data and images for computers and fax machines. This communications path may consist of wires (e.g., coaxial cables or fiber) or air (e.g., broadband cellular or satellite). As this transformation to the information age occurs, individual users will want and need more personalized communications capabilities, and smart cards can play a key role.

INDUSTRY TRENDS

The Telecommunications Reform Act, signed into law on February 8, 1996, is the catalyst in transforming the industry. Many of the changes slowly taking place over the past decade will be allowed and even encouraged by this new law. The Telecommunications Reform Act permits, for example, local competition, removing the monopoly that telephone companies have enjoyed. Telecommunications services could soon be offered by numerous providers, including cable TV companies. Similarly, television programs could be transmitted by local or long-distance telephone companies. The new law also permits local telephone companies to enter into electronic publishing.

Even before the Telecommunications Reform Act was signed into law, many types of alliances were being formed for the purposes of delivering services to customers and developing content. Regional Bell Operating Companies (RBOCs), for example, have formed alliances with Hollywood companies for program production and with cable TV companies for delivery of services. Several RBOCs have formed alliances to obtain licenses for Personal Communications Service (PCS), the newest form of wireless telecommunications. Another telephone company teamed with cable TV companies to obtain PCS licenses as well. Many long-distance carriers are providing access to the Internet, and RBOCs are following suit. Thus, as the following headlines indicate, there is tremendous convergence in the industry as many telecommunications companies try to get into each other's business:

- "Bell Atlantic to Buy Tele-Communications, Inc. and Liberty Media Corporation for $23 Billion," 10/13/93
- "Bell Atlantic - TCI Merger is Called Off," 2/24/94
- "Sprint Spectrum [Sprint Corp., Comcast Corp., TCI, and Cox Communications, Inc.] is Top Bidder in FCC Auction," 3/14/95 (winning 29 markets covering 145 million people and direct access to one-third of the homes in the United States)
- "MCI and Rupert Murdock's News Corporation Form Joint Venture," 5/10/95 (to provide electronic information)
- "GTE Joins Ameritech, BellSouth, and SBC Corporations in Alliance with Walt Disney Company," 8/11/95 (to develop and market video programs)
- "MCI and Microsoft Form Product Alliance," 1/29/96 (to market on-line and data networking services)

Players and Motivations The companies trying to expand beyond their traditional roles into information services can be characterized by the following industries:

- Telephone companies, including local, long-distance, cellular, and PCS carriers, interested in providing personalized and mobile voice

and data services, video services, and Internet access; developing video content; and electronic publishing
- Cable TV companies, interested in providing telephony services, including mobile services, and in developing video content
- Conglomerates that own cable TV companies, program-production facilities, and publishing companies, interested in expanding further into the telecommunications business
- Software companies, seeking to provide access to the Internet and other forms of information services

One of the greatest motivations for these companies is to gain larger market shares with one-stop shopping for more services than they provide today. By providing the information path into customers' homes and businesses and creating the content transmitted over those paths, a company could exert huge market leverage.

Little of the above discussion mentions smart cards, but they will play a key role as the industry transforms itself. Over the past few decades, the intelligence added to telecommunications networks through computers has tended to move both to the center of the networks and to the peripheries. Inside the network, computers do a tremendous amount of processing, not only to connect calls, but to offer a wide range of services, such as three-way calling and call waiting. In the peripheries, more intelligence has been appearing at the extremities: in telephone sets (including cellular phones), fax machines, modems, private branch exchanges, and even set-top boxes for cable TV customers. When smart cards containing telecommunications applications become available, the migration of intelligence will continue to move to the extremities, *viz.* into the smart cards. Smart cards are emerging as an enabling technology for the use of sophisticated telecommunications and information services.

TELECOMMUNICATIONS APPLICATIONS

Prepaid Telephone Cards   Prepaid telephone cards are purchased by consumers for fixed amounts (e.g., $5.00, $10.00, and $20.00) and used to pay for service from public pay phones equipped with smart card readers.

Players and Motivations   Telephone companies and telephone-service providers are the primary issuers of prepaid telephone cards. The first widespread use of such cards began in 1986 in France, when the French Post Telephone and Telegraph (PTT) decided to upgrade its public pay phones and equip them to read smart cards. The reasons the French PTT decided to make this investment were to reduce loss from vandalism and theft, to reduce operations costs associated with maintenance and coin collection, and to provide better service. Many countries have since followed suit, and the sale of prepaid phone cards dominates the industry today.

In 1995, 1.5 billion prepaid telephone cards were sold. Four hundred million of these cards were smart cards that can be accepted in one of every five pay phones in more than 70 countries. See Exhibit 8–1. The growth in the number of prepaid telephone smart cards has been 40 percent per year.

Convenience to Customers The reason telephone companies want to issue prepaid telephone cards is convenience. First is the convenience to customers. People who want to make telephone calls from pay phones and want to pay cash need exact change, and sometimes a lot of change for very long calls or international calls. The use of a prepaid smart card removes the need for change during the call since the cost of the call is deducted from the card as the call progresses. Should a card run out of money, most pay phones will allow the caller to remove the spent card and insert another to continue the call.

EXHIBIT 8–1

The Number of Countries Operating Smart Card Pay Phones

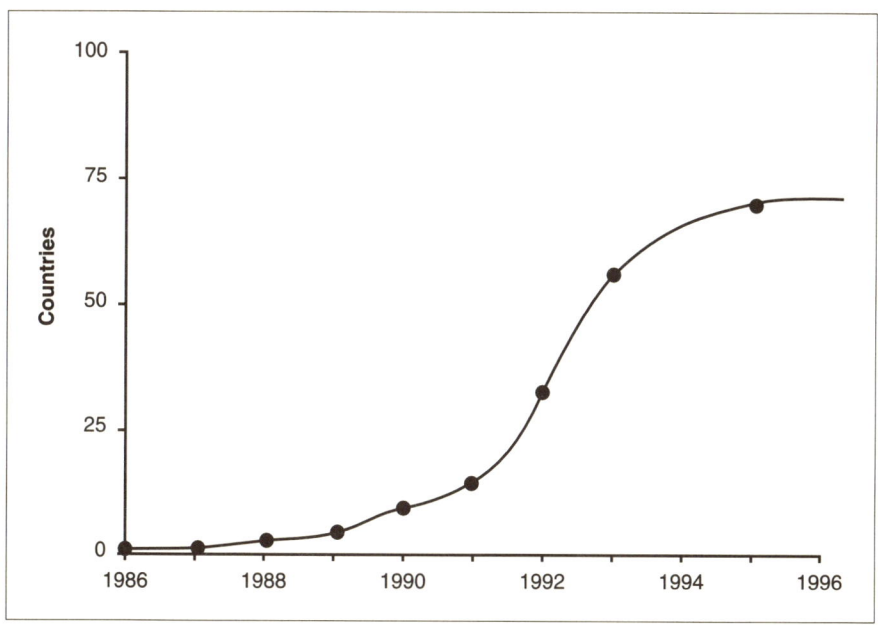

Many people today use pay phones and are candidates for the sale of prepaid smart cards. Some of these customers do not want to use credit cards or cannot get credit, and others are people who visit the United States and who are used to the convenience of prepaid telephone cards in their own countries.

Convenience to Telephone Companies The second reason for prepaid cards is convenience to telephone companies. The most obvious benefit is that the cards are sold before the service is provided. Many cards are purchased by collectors who never intend to use the cards. This results in millions of dollars of float or unclaimed funds.

Another benefit is that the cards help reduce the cost of cash collection, which is labor intensive. Periodically, telephone companies dispatch employees to remove the cash from pay phones and bring it to a collection center, where the coins are counted and packaged for shipment to a bank. Phones are sometimes vandalized for the coins they contain; so a coinless phone that accepts only smart cards would be a less attractive target and reduce repair costs. Such phones would also reduce maintenance costs for the mechanically complex coin phones.

Another reason a telephone company would issue smart cards is to keep customer loyalty. The cards could be branded with the name of the telephone company to remind customers where to use it. Alternatively, the telephone company could sell the advertising space on the smart card to another company.

Finally, telephone companies could charge exact amounts (to the penny) for calls made using smart cards. Costs of calls are now in increments of five cents because it was not economical to have pay phones accept pennies. In fact, telephone companies could even offer smart card users discounts since the use of the cards would identify the caller as a smart card user. Eric F. Ensor, President, BellSouth Personal Communications, notes that "smart cards can create a differentiation among wireless services, and we are excited about the opportunities they present to us at BellSouth Personal Communications. They will allow us to enhance our distribution plan by opening up a number of new channels and, over time, will offer substantial co-marketing opportunities.

"The smart card can do for telephony what the credit card did for finance. The flexibility that smart cards provide will be important as wireless services further penetrate the consumer marketplace. And since we anticipate smart cards only getting smarter, the potential uses will continue to expand."

Single-Application Prepaid Telephone Cards Today's prepaid telephone smart cards are disposable; they use wired logic and are inexpensive to make. The next generation of smart cards will be reloadable.

CHAPTER 8   Telecommunications and Information Services   133

Although they will be more expensive to produce, their reuse will more than make up the difference between them and the cheaper disposable cards.

Single-application smart cards are those that can only be used for telephone calls, and evolution of this telephony application can take several branches. First, the cards issued by one telephone company may be accepted by another. A person with a card purchased from US WEST, for example, may be able to use it in Atlanta in a BellSouth pay phone; and vice versa. Making this happen requires interoperability between the cards and the pay phones as well as a process to settle payments.

Another evolutionary path will be telephone sets with smart card readers in them. This would allow prepaid cards to be used from phones other than pay phones. The market exists for such uses and is exemplified by the growing number of people who use credit cards or prepaid "800" cards.

Unlike smart cards, prepaid "800" cards contain no technology. Instead, they access a remote database which tracks the remaining value of the account. Their advantage is that they can be used from any telephone with a tone pad; their disadvantage is the large number of digits a customer must enter, first to call the data base, second to enter the account number unique to each card, and finally, to enter the telephone number of the called party. These prepaid 800 cards do not have to be issued by the service provider, and about 40 percent of them are used as promotional means for companies and other organizations. Other cards are issued by service providers and often provide discounts for long-distance calls.

OPEN-SYSTEM ELECTRONIC PURSE CARDS

As mentioned previously, the next generation of telephone cards will be reloadable and, of course, reusable. The card holder, using a single-application card, would have to return the card to the issuer or sales outlet and pay to have more money loaded onto it.

A more likely scenario is that reloadable cards will have an electronic purse application that can be used to pay for a variety of services and goods, from pay-telephone service to candy from a vending machine. For these cards, the issuer does not have to be the same as the service provider, and the card holder would have a variety of choices for adding money to the card. One choice is to pay the issuer to add money, as described above. Another choice is to use an automated teller machine (ATM) to transfer money from a bank account to the card. A third choice, of interest to the telecommunications industry, is to perform this transfer by telephone. A pay phone that has a smart card reader could be used as an ATM machine. Screen-based telephones with smart card readers offer another option.

Players and Motivations

Open-system electronic purse cards and multi-application cards cross all boundaries, from financial services to telecommunications and retailing, from healthcare to government services, and from transportation to travel and entertainment. From a telecommunications-industry perspective, electronic purse cards bring many more players into the arena.

The telecommunications infrastructure, from international networks to telephone sets with smart card readers, becomes an enabling infrastructure that will attract many businesses to smart cards. As we will demonstrate, the telecommunications network will enable such applications as home banking and airline ticketing. Other uses are too numerous to describe, although major applications are discussed later in this chapter.

APPLICATIONS FOR ELECTRONIC PURSE TELEPHONE CARDS

Screen-based telephones are beginning to appear in retail stores. In addition to the normal functions of a traditional telephone, these phones have a small screen with buttons either below the screen or on each side. The functions of these buttons can change, depending on how the phone is being used at the time, and the screen can be used to label the buttons. When equipped with smart card readers, these phones can be used as household ATMs.

With a screen-based phone in your house, you would insert your smart card into the reader, and the phone would be programmed to display the telephone number of your bank next to one of the function buttons around the screen. You would call your bank simply by pressing the button. When the bank's computer answers the call, it would authenticate the card and display a request on the screen for you to enter your personal identification number (PIN). Upon receiving a correct PIN, the bank's computer would display labels for the buttons on the screen, similar to the way an ATM dynamically labels buttons. You could then request that a certain amount of money be placed on your card.

The use of screen-based telephones is not limited to placing money onto a smart card. A full home-banking capability is available without requiring you to have a computer. You could, for example, make a deposit by transferring money

> **MONDEX USES PHONES AS ATMS**
>
> In the Mondex trial in Swindon, England, card holders can add more cash into their Mondex cards using pay phones equipped with smart card readers. Money is transferred from their bank accounts to the card, which can then be used, for example, to pay for telephone calls made from the same pay phone.

from your smart card to your account. Without using the smart card *per se*, you could request to see account balances and transfer money from one account to another. Some screen-based phones have keyboards that can slide out from underneath or from a rear panel to provide a capability to enter detailed information for functions such as paying bills.

The role of the smart card for these applications would be in authentication and possibly encryption. So far, on-line home banking using personal computers has not caught on in the marketplace. Perhaps the advent of inexpensive screen-based telephones and smart cards will be the products that make banks and consumers re-think home-banking services.

A screen-based telephone can be used for many other applications besides home banking. Mondex envisions them used to transfer money between two people, who must each have a screen-based telephone with a smart card reader. You could make airline reservations using such a telephone, and the reservation information and tickets could be placed onto your smart card. You would then insert your smart card into a reader at the gate in the airport to receive your boarding pass.

MOBILITY AND PERSONALIZED COMMUNICATIONS

Smart cards can provide the means for a telecommunications subscriber to access and use the same services from any telephone that can read the smart card.

Players and Motivations The first instance of mobility and personalized communications using a smart card occurred in 1992, when the Global System for Mobile Communications (GSM) was introduced. The GSM specifications, a pan-European effort completed in 1990, were written because cellular systems in various European countries were not interoperable and travelers wanted a system that they could carry from one country to another.

At the beginning of 1996, 22 European countries had 35 GSM systems in operation and GSM systems are operational in 70 countries in all. The number of subscribers rose from 3.8 million at the beginning of 1995 to 8.8 million a year later, a growth of 130 percent. In Europe, multiple operators are beginning to appear, giving consumers a choice of service providers; and many countries outside Europe are planning or implementing GSM, too.

In the United States, American Personal Communications and Sprint Spectrum joined to introduce the first GSM system in the U.S., in the Washington-Baltimore area. Shortly, other holders of PCS licenses, which were auctioned by the Federal Communications Commission (FCC) in 1995, will introduce GSM systems in other regions in the U.S. The companies that purchased PCS licenses were some traditional cellular-telephone providers, some alliances of telephone companies and nontraditional companies, and some newcomers. Seeing the enormous growth of cellular telephony and knowing that the opportunity for the existing cellular business is quite limited, these companies saw tremendous opportunity for PCS, which allows them to add new markets.

An important reason for using smart cards in mobile communications is the security features they offer. Almost all information sent over the air is encrypted, including telephone numbers, voice, data, and control information. It would be very difficult to intercept telephone numbers and illegally program them into cellular phones as is done today. Even if it were possible to intercept and decrypt transmissions, GSM systems use only a temporary identification, which is changed with each use. Thus the impact on expensive theft of service would be significant.

MOBILE AND PERSONALIZED TELECOMMUNICATIONS APPLICATIONS AND SERVICES

As we describe the applications and services for mobile and personalized telecommunications, we shall often refer to GSM as an example. A primary benefit of using a smart card is that the user's identity is on the smart card and is physically separate from the telephone.

Unlike cellular telephones in the United States, which must have the user's identity programmed into the telephone, GSM phones are like appliances, differentiated by their features and qualities, but inoperable until a smart card is inserted. This means that a user is not confined to using just one telephone, but can use any GSM phone. If a phone needs repair, for example, any other phone can be used as a replacement. New subscribers could be mailed smart cards by the service provider and the subscriber could separately purchase or lease a telephone.

Sprint Spectrum sells telephones with smart cards already inserted into the phone in the Washington-Baltimore area. After you buy the phone of your choice, you dial a toll-free number, and the smart card is activated over the air. You can then use the phone you purchased or any other compatible phone to make and receive calls.

The smart cards used in GSM phones are single-application cards called Subscriber Identity Module (SIM) cards. In the United States, they will be called User Identity Module (UIM) cards. The use of a UIM card makes all components of a PCS system more independent of each other. This decentralization would simplify the distribution of services and telephones, resulting in less expensive service for the end user. As multiple-application cards come into use, the UIM function is likely to become an application on such cards, and UIM-only cards may eventually disappear.

It is important to separate the communications functions of a telephone from the applications and services offered. There are currently three technologies under serious consideration for PCS in the United States, and only one of them is compatible with GSM. The other two do not use smart cards, but require that phones be programmed as cellular phones are today. There is no inherent reason, however, that these other technologies cannot be designed for use with smart cards; as GSM grows internationally, market pressures may force them into compatibility.

The three categories of UIM capabilities are mobility management, security management, and subscriber management. As mentioned earlier, these features are not limited to GSM-compatible telephones, but could be available to any telephone and technology that takes advantage of UIM capabilities, whether it is wireless (mobile) or fixed. Let's examine each UIM capability separately.

MOBILITY MANAGEMENT

Mobility management includes nationwide and international roaming—the ability to have continuous service even when crossing state and national borders. Nationwide roaming is activated when a smart card is inserted into a telephone. The telephone can be programmed to send a registration message when the card is inserted to let the telecommunications network know where the user can be reached. This registration is not limited to wireless telephones. For example, in the morning, you could put your UIM card into your car telephone as you drive to work. You could remove it and take it with you to your office, where you could insert it into your office telephone. At the end of the day, you could reverse your steps, deciding if you really want to put your UIM card into your home telephone to receive business calls there. You could also take your UIM card on business trips, using it in the telephones on airplanes, in rental cars, and in hotel rooms to register your location to receive calls. Your services could also be available to you at each location, as described below under subscriber management.

International roaming extends the nationwide roaming features. As demonstrated by GSM, it can be made possible by conforming to international UIM card standards developed by the International Organization of Standards (ISO). If additional global standards can be achieved, service-profile downloading can be extended to mobile and fixed telephones all over the world.

SECURITY MANAGEMENT

The UIM smart card can play a significant role in security management. First, it offers protection and privacy for subscribers. Although the subscriber's identifier is transmitted over the air when the phone enters a new cell, this identifier cannot be used to clone a new phone without the secret key on the smart card. Further, in GSM, a temporary identifier is subsequently created and used in the cell, and this temporary identifier is discarded when the phone is turned off or a new cell is entered.

Second, when the telephone is switched on or when the UIM card is inserted, a personal identification number (PIN) is requested before any calls (except emergency calls) can be made.

Third, the subscriber is authenticated through an algorithm stored on the UIM card before a call is set up. For subscribers who are roaming, the visited network does not have to know this algorithm because the subscriber's home network sends enough authentication parameters to the visited network for the authentication process to take place.

Fourth, once the subscriber is authenticated, speech, data, and control information are encrypted to ensure privacy. The key for the encryption algorithm is securely stored on the UIM card. Finally, remote activation, deactivation, modifications, and corrections to the service profile stored on the UIM card, as well as limited modifications to the telephone software, can be made remotely. This would make it possible to take real-time fraud control measures by decreasing the time between detecting and acting on a fraud attempt.

SUBSCRIBER MANAGEMENT

There are two parts to subscriber management: the subscriber's viewpoint and the service provider's viewpoint. From the subscriber's point of view, the UIM card stores his or her personal and telephone identification, service profile, and other information, such as a personal list of telephone numbers and short messages. The service profile on the UIM card will permit the subscriber to use all telephones the same way. For example, if the subscriber is used to using a "speed-calling list" to dial frequently called numbers, the UIM card could store this information for the subscriber's convenience.

The UIM card also contains billing information so that when the subscriber is roaming, the local network knows how the subscriber will pay for the services and can render appropriate bills. The UIM card allows a user to change telephones conveniently and at any time without having to have the telephone reprogrammed. This allows full mobility and roaming, as described earlier, and also permits the sharing of telephones. For example, employees or family members can share portable telephones if it is uneconomical for each to have his or her own. People working different shifts can share telephones, yet personalize them with their own UIM cards. This would also help an employer allocate charges for shared telephones.

In addition, employer-provided UIM cards can impose calling restrictions so that employees do not abuse telephone privileges. GSM also offers a Short Message Service (SMS) in which the telephone can be used as a two-way pager for receiving and sending short messages. The messages are first stored in the service provider's SMS center until they can be sent to the subscriber's UIM card. Being stored on the card, the messages travel with the subscriber rather than stay in the phone. This SMS feature is also used to modify remotely the service profile stored on the UIM card.

From the service provider's viewpoint, activation of a subscriber's service can be programmed into the UIM card before it is sold or sent to the subscriber, or activation can be done remotely. Thus telephones can be distributed independent of service activation, making centralized, expert-driven distribution of telephones and services unnecessary. This will enable a service provider to increase the number of sales locations while decreasing distribution costs. Because the telephone is independent of the subscriber's services, it can be replaced immediately if it fails or needs repair. On the other hand, the telephone's software can be modified or corrected remotely.

Modifications to the subscriber's service profile can be distributed via a new UIM card, without having to change anything in the telephone, or modifications to existing UIM cards can be done remotely. For mobile telephones, the most often used base-station frequencies are stored on the UIM card to shorten connection times.

MOBILE COMPUTING

The use of smart cards is not limited to mobile telephony. The popularity of laptop computers and mobile computing applications has made such devices indispensable in some businesses. Portable computers can be equipped with modems that attach to cellular telephones so that the computers can be used even when a connection to the fixed telephone network is not available.

One of the limitations of equipment available today is that data sent over the air with cellular telephones are not encrypted. Some of these contain sensitive, proprietary business information that could be received by anyone with an appropriate receiver.

Smart cards, similar to or the same as UIM cards, offer a solution. As discussed previously, everything sent over the air in a GSM system is encrypted, including authentication messages. The UIM card uses its encryption algorithm to encrypt speech and control information. In the same way, a UIM card could provide these capabilities for mobile computing.

A portable computer connected to a UIM-equipped telephone via a modem would have all its data encrypted in the same way voice is encrypted.

Received data would also be encrypted before transmission and decrypted by the UIM card. An additional level of protection could be provided by using a modem driven by a smart card. Such devices are being developed, and AT-type modem commands would be used to access the smart card.

ENTERTAINMENT

Smart cards can be the means of accessing entertainment services over a telecommunications or cable TV network.

Players and Motivations Providing home entertainment, originally the realm of radio and television broadcasters and later cable TV companies, has attracted other players because of anticipated growth in the home entertainment area. Traditional telephone companies are interested in providing television programs and movies over the telephone network, which may have its pairs of wires supplemented with coaxial cable, fiber-optic cable, and microwave transmission facilities to handle the higher bandwidths required. Direct-broadcast satellite companies have begun to offer up to 150 channels of programs over satellite receivers only 18 inches in diameter.

Because of the rapidly evolving infrastructure, other companies, including networks and movie studios, have become interested in providing programming. Software companies want to provide interfaces to make it easy to access the many choices that consumers will have and are interested in other forms of entertainment, such as interactive games.

Finally, equipment manufacturers see tremendous growth in new types of televisions that may also serve as computer screens, modems that will work on the coaxial cables of cable TV companies, more sophisticated set-top boxes, and new types of receivers and transmitters.

Besides the expected growth in home entertainment, there is likely to be a convergence across the three industries of telecommunications, cable TV, and computing. Today, each has its own networking infrastructure; yet companies in each of the industries are trying to expand into the others' territories. Cable TV companies are offering telephony services over cable TV networks, and telephone companies are offering cable TV services over telephone networks.

Today, the telephone network is used for remote access to computers, computer networks, and the Internet. However, cable TV companies are trying to provide such access with the use of cable modems, a relatively new product with the immediate advantage of substantially higher data rate—even higher than the ISDN access rates (128 kilobits/second) offered by telephone companies. This means much faster transmission of data and the ability to download higher bandwith video products such as movies and games. In response, telephone companies are deploying even higher-speed access technologies, such as Asymmetric Digital Subscriber Lines (ADSL).

SMART CARD-BASED APPLICATIONS

Smart cards can add substantial value to this growing industry by providing payment options, access authorizations, personalized services, and security. We shall assume that in the future, set-top boxes (or televisions with integrated set-top box functions) will include smart card readers. Payment options are not necessarily an important service when watching television at home, but people who travel may find them useful. The smart card could have a prepaid application and be used much like a prepaid telephone card, or it could contain billing and authorization information so that a service provider could get paid.

There has been much discussion about the television V-Chip, required by the Telecommunications Reform Act of 1996. This will allow parents to prevent their children from watching programs with violent and sexual content. An alternative to the V-Chip would be to use a smart card in the set-top box to gain access to television programs. Parents could give children their own smart cards, which could be programmed to permit the child to watch only what the parent feels is appropriate. Young children might have rather restricted access to television shows, while teenagers would have wider choices.

Smart cards could also be used to limit the amount of television children watch. Besides limiting the specific types of shows, the smart card could have a "TV budget," equivalent to a stored value in an electronic purse application. When the week's budget of, say, five hours is used up, the child would not be able to access any more television for that week. Children may be able to pool their resources with their friends, of course, but this approach provides a great deal more control than is now avaliable.

Smart cards can also be used to personalize services. The future will bring a bewildering number of television channels into the home, and viewers will likely have their favorite channels. A smart card could store the viewer's list of favorite channels and display those choices first, much like a telephone card would carry a speed-calling list. Each viewer would have a customized card; so compromises on the channel lineup that is displayed would be unnecessary. Furthermore, these smart cards could allow roaming, much like telephone cards. When you check into a hotel, you could place your smart card into the television set and see your favorite channel lineup as you do at home.

Finally, smart cards could provide security features. As television becomes more interactive, the smart card could be used to encrypt information you wish to send. Home shopping, for example, uses the telephone network today for ordering products. With interactive television, this would not be necessary. Since cable TV transmission technology is not secure (all information is broadcast to everyone on the cable system), consumers may be reluctant to send ordering information and credit-card numbers over the cable. By encrypting the information as is done in GSM, smart cards could make all transactions over interactive television secure.

COMPUTING

People are accessing computer services and the Internet in growing numbers, and smart cards can provide easy, secure access to these services.

Players and Motivations With over 30 percent of the households in the United States with personal computers (PCs) and a large percentage of PCs equipped with modems, many companies are trying to take advantage of related commercial opportunities. In addition, new Internet terminals, possibly selling for as low as $500, may be introduced in 1996. They will allow users to access the Internet to send and receive electronic mail, access the World Wide Web, and run certain applications based on new Internet environments. Companies interested in capitalizing on this growth are:

1. Hardware manufacturers of computers, terminals, modems, and other peripherals
2. Software companies that provide the applications that enable and increase the use of computers
3. Service providers that give access to networks and applications, from simple Internet-access providers to value-added providers such as America Online, CompuServe, and Prodigy
4. Commercial businesses that permit remote services, from banks offering sophisticated money-management applications to small businesses that advertise on the Internet.

Another industry that seems to be taking hold is providing public access to the Internet. Coffee shops and libraries are being equipped with PCs, and the public is invited to use them, usually for a fee.

Computing Applications
Several applications enabled by smart cards—mobility, access, personalization, payment, and security—have parallels in telecommunications applications. Although mobile computing was discussed earlier, there are several other uses for a smart card in mobile computing.

In mobile telephony, such as GSM, all the security features are in the smart card, not the telephone. This would allow portable computers to be shared, yet made individually secure with a user's own smart card. With smart cards, computer users would not be restricted to using their own computers. Personal computers on a network can be configured to allow any user to use any computer. A smart card could facilitate this by helping to authenticate the user: a user would insert the smart card into a reader, the PC would initiate an authentication procedure, including asking the user for a PIN or password, and would then configure the PC according to the user's profile.

For public access to the Internet, from a coffee shop for example, a smart card could be used to provide payment for the service in addition to personalizing the PC for the card holder.

The powerful authentication and encryption capabilities of a smart card would benefit traveling and mobile employees greatly. They would be able to establish their own telecommunications and computing environments wherever they are, and would be able to access even the most sensitive information in company data bases. All transmissions, including voice and data, would be encrypted, and employees would know that even their electronic mail could not be intercepted and read, especially when transmitted over the air. Smart cards could also be used to keep data secure.

By authenticating specific users, computer applications could restrict access to those who are authorized. One benefit of using a smart card is that multiple authorizations for different applications could be stored on it, but the user would have to remember only one PIN or password rather than the multiplicity of passwords required by today's multiple systems.

Finally, smart cards could alleviate the concern about sending credit card numbers over the Internet. A smart card could be used as a direct payment mechanism (via an electronic purse application) or as an encryption device to authenticate and secure credit card numbers sent over the Internet.

Network-Based Services Telecommunications networks can serve to enable other applications of smart cards, such as home banking and remote access. Although some of these applications were discussed earlier, the functions that the telecommunications network performs to add value to these applications were not.

Players and Motivations The parties interested in network-based services are the network-services providers, viz. the telephone companies. These include both local and long-distance service providers and, in the future, other providers such as cable TV operators. These providers are interested in network-based services for two reasons. First, they are interested in increasing the use of their networks; second, they can provide value-added services.

Directory Applications Directory applications allow smart card users to easily find the services and applications they want to use when they want to use them. Their primary purpose is to add convenience for the user, particularly when the user is traveling and wishes to locate a specific service or application. They also offer the user the option of establishing a connection to the application or service.

The application may work as follows: When you insert a smart card into a telephone (or a computer or set-top box) and access the directory application, it asks you to make a specific request (e.g., a person's name, a smart card-accessible banking application, or the nearest pizza store), which may include specific parameters chosen by you (e.g., price or location). The directory executes a search and presents you with the results, possibly asking you for more information or to make a selection among the choices presented. The method of accepting requests and supplying information depends upon the capabilities of the telephone or terminal you are using (e.g., voice response or screen-based). Once you have selected a specific service or application, the directory application may give you a price for establishing a direct connection to the service or application. You then have the option of either proceeding and establishing the connection, saving the information on the smart card, or starting over with a new request.

Security Applications Security applications in the network include key management, authentication, certification, and fraud control. The purpose of key-management applications is to ensure that cryptographic keys used by secret-key encryption algorithms on smart cards are correctly generated and issued and that these keys are known only to the parties who should legitimately possess them. Smart card users need private keys to encrypt and decrypt data and to access various applications in the authentication process. Such privacy and secrecy are required by certain applications, such as financial transactions, particularly when they involve an exchange of money using an electronic-purse application.

INFORMATION MANAGEMENT APPLICATIONS

Information stored on a smart card is quite valuable to the card holder and to the service providers whose applications may be resident on the card. If a card is lost or damaged, the information may be irretrievably lost as well. Information on a smart card may be established through a variety of applications, which may be independent. Because of multiple applications, some of which may be used off-line, it may be difficult if not impossible, to re-establish the exact state of the card if it is lost, stolen, or damaged. An information-backup application can take a snapshot of the card (i.e., make a copy of the contents of its memory) at particular points in time and store it in a secure medium. If it becomes necessary to replace the card, the information-backup application could be used to initialize the new card to that same point in time if the information could not otherwise be recreated.

The information-backup application could be accessed by a card holder as often as needed to copy the contents of the card, and the frequency of use would depend on the nature of the information on the card and the comfort level of the card holder in keeping information on the card. Because of possibly independent applications on the same card, a neutral third party, such as a network provider, would be the appropriate choice to store the information securely.

During the life of a smart card, its memory will often be changed through the use of particular applications. In addition, other changes may have to occur at either the card level or within individual applications. As smart cards become more sophisticated with more complex operating systems, memory management will become increasingly important. At the card level, the total number of applications on the card can be increased or decreased, or an existing application may be overwritten with an update or a different application.

Application-independent information, such as card serial number or card holder name, is also managed at the card level. These data may be accessible by all applications, but cannot always be updated or modified by any one application or application provider. This information can either be updated by the card holder or by the card issuer, depending upon the specific data items. The card holder may be able to update certain card holder-related data by inserting the smart card into a terminal with a keypad or alphanumeric capabilities and accessing an update application. This can allow the user to update information, such as a change of address.

Some card-related data may be updated by a card issuer using an appropriate terminal and update application. The card holder could also use an update application to add yet another application to the smart card. However, the application provider would have to be contacted for specific application details and customization. Updates to specific applications (e.g., obtaining a newer version of the software) would be made by contacting the application provider, possibly with remote access through the telecommunications network.

TECHNOLOGICAL ISSUES

The technological issues fall into two major categories: interoperability and evolutionary directions. As the first telecommunications applications in the

United States become established, the question arises as to whether the smart card used in one application could also be used in another. There are two aspects to this question. First, can a smart card used in one application (e.g., the US WEST Telecard) be used in another similar application (e.g., pay phones provided by another service provider)?

The answer to this question involves not only the acceptance of "foreign" smart cards by a service provider in a technical sense, but also the payment mechanism for providing the service. The technical questions center around the representation of money and the security mechanisms built into smart cards and smart card readers. Prepaid cards used today represent the lowest denomination of money needed for the particular application as a single bit. For pay phones, a bit usually represents five cents, but it could represent, instead, one cent (requiring five times the number of bits). This representation of money may not be uniform throughout the country and across different applications (e.g., a parking-meter application may represent 25 cents as a single bit). Security mechanisms are designed to prevent unauthorized cards from being used, but they were not designed to accept smart cards from a large number of card issuers. Payment mechanisms would also have to be established.

If you buy your card from one service provider but use the services of another, the first provider would need to pay the second. This requires establishing business relationships and mechanisms to guard against fraud by card users and by service providers.

The second aspect of card interoperability involves open-system electronic purse cards. A bank, for example, may issue a stored-value card with an electronic purse application. If this is used in a pay phone, the questions of acceptance by the security mechanisms and establishment of payment mechanisms also arise. The difference is that such cards are no longer simply a single-application telephone card, and the pay phone would have to be built to accept a wider range of payment choices by the consumer. The other difference is that payment agreements are already in place between telephone companies. Electronic purse cards would require that new relationships be established with other parties. As the number of card issuers grows, clearinghouses will be needed to handle the payment transactions.

Achieving international interoperability adds new challenges to those discussed above. The most obvious challenge is to account for the different monetary systems (e.g., converting Canadian dollars to U.S. dollars and vice versa). Another challenge is that there are fundamental differences in the way pay phones are built and operated in different countries. These differences may affect the interoperability of smart cards.

EVOLUTIONARY ISSUES

The issues surrounding evolutionary directions today primarily involve wireless telecommunications. There are currently more than three technologies under consideration for PCS, and only one of them can accept smart cards and is compatible with GSM. The other technologies would require significant changes to be compatible with a smart card. Evolution issues are not limited to mobile telephony. As discussed earlier, mobile computing requires over-the-air data encryption, and a smart card could provide the encryption key. It is not yet clear whether the encryption should be done by the cellular phone or by the modem. Using a smart card in the modem would add versatility by providing encryption when the modem is used with a fixed, wired connection. Evolution of fixed telephones, cable-TV set-top boxes, and computers could also include plans to incorporate smart cards for the convenience of users and protection of information. Again, national and international standards bodies need to start addressing these issues.

A final technical issue is to determine how much information should be (or can fit) on a smart card and how much should be in the network. The applications affected by this have to do with user profiles, backup and storage of information, and security. For some services, user profiles may require more information than can reasonably fit onto a smart card. For these, the smart card could be used to identify and authenticate the user, and the network could be used to retrieve the user's profile information and to convey it to the application being accessed. This would allow, for example, a user to personalize a networked computer by activating it with a smart card. Information backups were discussed earlier, but it may be possible for the network to supplement the storage on a smart card with storage in the network. This, too, would be useful for applications that require too much user-specific information.

The question of security has to do with how much can be done at the periphery of the network and how much is appropriate in the network. Public keys, for example, could be stored as part of a network directory service.

LEGAL, REGULATORY, AND PUBLIC POLICY ISSUES

A number of issues in the public policy arena concern the telecommunications and information services industry. The first issue deals with prepaid telephone cards. While today they are considered a cash equivalent and guaranteed by telephone companies, regulatory pressures may come to bear if unscrupulous parties sell cash cards that do not work and disappear with the money. As multi-application cards put electronic purses into widespread use, what regulations will apply? Will pay phones of the future have to print receipts?

Although card ownership may largely be a business issue, the future may see regulations governing this. This affects the telecommunications industry not only because of telecommunications applications on the card, but also because the telecommunications network may be used to update the information on a card. For example, the Telecommunications Reform Act of 1996 places more decision making at the federal level (i.e., the Federal Communications Commission) and less at the state level (e.g., public utility commissions). It is not clear at this time whether these regulatory bodies will want to regulate the use of smart cards in telephones.

BUSINESS ISSUES

Several business issues are associated with the technology issues described above, including security and payment mechanisms. Although the technical security issues can be resolved, solutions may require that service providers and card issuers share secret keys. This may not be acceptable to some companies, and relationships will have to be found to deal with it. Perhaps a trusted third party will act as a secure clearinghouse. Similarly, while payment mechanisms can be solved technically, business issues may be more cumbersome. In the telecommunications business today, carriers exchange payments with each other for services rendered; for example, services to customers traveling and using their telephone credit cards, or long-distance calls connected through several carriers.

With prepaid smart cards, these relationships can still be used to exchange payment. In fact, the security mechanisms built into pay phones will help validate calls and reduce refunds due to repudiations. With electronic purse applications and a large number of issuers of stored-value cards, the number of business relationships would increase by orders of magnitude. It is likely that clearinghouses, like those used in the financial services industry, would have to be involved in settling payments.

Another issue alluded to earlier is one of card ownership. If a multi-application or electronic purse card is issued by a bank, how can the cardholder add a telecommunications application to it? Can the telecommunications provider do it or must the cardholder return to the bank? Similarly, if a telecommunications provider issues a card, can the cardholder add an electronic purse application? If so, how? One way to frame this issue is with an analogy to screen-based telephones. Suppose you go to a store and buy a screen-based phone; you then own it. When you contact your phone company to obtain the services available for it, the phone company will remotely send a telecommunications program to the phone, where it is stored. If you then want to do home banking, you would call your bank, which would download its program into your phone. In this case, you own the phone, and the service providers own the applications. You are responsible for managing the number of applications you store in the phone because storage is limited. Should smart cards perhaps also be owned by card holders responsible for managing the applications they put on them?

High infrastructure cost as an entry barrier raises still another issue. Depending on the universe of potential customers, the infrastructure might be quite limited, such as on a college campus, or it could be quite broad (e.g., US WEST is deploying 16,000 pay phones with smart card readers in its 5 largest markets). In the telecommunications industry, public pay phones appeal to a mass market and would involve a large upgrading expense. A more limited application would be screen-based phones with smart card readers. The market for these may be manageable in terms of size and scope, since the primary applications might be for home banking, travel reservations, and others services obtainable from home. Another entry barrier is the potentially high cost of upgrades. The next generation of pay phones will have improved security modules. Today, these are hardware modules and have to be changed manually. In the future, it is expected that many upgrades will be able to be done remotely through software.

Another barrier to entry is the lack of industry-accepted standards. Many businesses are reluctant to make a significant investment if it is uncertain what technologies will be standardized and accepted in the marketplace. Most smart cards used today for telecommunications are contact cards; but contactless card technologies are still around. Prepaid telephone cards are not necessarily compatible with certain electronic-purse, credit, and debit applications, which are becoming widely accepted in the financial services community. Smart cards used for GSM are not compatible either, and it is not clear whether any infrastructure (e.g., pay phones and GSM phones) will have to be changed to achieve compatibility.

CONCLUSION

Despite some of the challenges that lay ahead, there is a big telecommunications market for smart card issuers and service providers. Judging from the "800" telephone card market, which does not use smart cards yet, issuers who are not service providers seem to have found a growing business. We may conclude that the next wave of growth in this area will be in issuing smart cards. More important, the rapid growth of GSM and the convenience of global roaming has guaranteed a place for smart card in the cellular phone business. Applications of GSM cards in wired telephones are likely to appear soon because the roaming infrastructure is already in place. In addition, telecommunications networks provide an enabling infrastructure for open-system electronic purse cards and multi-application cards across all businesses, including financial services, retailing, healthcare, government services, transportation, travel, and entertainment. This infrastructure will attract many businesses to smart cards and help ensure their success.

CHAPTER 9

Healthcare and Smart Card Technology

Lorraine Brainerd
Kaiser Permanente

Judy D. Tarbox
Thornebrook Associates

Political, social, and economic pressures are exerting strong demands on the healthcare industry to reduce costs, increase the availability of information, expand coverage, and improve the quality of care. A national movement aimed at cost-cutting via automation means advancement toward implementing efficient methods to manage the business of healthcare.

Until now, the healthcare industry has notoriously lagged behind other industries in using technology effectively to reduce administrative costs and fraud. Pressure to reduce costs and fraud as well as to improve the communication of information will promote the use of advanced card technologies in the healthcare industry.

In fact, the cost of medical care in the United States each year is $1.2 trillion. The 1992 and 1993 Health Insurance Association of America Survey of Health Insurance Fraud showed that approximately 9.3 percent of all claims paid were fraudulent. This amounts to over $100 billion. "With secure identity verification and automated eligibility verification, fraud could be reduced well over 50 percent," according to Jim Lout, CEO of Advantage Data Systems in a recent *World Card Technology,* article. A reduction of only 10 percent would amount to over $10 billion per year in savings.

In addition, in today's medical environment the patient is the only one involved who does not have access to his or her own personal data. Records are maintained by each physician treating the patient, by every institution servicing the patient, and by any insurer that covers a service. Medical records are often processed through clearinghouses used by providers and transmitted over normal telephone services. Although today's system does provide many places where redundant information is stored and available, it poses major problems in consolidating all information concerning a single patient. And as stated earlier, the patient has virtually no access to the data, no ability to determine what is in the various data bases, and no process for changing anything inaccurate.

The one item that nearly every patient does have is a health access card (also termed health identification card). Many individuals carry a health access card because they are instructed to by their employer or health benefits carrier. Other individuals view the card as a symbol of having health insurance coverage. Still others feel that the card is the key that unlocks the door to medical treatment.

In its simplest form, a health access card is a credit card-sized patient card made of paper or plastic that contains identification information. These cards allow a means for providers to gather limited information, to verify eligibility and coverage, as well as to submit claims. Even this limited usage of current health access cards has made them the centerpieces of several healthcare reform proposals.

In fact, health access card technology could help improve timely access to health information such as demographics, insurance, and basic medical information needed for emergency treatment. Further, many of today's technologies will enable a card to house a patient's entire health history.

HEALTHCARE TRENDS

Per capita healthcare spending in the United States ranks among the world's highest. This is due to many factors including the high cost of equipment and personnel, and the high cost and fraudulent claims common to insurance. In order for the United States to reduce per capita healthcare spending to the level of other developed countries such as France, Canada, and Germany, it will have to reduce systemic costs.

Many industry experts believe that one way to do this is to automate the Health Access Card to allow for electronic verification of eligibility, plan benefits, and deductibles, thus reducing administrative costs significantly.

This healthcare technology actually encompasses a wide range of currently available applications. Healthcare *smart card* technology is nothing new to the United States and is even more familiar in Europe and Canada where smart card healthcare programs have been in place for several years.

In the United States, health smart cards have been introduced in Oklahoma City and Florida on a pilot basis.

Since 1986, France has been promoting a healthcare smart card called Vitale to streamline the administration and reimbursement procedures for French Social Security services by:

- Replacing the 800 million paper claim forms produced yearly
- Eliminating use of medication labels for reimbursement
- Cutting reimbursement times from weeks to days
- Making substantial savings in Social Security costs
- Offering cardholders other services

In the Vitale system, patients carry cards with their identification, eligibility information, a record of services rendered and fees earned. The information is validated by the healthcare practitioner and electronically processed for payment. The full-scale system envisions a dual card system with 50 million patient cards and 1.2 million health professional practitioners' cards. These will be used in over 600,000 terminals and will be renewed every 4 years.

Worldwide, healthcare smart cards are raising the quality and reducing the cost of healthcare by providing efficiencies in the administration and handling of medical information. We find other examples today in Canada, Finland, Japan, Austria, and Germany, to name just a few.

PLAYERS AND MOTIVATORS

Obviously, the three groups likely to extract significant efficiencies and improved services with the use of healthcare smart cards are patients, providers, and payers, each from a specific perspective.

Patients Perhaps the most significant advantage to using healthcare smart cards is the improved quality of patient care. The cards' ability to store pertinent medical records gives providers immediate access to medical histories, current conditions, and prescription drug information, making the most effective treatments possible. Availability of recent lab test results may eliminate redundant testing and the wait for existing medical records. In emergency situations, knowledge of pre-existing medical conditions and known allergies allows the treating team to avoid inappropriate remedies.

Cardholder demographics stored on the smart card, including primary physician and coverage information, improves access to treatment when traveling, moving, or when changing primary providers. This is especially valuable for patients with chronic or recurring illnesses. The smart card eliminates the need for transcription of medical history and/or insurance information and informs provider office staff of the extent of coverage, thus streamlining service.

Providers Healthcare smart cards possess significant potential for reducing administrative cost and improving efficiencies. With accurate coverage information provided on the card, providers reduce costs for rework due to errors, need fewer communications with insurance personnel, and have more time to devote to the medical practice. Patient information obtained from the smart card allows providers to immediately verify coverage, benefit contract levels, deductibles, and co-insurance. It also eliminates the need for medical records transfer requests. Thus, new patient data capture time is greatly reduced.

Healthcare smart cards could eliminate some costly and frustrating practices completely. One of these, verification of patient eligibility, is performed every time a patient visits a provider. This is particularly true at HMOs. In the case of dependent identification, for example, the smart card could uniquely identify each dependent with a full name, date of birth, sex, and social security number, eliminating the need to check and recheck records or coverage information.

Payers Many of the smart card benefits cited above accrue to payers as well. Electronic Data Interchange (EDI) via the smart card reduces administrative costs by allowing for less "keying" of information and for more direct transfer of provider information that is complete and consistent with the payers' database. It also promotes reduced claim costs in treatment proficiencies and the elimination of redundant testing. This results in an overall improvement in the quality of care. With less manual intervention and rework from improved accuracy of coverage and benefit levels, fewer claims will be suspended for incomplete or inaccurate data. Thus claims examiners are able to focus on more complex claims and speed up processing.

The benefits (motivators) listed in Exhibit 9–1 are possible through the integration of a smart card with an on-line system maintained by either the insurance carrier or the healthcare institution itself. It assumes that the card will be updated by the carriers each time it is used before the data are presented to the requesting medical staff. (This may or may not be true in a transient facility such as an ambulance or paramedic unit.) See Exhibit 9–1.

IMPORTANT ASPECTS OF THE HEALTHCARE SMART CARD

Access and Security A healthcare smart card can be used either as an access key to centralized databases or as a standalone medical file. Both applications require system support but each provides a unique approach. Although the smart card is an effective access key to a centralized database system, its capabilities are better served when the card is used to store the patients' medical files. What distinguishes the healthcare smart card from other types of cards is its ability to transport confidential data securely from cardholder to practitioner

EXHIBIT 9-1

Players and Motivators of Healthcare Smart Cards Table

Players	Motivators					
	Quality of Care	Access to Critical Information	Improved Security	Eligibility	Tracking Medications	Administrative Cost
Patients	Holistic treatment based on patient history as well as current conditions	Medical records would be available in real time regardless of patient condition	Medical records maintained privately not by multiple institutions	Positive verification of eligibility and benefits without filling out paperwork	Easy check for conflicting medications	Less time in filling out forms at provider locations
Service Providers	Additional data would increase probability of most effective diagnosis and treatment	Access to real time patient medical history and drug use would save lives	Records would not get lost or delayed during patient care	Reduces office clerical support	Medication history for diagnostic assistance	Reduced time in filling out claims forms and in verifying eligibility
Payers	Superior patient outcomes due to more information would reduce the overall cost of care	Minimize repetition of diagnostic tests. Improves the quality of care	Patient verification (PIN) required for non-emergency treatment	Reduces the clerical support for the inquiry process. Ensures data on patient is complete and current	Provides the most cost effective delivery of prescription drugs	Clean claim data reduces suspense. Telephone verification of eligibility is reduced

and the convenience of having that data available immediately. Access to data on a smart card could be controlled by the patient. Audit trails, of both access and modification of the card database, document who used the data and why. This improves both privacy and security of patient records.

Recently, PCMCIA (Personal Computer Memory Card International Association) created a widely adopted standard that enables cards to store a complete medical record including digitized images (X-ray, sonograms, computerized topography, magnetic resonance imaging(MRI) and electrocardiograms) as well as demographics and basic medical information. These can be transported with the cardholder. As storage capabilities for smart cards increase, many of these records will be capable of being stored and transported in the more convenient smart card form.

Healthcare smart card security features restrict access to data stored on the chip through use of a password or PIN. The microprocessor compares the password encrypted on the chip to that entered in the reader device. This comparison feature makes the smart card a more secure method of verifying a patient's identity and reduces the overhead associated with centralized password management systems. The local PC or mainframe access control system still requires a unique sign-on code from the user. This is generated by the card using cryptographic authentication routines. The process is transparent to the user and the user's password is never revealed openly once loaded onto the card. Similarly, healthcare smart cards may employ a series of sign-on privileges that determine which host to access while restricting users to the information required to perform their tasks.

Consequently, healthcards would allow individual patients to maintain their own medical records, empowering the patient to consent to any access of the data by authorizing access to the card.

Data Storage Healthcare smart cards can help alleviate the public's concern about easy availability of personal and financial information housed in large, centralized databases. As a repository for healthcare data, a card may act in lieu of a computerized centralized database or linked network of information.

Clinical and administrative data repositories would also need to be developed and maintained as backups to the information stored on an individual card. These could be housed in the primary care physician's office with limited and restricted availability. Remote access to this information could be controlled by the patient through keys stored in the card.

The healthcard, as a patient-borne record, would represent a distributed database with the advantage that real-time access to information is available only with the informed consent of the patient.

Pilot studies are proving the potential of health cards. One conducted in England, called the Exeter Care Card Project, involving 12,000 Care Cards, proved the Care Card a reliable means of patient retained data transfer and has also shown the potential for reducing the costs of healthcare delivery and aiding overall service efficiency.

One major issue that needs to be addressed in this type of open architecture system is the design of a set of unique identifiers for providers, payers, employers, and patients to avoid redundancy and errors. For example, the largest open architecture smart card program in the United States, the Oahu Test, is being performed in Hawaii by the United States Department of Defense (DOD). The test demonstrates the benefits of smart card technology in multiple functional areas including soldier readiness processing, transportation manifesting, food service, patient reception, field medical support, and patient evacuation. Nearly 50,000 cards will be issued by the end of the project in 1996. This pilot is part of a larger information contract between government and multiple vendors. It is also part of a DOD-wide corporate information management program aimed at standardizing data elements and language within an open systems architecture. Central and individually carried data storage are seen as supplementary and complementary. The DOD smart card prototype, termed Multi-technology Automated Reader Card (MARC), contains bar code and integrated circuit chip technologies.

The initial field medical component of the MARC Test demonstrated substantial business process improvement over current practices. While the current cardboard field medical cards literally disintegrated in wet conditions, healthcare smart cards quickly captured data and reliably moved it with the patient from foxhole, to battalion aid station, to field hospital.

Payments Consortia of providers, insurers, and financial institutions could significantly streamline the financial administration of a medical situation. The service provider could submit a record to the insurer, who would process and pay the provider according to the prevailing contract. The insurer could then determine any patient responsibilities such as co-payment or deductible. Patient charges would be collected directly from the financial institution which would then bill the patient. The provider would not have the overhead of accounts receivable. The insurer would continue to process claims and data. The financial institution would provide a value-added service to its customers. For example, a doctor provides a standard office visit to a patient. The doctor files a claim for $100 against the patient. The insurance provider pays the doctor $80 (the negotiated amount for a standard office visit). The insurance company checks the patient contract and determines that there is a $20 co-pay and a $50 deductible which has not yet been satisfied. The insurance company collects $70 from the financial institution which subsequently collects from the patient.

Healthcare Smart Card Applications Worldwide, healthcare smart cards are raising the quality and reducing the cost of healthcare by improving the efficiency of administrative and medical information handling. They are being implemented across a broad range of applications, from simple insurance cards to high security medical record storage.

Insurance healthcare smart cards provide substantial labor and cost savings by reducing the time spent on routine paper work, eliminating transcription errors, reducing fraud, and expediting the payment process for both medical professionals and patients.

According to the Institute of Medicine, the U.S. General Accounting Office, and the Journal of the American Medical Association:

- During 30 percent of office visits, doctors cannot get access to the patients' medical records
- 11 percent of laboratory tests are duplicated needlessly
- Medication interaction causes 33 percent of emergency room visits by elderly patients
- Physicians spend 38 percent of their time writing up patients' charts
- Diagnoses are omitted from patients' records 40 percent of the time

Healthcare Smart Cards could significantly reduce these costly and dangerous inefficiencies.

The following sections examine more closely various applications that can be performed by smart cards for each of the groups mentioned earlier—patients, service providers (including physicians and medical care facilities), and payers (including group administrators and insurance companies).

PATIENT APPLICATIONS AND BENEFITS

Improved Quality of Care Perhaps a healthcare smart card's most significant advantage is its overall impact on the quality of a provider's diagnosis and the resultant quality of treatment. Real-time access to medical records permits providers to refer to patient history as well as current conditions to assist in determining a holistic treatment program. Records of recent lab tests will be available, eliminating the need for re-testing or the delay of ordering existing records. Prescription drug information and known patient allergies will be available to assist the provider in selecting the most effective treatment.

Improved Service One of the healthcare smart card's primary strengths is its ability to facilitate "hassle free" service at the patient/provider interface. The card eliminates the need for transcription of medical history and/or insurance information by the patient. It ensures the provider office staff not only of benefit coverages but specifically what contract benefit levels, deductibles, and co-insurance levels exist from multiple insurance companies. It also includes the effective dates for any optional coverage that the patient may have selected. Use of the healthcare smart card will eliminate the manual forms update process that precedes many office visits.

The promise of improved service is indicated by a recent Canadian project. The Ontario Ministry of Health conducted a pilot program, called Service Encounter Card, from June 29, 1992 to March 31, 1993 in the Rainy River District of northwestern Ontario. Over 2,500 volunteer patients carried a smart card containing their personal health records. The card was presented to participating providers of healthcare services. Participating healthcare agencies included a hospital, two clinics, four pharmacies, a district health council, two home care groups, laboratories, and an optometry group. Participating providers included registered nurses, laboratory and diagnostic imaging technicians, physiotherapists, speech therapists, community counselors, chiropodists, optometrists, nutritional counselors, diabetic educators, health records clerks, pharmacists, and physicians.

At any time, patients were able to view everything contained in their cards using public viewing stations. Patient data were protected at the application, file, record, and field levels. Access was controlled by passwords, PINs, and keys. Patient data were also encrypted, using a DES security algorithm on cards, disk files, diskettes, and during any communication process. The Ontario Ministry of Health had access only to data according to access assigned rights, carefully defined by the project's advisory committee.

Each patient's card contained three categories of data: demographic, health status, and encounter information. The demographic data included name, address, health identification number, date of birth, gender, and primary physician, etc. Health data included information on allergies, medical problems, drug sensitivity, significant test results, and home care status records. The encounter information included records for allied health service, hospital inpatient, diagnostic imaging, laboratory, medication, and optometry.

This project was a unique opportunity to provide all parties concerned with immediate information needed to improve the quality and availability of healthcare services while reducing overall cost. If the Health Ministry's overall evaluation of this smart card system, results of which are not yet available, is positive, then the province-wide use of personal, portable health records can be expected to contribute significantly toward higher quality healthcare while lowering costs.

Emergency Access to Medical Records In a medical emergency where the patient and emergency worker are not able to communicate with the provider, a healthcare card may show any pre-existing medical conditions, such as diabetes, pacemaker, hemophilia, etc. It could also provide a current history of the patient's prescription drugs, as well as a list of known allergies. While this information may not always be necessary to diagnose the cause of the current patient condition, it could prevent aggravating an existing condition.

Traveling/Moving/Multiple Physicians Using the healthcare smart card as a portable medical history facilitates patient movement among providers for any number of reasons: traveling, moving, referral to specialists, or changing primary providers. The card gives the receiving provider all the information needed to dispense quality medical service. This is especially valuable when the patient has a chronic or reoccurring illness.

For example, another government healthcare program is being studied in five states (Wyoming, Nevada, Idaho, North Dakota, and Montana). These states are working toward a regional system using the same cards and systems so that people can carry their medical records with them when they cross a state line to receive covered services. The goal is to eventually issue a health card that contains both medical records and insurance benefit information. If a single card-based system can be used by several different programs, the overall savings can be significant. Some of the savings will be experienced at a state level, while other savings may be found at the federal level. The savings may be realized at different times for different programs.

Improved Medical Record Security Using the smart card as a personal medical history also ensures both the security and privacy of the data. Unlike a "National Electronic Patient Record" where the patient has no control over who accesses the data and for what reasons, access to the data on the card would be controlled by the patient. Audit trails of both access and modification of data can be maintained on the card to document who used the data and for what reason.

Single Card with All Insurance/Medical Information In today's work environment a large number of patients have multiple insurance policies. This is true in families where both husband and wife work and it is especially true in the over-65 market where most patients have a Medicare supplement policy. Having all insurance information on the same card reduces the potential for missing information at the provider location and makes record keeping easier for both the patient and the provider.

Medical Device Tracking To maintain compliance with the Medical Device Safety Act of 1992, "life giving" devices such as pacemakers, heart valves, etc. need to be tracked and reviewed periodically. The healthcare smart card could provide a record of the patient devices with information relative to their model identification, date of manufacture, serial number, etc. Information relative to the maintenance of the devices such as adjustments, follow-up checkups and/or any required modifications could also be maintained on the card and made available to any provider without the delay of a patient record transfer.

Additional Services Available One advantage of the healthcare smart card is the ability to develop new products and services by the insurer. These could take the form of new business for the insurance carriers or additions to existing business. Inclusion of additional information such as medical power of attorney, living wills, and organ donations are just a few of the possibilities that would add value to the patient.

PHYSICIAN APPLICATIONS AND BENEFITS

Reduced Administrative Cost One of the most significant advantages to the provider is the impact on the amount of office work. Reduced administrative overhead, fewer personal communications with insurance office staff, and reduced rework due to errors, allow more time to be devoted to the medical practice.

New Patient Data Capture All relevant information concerning patients could be obtained from the card. This includes not only information from multiple insurance companies but also a complete medical history. With this information immediately available, verification of insurance eligibility, contract benefits and coverages, as well as requests for medical records transfer, will be eliminated from standard office practices.

Existing Patient Validation One of the most time consuming and frustrating practices in a provider office is the verification of existing patient eligibility and benefits. Even in the case of an HMO this process is performed every time a patient visits a provider. In some cases this increases the required size of clerical office staff. Using the healthcare smart card would eliminate the need for such verification.

Dependent Identification Proper dependent identification is becoming more of an issue with insurance companies and companies with

ASO (Administrative Services Only) self-insurance. Being able to keep track of dependent level benefits and additional dependent level coverage requires the accurate tracking of medical events by dependent. The card could uniquely identify each dependent with full name, date of birth, sex, and social security number. This ensures positive patient identification and clean consistent data for the processing systems.

Increased Information for Decision Making The quality of any decision is greatly influenced by the amount of relevant, available information. The healthcare smart card enables the provider to review relevant patient data over an extended period of time and treat the illness—as opposed to treating only the current manifestation or symptoms. Medical records such as a normal or irregular EKG would enable the provider to eliminate many possibilities and save time in reaching a proper diagnosis. Additional historical data could assist in identifying previous similar conditions as well as what treatment worked well for this patient and what did not. They could also be used to aid special types of treatment such as dieting and sports medicine.

Improved Cash Flow Reimbursement for services rendered is based on accurate and complete submission of data. Inaccuracies and/or incomplete data cause human intervention between the insurance carrier and the provider. This delays the processing of data and in the subsequent expense reimbursement. With correct information, electronic processing is facilitated and reimbursement is predictable.

In addition, complete and accurate information will enable the provider to collect co-payments, co-insurance, deductibles, and non-covered services without the necessity of waiting for an EOB (explanation of benefits) and subsequent patient billing.

Reduced Medical Malpractice Insurance Information available on the card will enable the provider to make better decisions for the patient, resulting in higher quality outcomes with less defensive practices. This, in turn, can reduce the risk of medical malpractice lawsuits and *in time* may reduce the cost of malpractice insurance.

MEDICAL CARE FACILITY APPLICATIONS AND BENEFITS

Eligibility and Benefits Determination Medical care facilities face the same challenges as physicians when it comes to verifying a patient's eligibility and benefits. A significant amount of work is performed by the back office staff, especially during admission. All relevant information could be obtained directly from the patient card (or the card could be used as a key to the insurance companies' computer data banks) and the information transferred to whatever format needed by the medical care facility. This would result in reduced administrative overhead and expedite the admission process. It would also ensure accurate and complete data for subsequent submission to insurance company claims processing systems. This would, in turn, reduce additional clerical work (resolving claims suspended for lack of such information) and reduce reimbursement delays.

Patient Tracking As a patient moves through a facility, the smart card could be used to verify such items as check in and check out for each service area (i.e., transport services, operating room, recovery room, X-ray, etc.). This could permit the facility to analyze patient movement and the time spent at each location. These data could also be fed into an automated billing system.

Specialty Treatment Patient-carried information on chronic disease and regular treatment of disabilities would expand the scope of coverage available to the patient. In today's environment, a patient with a need for dialysis is confined to one dialysis center which would hold his or her medical records. If the patients carried the information, they would be free to travel and to seek alternative facilities. In the case of an emergency, the information would be available to an emergency medical provider. This particular function is currently being tested in France, Japan, Spain, and Canada.

Medication Tracking The use of a healthcare smart card instead of a manual log would not only enable entry and storage of medication data, but would facilitate cross-checking the type and quantity of medication for overdosage and negative interaction. Date, time, who ordered the medication, and who administered it could be captured for later review. Medication history would be available regardless of patient location. Doctors would have an up-to-date analysis of all medications a patient had received and of when they were administered. Use of a dual card system, one for the patient and one for the doctor or RN, would also prove that the medication was administered by an authorized staff member.

For example, in the United States, there is a cooperative project between Alliance, an organization dedicated to improving quality care to its 60,000 members in Madison, WI, and ASI to create an interactive patient record. This will facilitate prospective drug utilization review (DUR) by physicians and pharmacists before they write or dispense a prescription. The ultimate objective is to use a healthcare smart card as a portable patient profile. The card will be issued by insurers or employers, carried by patients and used by practitioners to reduce drug-caused death, prevent hospitalization, and forestall premature entry into nursing homes. It will also improve claims processing, and is expected to save billions of dollars in annual expenditures.

Blood Bank Cards Healthcare smart cards containing information on an individual's blood type would allow the institution to bypass certain tests and pre-code the donated blood (this process does not bypass all testing, it just minimizes the need for certain types of testing). Patient records on dontation frequency and dates could be maintained.

Nursing Cards Nurses who carry healthcare smart cards could log information on the patients they see, why they are seeing them, and what treatment is performed. This could reduce the nurse's manual paperwork and allow more time for care delivery. These cards could also be used to record time and attendance automatically, reducing the time spent on internal record keeping.

Emergency Medical Treatment Accurate and complete medical information would speed delivery of medical services in an emergency situation and could save lives, particularly in an ambulance or emergency room. If the patient can't communicate with the medical staff, the information on the card might be invaluable in choosing proper treatment. In addition to medical information, the healthcare smart card could carry emergency contact information identifying a medical power of attorney, a living will, an organ donation agreement, or any number of non-medical agreements that would reduce clerical overhead.

School Vaccinations Patients who carry healthcare smart cards could carry immunization history including the type, dates of vaccinations, and location. For instance, children inoculated at a hospital or physician's office could have their records updated. Public schools could then use the information for vaccination verification. This would minimize administrative overhead for the school and reduce the hassle for the student or family.

Laboratory Results Results from an internal (or external) lab could be electronically transmitted to a central location to be available for medical staff review. The information could also be downloaded from this central source to the healthcare smart card the next time it is used. Paper copies of floor records would not be required and the paper files maintained throughout the institution would be reduced. The electronic process would ensure rapid information availability for all those with a legitimate need to know.

Another program demonstrates the potential lab benefits: Since 1989, clients of Labor Birkmayer Blood Laboratories in Vienna, Austria have been able to receive a 32 Kbyte MEDiNFO healthcare smart card on which they can confidentially carry their clinical laboratory results to healthcare providers. There is a one-time fee of $200.00 to issue the card, for which the patient also receives an annual exam. Patients can also buy their own portable readers so that if they travel outside Vienna, the card still can be read by doctors who do not have readers. Doctors and several hospitals are currently participating in the program. Due to the success of this project in Vienna, as well as the feedback of doctors in the United States, Georg Birkmayer, M.D., Ph.D., has opened an office in the United States to market Birkmayer Smart Cards.

GROUP ADMINISTRATOR APPLICATIONS AND BENEFITS

Dynamic Benefits Management Using the healthcare smart card, the group administrator is able to modify the benefit structure according to company schedules without reissuing ID cards. This is true whether the benefit level changes are for the primary patient or any dependent. Benefits take effect when the group administrator identifies them to the system and may even be communicated to the providers through the insured's card.

Automatic Prescription Routing Addresses of approved mail-order pharmacies could be maintained on the healthcare smart card so that medication that is periodic or not immediately needed could be ordered and delivered to the patient. This would save the patient time and ensure minimum cost for the group and insurance company, without sacrificing quality of care.

INSURANCE COMPANY APPLICATIONS AND BENEFITS

Reduced Administrative Costs Information received from a provider using the healthcare smart card could be received through an EDI system. The information about the patient could be transferred directly from the healthcare smart card and would eliminate abbreviations in names or the use of initials. Valid gender codes and birth dates would uniquely identify the patient and would match enrollment files.

Reduced Claims Costs In addition to reducing administrative overhead, rapid data access could lessen actual claims cost by avoiding unnecessary medical treatment. Additionally, access to current medical lab tests and

X-rays could eliminate the need for additional or repetitive testing. Overall, improvement in quality of care could result in a long-term reduction in medical cost. Use of the healthcare smart card by patients would enable providers to more easily recognize abuse: Since all patient history would be on the healthcare card, the provider would be aware of recent treatment, history, and current prescriptions. Although the provider may not be able to gain specific access to some records due to patient privacy concerns, he or she would have access to treatment conditions conflicting with the current diagnosis and treatment. This can prevent drug overdose or incompatibility.

Finally, a healthcare smart card could help reduce costs by reducing fraudulent claims. And, without a valid healthcare smart card, the provider would not be able to generate fraudulent services. With a valid healthcare smart card, an audit trail outside the provider's control would uniquely identify when and where the access was obtained.

Reduce Manual Intervention In a non-emergency situation, the use of a healthcare smart card in a provider location requires one on-line transaction with the home office network. This simple electronic transaction could contain all of the information necessary to support electronic claim submission. The use of such an EDI facility for claims submission (or data collection in the case of a managed care medical event), directly reduces manual processes in the home office.

Allocate Proper Resources for Difficult Cases With fewer claims suspended for incomplete or inaccurate data, the claims examiners would have more time to spend on difficult cases requiring medical review or policy interpretation. This would speed up the processing of these claims and potentially reduce overall manpower requirements.

Additional Services The use of healthcare smart cards allows for the expansion of corporate services to areas that would be considered new business. They could be revenue-producing services or they could be free and be available to either the patient or the provider. They include such things as living wills, medical power of attorney, or organ donations.

Membership and Billing One benefit to the operations area is the healthcare smart cards' reusability. This would include any adjustment to contract benefit changes from existing groups, mandated governmental changes, or changes in the individual coverage (i.e., single to family).

Enhance Product Development and Strategic Planning

Patients' data obtained from the card during initial processing ensure accuracy for statistical manipulation and reporting. This forms the basis for product development, underwriting, and general product performance reporting. Consistent and accurate data will yield better historical models and a more accurate forecast for strategic planning.

Rapid Implementation of New Products and Services

Deployment of a new product or service no longer needs to wait for distribution of new healthcare smart cards—functions may be added to the card any time it is used after support system changes are made.

Looking Ahead

Some predictions for the future of healthcare cards include:

- The Clinton Administration has several high ranking executives, including Vice President Al Gore, who think smart cards are the way to go nationally. Implementation by 2000 is a real possibility if the president is re-elected in November
- Consumers' privacy concerns may create resistance to smart cards; this has happened in Germany
- More HMOs and insurers see the administrative benefits of health smart cards and may be the ultimate card drivers in the United States

The healthcare industry presents an excellent opportunity for the implementation of smart cards. In Europe, healthcare smart card programs have been in place for several years. In France alone, for example, it is estimated that approximately 500,000 French citizens are now carrying healthcare smart cards in their pockets. While the majority of these cards are being used to carry insurance details, some cards also contain more important medical information.

In moving to a smart card based system, the minimum information stored on the card should contain the necessary data to verify eligibility and coverage. These include:

- Name and address of card holder
- Emergency contact and phone number
- Medical plan number and effective dates
- Plan deductible and co-payment amount
- Primary care physician name and phone number

Since the smart card technology will handle the medical data storage and retrieval functions, more detailed and confidential information can be housed on the smart card. This medical information should be determined by the patient and could include the patient's personal characteristics such as:

- Age, height, weight, eye color, and other identification items
- Blood type
- Allergies
- Current prescriptions and ethical drugs
- Surgical history
- Up-to-date chronic illness treatment history
- Most recent encounter information
- Test results from the past three encounters
- Pertinent emergency information

CONCLUSION

From a global perspective healthcare smart cards unveil opportunities for healthcare providers and payers to establish an access vehicle that enhances efficiencies while improving patient care. The smart card's ability to manipulate variable data in a secure environment strongly suggests interchangeability, open architecture, and shared access. Managed properly this could lead to substantial cost savings, ease of use, improved access, and better medical care.

CHAPTER 10

Smart Cards in Government

By Joseph R. Zimmerman
Seimens

John Moore
U.S. Department of the Treasury

Judy Tarbox
Thornebrook Associates

Government has been assailed by a host of critics citing everything from unbridled spending and narrow vision to serious breaches of privacy. These critics have not only included politicians, journalists, analysts, consultants, and business leaders, but interest groups and individuals as well.

Today, people are calling for government to operate with greater efficiency and security and to conduct its health, finance, and transportation functions at new levels of fail-safe performance for an increasingly mobile group of citizens. Smart card technology will become an important part of this process.

Over the past 30 years, government has used card technologies with magnetic stripe cards and various other types of media, such as bar codes, for identification and payment purposes. (See Exhibit 10–1, following page.) While this has worked fairly well, there have been problems of fraud, security, privacy, limited use, and little interoperability among the various systems. Because of this, federal, state, and local governments are exploring smart card technology to help address these problems. Government agencies are gaining greater control in management and administration using smart cards. In fact, government research shows that over the last 10 years smart card technology has shown significant growth and will most likely continue this trend over the next several years.

GOVERNMENT AND TECHNOLOGY

Over the past several decades, governments have adapted the most current technology in order to improve its services. In fact, we can go back to the 1890s when the federal government made use of the first "tabulating" machine

EXHIBIT 10-1

Trends in Government Computer Card Technology Applications

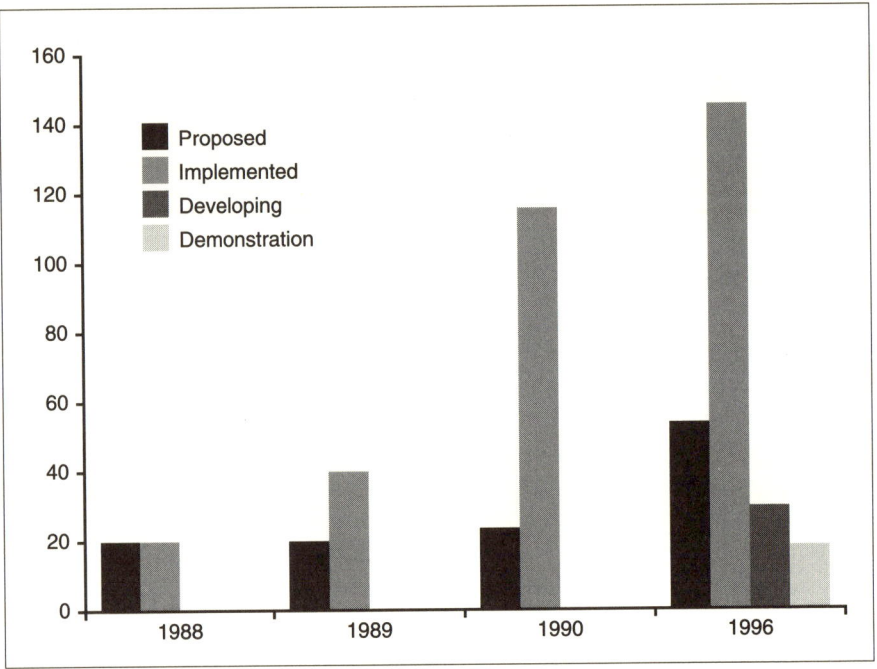

in order to complete the 1890 census. During the early to middle 1900s, great strides were made in the defense industry with the invention of early computers that were able to go on-line and transmit data simultaneously.

As we progressed into the late 1900s, most government departments became automated and used the latest technology to perform bookkeeping, accounting, and various other types of functions. Unfortunately, different departments often used different types of systems to perform similar functions and very often added more layers of impersonal bureaucracy.

Today—on the threshold of the next century—the efficiency, speed, and interactive capabilities of the new computer card technologies are enabling government at all levels to develop systems that interact and respond to the citizens. The *Debt Collection Act of 1996* mandates that all federal government payments be made in electronic form (EFT) by the year 2000. This law is transforming government agencies overnight and will serve as the impetus for government adoption of smart card technology. According to the Department of the Treasury Financial Management Service Report, *Government*

Applications of Computer Card Technology, 1996, this is happening in several areas including:

- Benefits delivery
- University services
- Toll collection and traffic management
- Financial services
- Access/security

The following is an explanation of the report's findings:

Benefits Delivery According to this latest research, implementation of benefit delivery projects has been accelerating to the point where on-line benefit transfer systems with point of sale terminals have been recognized by law as an alternative delivery system.

University Services There has been a wide acceptance of card technology in this setting, specifically in the areas of access limitation and payment for services. It has resulted in a greater accountability, reduction of fraud, waste, and abuse.

Toll Collection and Traffic Management Projects in this area have demonstrated that card technology systems have increased revenue while reducing traffic congestion and gridlock in critical locations like bridges and airports.

Financial Services The use of card technology to support payment based activities is expanding not only in credit and debit applications, but in areas like fuel management, and inventory control. This has contributed to substantial cost savings and improved management.

Access/Security This area includes airport security, communications, computer access and access control. Terrorism and computer security breaches, and the increased use of public communication systems (like the Internet) have caused it to grow rapidly. For example, airports all over the country are actively installing card technology security systems in response to the FAA's lead. Many of these are being designed to cover more than just access control.

The Treasury study concludes that the use of computer card technology in the government has shown enormous growth in recent years, and adds that the real growth is just beginning. Research shows that there are over 200 various government applications in one stage of development or another today

EXHIBIT 10-2

Smart Card Trials in the United States:
U.S. Government/Military

- California DOT training scheme
- Dept. of Veterans Affairs Medical/Access Card
- Falcon Card—U.S. Air Force Academy Cadets
- DOD MARC Card
- Marine Corps Parris Island
- Soldier Readiness Card
- St. Louis Benefit Card
- Supplemental Food Program—Wyoming
- U.S. Air Force Card
- U.S. Army Soldier Support Center
- U.S. Department of Defense
- U.S. Michigan Opportunity
- U.S. North Carolina Dept. of Transportation
- U.S. Peanut Program
- U.S. Wisconsin Hunting and Fishing License Control
- E.S. EBT—Ohio
- U.S. Navy Recruit Card
- Wyoming Food Stamp Program

utilizing the latest technological devices. Exhibit 10-2 shows a sample of those programs. What's behind these trends? Let's examine some of their prime motivators.

MOTIVATING FACTORS

Government use of smart card technology offers individuals direct and quicker access to service with greater security and at their convenience. It also offers other benefits such as fraud reduction, automated internal administration of documents, and cost savings.

Fraud Governments have been aware of the chronic fraudulent procurement of issued benefits for many years. However, this abuse has grown monumentally over the past two decades. When caught, the violators consistently agree that they had no trouble scamming the system. There was no serious challenge in the application process, and no cross-checking for duplicity. Ultimately, smart cards provide real time cross-referencing of applicant benefits, applications and entitlement. It also provides an effective method for auditing distribution and redemption, and monitoring merchants for unusual transactions.

Multiapplications/Documents This book frequently discusses the merits of having multiple applications on one smart card. This technology benefits the internal administration of government social programs and documentation. Smart cards can and are being used to automate such things as drivers' licenses, social security cards, passports, recreational and professional licenses and certifications, unemployment benefits, food stamps, and military identification and benefits. The state of Ohio has led in this area and six other states are following suit with RFPs for multiple applications government services cards.

Reduction of Administrative Costs Keeping this small sampling of government services and documents in mind, consider the gigantic volume of checks that local, state or provincial, and national government administrations issue on a daily basis. Compound these figures with the number of benefits transactions that occur, the services that are applied for or rendered, and the daily interactions that citizens have with their government. If smart cards were used to automate even a small number of these service applications, the administrative costs of creation and delivery of these programs would be dramatically lowered. Even more money can be saved by another intrinsic asset of the smart card—the electronic audit trail and related administrative process.

Market Segmentation and Implementation Capitalizing on the growth of smart card technology in the United States private sector, government can "ride" on the introductory wave and take adavantage of preexisting market acceptance during its initial "gestation period." The public will begin to demand the same accessibility, convenience, and speed of smart card technology that they will take for granted in the private applications. Moreover, the government is also developing its own applications, such as Electronic Benefits Transfer (EBT). Additionally, smart card technology not only makes these services portable, it also empowers citizens to gain needed access to the government and to protect their individual information.

Depending on the perspective, government will play a significant role as an accelerator or as a barrier to rapid global implementation of smart cards. A couple of factors which affect the impact of government on United States implementation of smart cards include administrative momentum and sheer size. As a customer, government will influence financial operations, currency manufacture, citizen protection in applications, and dispersal of privileges and benefits. As a governing body, it must simultaneously be an enforcer, a policy maker, a diplomat, and a guardian of public trust and privacy.

GOVERNMENT APPLICATIONS

State Administered Programs In the past few years, individual states have exhibited a great deal of interest in the smart card possibilities for EBT. As mentioned, this interest is driven largely by the need to prevent fraud. However, there are a variety of other assets that need to be addressed. Distribution of benefits can now evolve into a process that will not require regular interface with a government employee. The paper trail of these programs will essentially disappear as checks become electronically based, and retailers capitalize on the tremendous advantages of electronic based transactions at the point of sale (POS). States now realize that even greater savings and administrative improvements can be realized through the technology. States issue many kinds of documents—license vehicle registrations, benefits entitlements, identification, professional and recreational licenses, law enforcement needs, and much more. All these documents are for the most part originated and issued by individual departments through conventional methods: service counters, the mail, private state agencies, and paper applications. Through the use of smart cards, much of the cost of EDI-based service applications, and electronic interfaces (ATMs, kiosks, personal computers, and devices), can be drastically reduced. These costs can be cut even further through the combination of these programs on multiapplication smart cards. Merging these applications provides a single contact source for many programs. The natural place for all of these applications to reside is the driver's license. For citizens who do not have a driver's license, a state issued alternative ID card could be distributed. Hence, a single state issued card already issued in a more fundamental form could consolidate many services into an organized and practical device-driven document.

The State of Ohio is currently piloting a multiple application smart card that will be used for benefits, vehicle registration including license plates, water craft drivers' licenses, game hunting licenses, professional licenses, a senior citizen retail discount program, inquiries for state services information, and federal applications. The anticipated statewide rollout will occur by the year 2000.

Ohio is also instituting a system called "Pay Ease Food Stamps." This program uses USDA smart cards issued to replace Food Stamp coupon books. The pilot is a fully off-line electronic benefits system with recipients carrying their monthly benefits in the smart card's memory. Currently, there are over 25,000 cards in use at approximately 200 different Ohio retailers.

FEDERALLY ORIGINATED PROGRAMS

Many of the cited state programs receive some funding from the federal government. It seems natural that if the states, individually or collectively, are to issue multiapplication smart cards, these cards should be a compendium of all government services. They can be a key to benefits and interaction as well as providing a gateway to structured informational resources and communications. Efforts through such organizations as the Federal Smart Card User Group, the Western Governors Association, and the National EBT Task Force have provided educational networks and collective focus on many of the issues that government is facing and will face in this technology.

Concurrently, smart cards are recognized as an important internal, administrative and security tool for the federal government itself. Financial transactions, access, identification, and a multitude of individual personal services are intrinsic lifeblood to the interactive business of internal government. The Military, the Treasury, the U.S. Postal Service, and Departments of Agriculture and Transportation—as well as many other departments and agencies—are exploring the vast possibilities of smart cards. The Department of Defense is developing identification, logistics, security access, medical services, and other applications. The Treasury is exploring funds transfer, authentication and electronic funds transfer, benefits transfer, and tax processes.

The Department of Agriculture has issued over 200,000 cards to peanut farmers throughout the country. These cards are portable databases used to monitor and control crop sales. The card's memory stores crop quota and loan information, and allows the USDA to receive accurate, timely data about all crop sales for price forecasting. This is one of the first and largest live United States smart card applications.

PRIVATE/PUBLIC SECTOR PARTNERSHIPS

Private/Public partnerships are highly likely to occur in healthcare, financial services, and travel. Just as corporations are learning to be more adaptive and quick to market, the public sector is learning to attract viable partners. For example, American Express/U.S. Postal Service partnership on prepaid phone cards has been a financial and implementation success story. More will surely follow.

The Smart Card Forum has created a Government Unit that addresses public sector needs in implementing smart cards. A Government Advisory Council administrates the unit. Benefits include meetings both with, and separate from, the Smart Card Forum Working Groups, a centralized information distribution point; development of de facto standards and specifications; focus on multiple application cards; access to legal/regulatory issues; discussions; and networking. This unit will promote public/private sector partnerships.

The private sector can provide many valuable tools in developing these services. Forging the public-private partnership will be important as we migrate toward fully implemented smart card technology.

MILITARY APPLICATIONS

Smart card applications in the military are also multiplying. The U.S. Marine Corps is piloting credit/debit smart cards in bases on Parris Island, South Carolina and San Diego, California. Marine recruits have their pay entered onto smart cards which are then used to make purchases and cash withdrawals at all post exchanges. This system reduces manpower and material costs required to administer the previous paper coupon process. There are 10,000 cards in Parris Island and 7,000 in San Diego. The system is semi on-line; that is, stored data for each transaction are relayed from POS terminals to a microcomputer in the base comptroller's office each day.

The MARC card, discussed earlier, is another example of the military's smart card interest.

Smart card predictions for the future include:

- Federal smart cards for healthcare, identification, and access will emerge by 2000.
- EBT and other benefits programs will be implemented via smart cards in the same period.
- Private/public sector smart card alliances will grow.

CONCLUSION

Our society has too often viewed our government as large, inconvenient, and unresponsive, and has begun demanding that this be changed. Through the use of smart cards, the government is making great strides in improving communication and convenience, while reducing costs for its citizens. These enhanced systems and programs will not only improve the way the government does day-to-day business, but will also help improve overall relationships with its citizens.

According to the latest government research, there will be significant growth of card technology systems in the public sector over the next several years. The rate of this growth will either be explosive or slower and more restrained depending on the health of the economy and budget constraints. Research demonstrates the reason for this growth toward card technology systems is simply that they work. Also, declining hardware and software prices are making these solutions not only easier, user friendly, and efficient, but cost effective as well. Finally, studies have also concluded that the participants in card system programs prefer them to the previous paper-based systems, a fact that also bodes well for future expansion and implementation.

CHAPTER 11

Transportation

Michael Dinning
Volpe National Transportation Systems Center

The transportation industry offers one of the largest potential markets for smart cards. Electronic payments featuring smart cards are being implemented on public transit systems for fare payment on buses, subways, ferries, van pools, and parking. In addition, opportunities for smart card applications are emerging in highway toll systems, electronic drivers' licenses, and as a way to electronically identify travelers, vehicles, and cargo. Smart cards are a key element of the Intelligent Transportation System (ITS) concept, which seeks to improve the nation's transportation system through innovative applications of information and telecommunications technologies.

Public transit systems have been using electronic stored value cards since the Bay Area Rapid Transit (BART) system introduced paper magnetic stripe tickets in San Francisco in 1972. More than 50 major transit systems use electronic fare media worldwide, accounting for 23 billion low-value transactions annually.

The transportation industry is aggressively introducing many new telecommunications and information technologies. The Intelligent Transportation System (ITS), an industry/government initiative established in 1991 to maximize the productivity of all types of transportation, is spearheading many of these developments. Because future expansion of the physical transportation infrastructure will be severely limited by budget and physical space restrictions, the ITS is being designed to increase the throughput and capacity of existing systems. An ITS architecture has been developed that weaves together many advanced technologies for monitoring, controlling, and providing information about transportation conditions. In addition to electronic payment systems, new technology is being implemented for tracking vehicle locations, and providing traffic and transit information to customers at home, at work, or in their vehicles. ITS technologies are being developed to automate highway and transit systems, and improve safety as well as capacity. ITS is an intermodal concept, with applications on private vehicles, public transit, and commercial vehicle operations.

SEAMLESS, NON-STOP MOVEMENT

In both public and private transportation, initiatives are underway to provide seamless, non-stop movement throughout transportation corridors. Public transit systems are implementing electronic fare cards for use on any type of transit services in a given region. Similarly, airlines are introducing paperless ticketing and loyalty programs. Regional information networks are being developed to exchange data needed for commercial freight transportation. When combined with automated weigh stations and toll booths, these advances are enabling non-stop commercial corridors which are thousands of miles long. Automated immigration clearance systems expedite movement across international borders. Smart cards, combined with other ITS technologies, provide the flexibility and information processing power which will help link together these many types of transportation services.

TRANSPORTATION TECHNOLOGY TRENDS

The Intermodal Surface Transportation Efficiency Act (ISTEA) of 1991 established national goals for improving transportation operations. ISTEA endorsed the concept of intelligent transportation systems, and set aside federal funding for innovative transportation system research, development, and demonstrations. The ISTEA legislation is currently being reauthorized, sharpening focus on using technology to increase transportation efficiency.

In January 1996, the Secretary of Transportation launched Operation Time Saver. The goal of this initiative is to implement ITS technology in 75 metropolitan areas in the United States within a decade. In conjunction with Operation Time Saver, federal funds are being awarded for demonstrations of integrated ITS technologies, which could include electronic payment systems.

The goal of transportation planners at all levels is to provide a seamless transportation system for the traveler. Strategies for integrating operations throughout a region are being developed and implemented for highway and transit systems. Systems for transportation monitoring, control, traveler information, and electronic payment are being coordinated. In many urban areas, transit system planners and operators are developing fare integration plans using smart card technology. These initiatives will enable consumers to use the same card for payment of transit fares throughout the region regardless of service provider or mode of transit. Operators of toll roads, bridges, and tunnels are also coordinating their electronic payment systems. Electronic payment systems on toll roads not only increase traffic throughput, but also allow application of transportation control measures, such as peak hour pricing, to ease congestion.

Budget Pressures Public transportation agencies are experiencing severe budget constraints, and operating budgets are expected to decrease. Electronic payment systems and other ITS technologies will enable transportation system operators to reduce costs and improve overall productivity. This is essential for an industry which traditionally operates at a deficit.

Productivity Pressures Similarly, commercial freight operators are under increasing pressure to increase productivity. The number of major commercial trucking fleets has fallen from over 500 in the mid-80s to less than 100 in 1995. While the operating environment for the surface freight industry as a whole has become severely competitive, many operators employing advanced systems, such as satellite communications, vehicle location systems, and electronic data interchange, have flourished. Electronic payment and data processing technology is being used to reduce administrative costs and expedite commercial freight operations. National initiatives have been demonstrated to provide seamless electronic transfer of commercial transportation information for intercity rail and highway systems across the country. These initiatives complement private industry trends toward adopting just-in-time manufacturing and logistics systems.

International Transport The North American Free Trade Agreement, and the general globalization of trade has extended the need for seamless transportation across international borders. International trade has increased; for example, U.S. merchandise exports to Canada and Mexico were up 14 percent and 22 percent, respectively, in 1994. International tourism is also expected to increase dramatically over the next two decades. Electronic identification and data communications technology are being explored to simplify movement across borders by both commercial carriers and individual travelers. Automated systems for immigration and customs clearance are being implemented for air, ground, and marine transportation. These systems will not only increase convenience and throughput for travelers, but will also significantly reduce the manpower costs of border inspections.

Partnerships New partnerships are emerging along with the implementation of advanced technology systems in transportation and logistics. A goal of the national ITS initiative is to stimulate private sector investment in transportation. Public agencies are outsourcing to "turnkey" contractors and private consortia to design, build, and operate new transportation systems such as toll roads and rail transit systems. Similarly, transit and toll agencies are contracting with third parties to implement and operate electronic payment systems. Financial institutions see public transportation as a prime market for stored value products, and are seeking to develop relationships with transit agencies. In turn, transit agencies, particularly those involved in large-scale fare integration efforts, would like to take advantage of the large infrastructure which financial organizations have in place for payment settlement and revenue management. Third party logistics operators are also emerging in commercial transportation. These organizations are using satellite and land-based vehicle and cargo tracking technologies to provide transit visibility and global logistics management services.

Players and Motivations Public transportation agencies are seeking to provide increased convenience to the traveling public and to attract ridership. At the same time, operating subsidies are shrinking, and public agencies are under increasing pressure to reduce operating, maintenance, and administrative costs. Public transit and toll facility operators want to reduce fare collection and administrative costs through smart card implementation. Some organizations, such as private toll road operators, have used electronic payment as a key marketing element to provide customer convenience and differentiate their service. In addition, operators are intrigued by potential new revenue generation possibilities, partnership agreements, and the transaction data captured by smart cards, which will enable them to plan services better.

Regional transportation planners see electronic payment systems as ways to facilitate coordination of transportation services regardless of mode or operator, and provide seamless public transit to the user. Planners concerned with congestion want to consider electronically-based variable tolls and fees to reduce congestion.

Financial institutions see public transit as a vast market for their stored value products, behind only banking and telecommunications. Transit systems provide widespread visibility of their product, and may generate significant revenues because of the large transaction volumes.

Third-party system integrators and clearinghouse operators are interested in providing turnkey systems. These organizations will often take on the cost and risk of implementing and operating an electronic payment system in return for a fee or percentage of the revenues generated.

Large employers and institutions such as universities also see themselves as partners for transit smart cards. These organizations would like a single multi-use card for identification, access control, and payment. The transit card initiative is often the dominant activity in the region for them to team with. Some universities are issuing their own payment cards in conjunction with a bank, and will provide their cards to transit operators as if they were another merchant.

In the commercial freight transportation world, operators are similarly motivated to reduce administrative costs and provide shipment security. Regulating agencies, such as state transportation departments, would like to streamline, and where possible regionalize, administrative services such as licensing and taxing to reduce labor requirements and costs. Agencies regulating international movement, such as immigration, customs and agriculture, have similar incentives. Carriers or third party logistics operators may view smart cards as a way to provide shipment visibility needed for specialized just-in-time operations.

The following sections will present more detail on smart card applications for:

- Public transit and parking
- Electronic tolls on highways, bridges, and tunnels
- Commercial vehicle operations
- Traveler identification at international borders

PUBLIC TRANSIT APPLICATIONS

The transit fare payment market readily lends itself to applications of smart card technology. Fare payment transactions are typically low value, and require high throughput. The transit industry has a long history of using stored value, magnetic stripe tickets for payment of fares. Unattended ticket vending machines are used extensively by many systems; some now accept debit or credit cards for purchase of fare cards. Subway riders are also used to unattended electronic fare gates at most systems. Despite extensive experience with electronic fare media, most transit agencies still also use cash, tokens, or paper tickets or transfers—all labor intensive and expensive to handle and administer. Current worldwide application of smart cards for fare payment is shown in Exhibit 11–1, on the following page.

Dozens of transit agencies around the world are implementing smart cards for payment of transit fares. Most transit operators would prefer a contactless, or proximity card, where the card is read when passed within about four inches of the card activation device, or target. Contactless smart card technology has demonstrated high reliability, and promises lower maintenance costs than some existing magnetic stripe card systems. In addition, operators

EXHIBIT 11-1

Leading Transit Smart Card Fare Systems Worldwide

Region	Programs	
North America	■ Montreal	■ Los Angeles
	■ Toronto	■ Ann Arbor
	■ Washington, D.C.	■ Atlanta
South America	■ São Paulo	■ Mexico City
	■ Buenos Aires	
Europe	■ London	■ Paris
	■ Oslo	■ Marseilles
	■ Manchester	■ Barcelona
	■ Liverpool	■ Berlin
	■ Helsinki	■ Ostersund, Upsalla, & Luela
	■ Amsterdam	■ Copenhagen
Asia	■ Tokyo	■ Sydney
	■ Hong Kong	■ Melbourne
	■ Singapore	

Source: SCF Working Group on Transportation

feel that contactless cards will reduce the "fumble factor" and increase throughput at the turnstile or farebox. Contactless cards would be particularly beneficial to physically challenged riders. These cards are being used in buses, subway stations, trolleys, commuter rail systems, ferries, van pools, taxi cabs, and at parking lots on transit lines. In most cases, the transit agencies have implemented a closed system card for use only on the transit system or nearby retail sales. Some transit authorities also issue smart cards to employees to control access to facilities or specialized equipment such as fare boxes.

Some transit authorities are exploring the use of contact cards, such as those used by banks, universities, and retailers for payment of transit fares. In Atlanta, contact cards were accepted on the rail transit system during the 1996 Summer Olympics. While transit operators want to take advantage of bank card programs, many are concerned about the transaction times, maintenance, and reliability of contact cards in the mass transit environment.

Contact cards could be used as a contactless card if the card was inserted into a specially designed sheath or pouch. These sheaths contain antennae and transmitters so that the contact card will be able to exchange data with a contactless card reader. Card sheaths often also have LED panels which display the value remaining on the card, and can sometimes display a record of past transactions.

In addition, many smart card manufacturers are developing dual mode or "combi cards". The dual mode card will operate with both contact and contactless readers. Most developers are trying to integrate the microprocessor and memory on the card. This would reduce manufacturing costs, and would enable a user to access a single electronic purse in either the contact or contactless mode, if desired.

Regional fare integration projects are underway to use the same card for any transit service in a region regardless of operator or mode of transportation. Participating transit operators will use a common payment clearinghouse and often will share in fare media production and distribution.

Many transit programs are also issuing multi-use cards, so that the card can also be used for purchases outside the transit system. Some transit systems are teaming with large employers, universities, and sports facilities in a joint card, which would be used for purchases, identification, and access to facilities and computer systems. These systems are usually designed as "closed" systems, and the use of the card is controlled by the transit agency, which issues the card. The majority of these are contact cards.

Some transit systems, such as the one in Atlanta, are considering "open" systems. In an open system at least one of the fare cards which is accepted on transit would be a smart card issued by a bank or credit card company and accepted for payment at many locations. In a similar fashion, a few transit systems, including the bus system in Phoenix, accept credit cards for payment of fares, but without real-time card validation. The open system concept is attractive to some operators because customers who ride transit

U.S. TRANSIT OPERATORS MOVING TO CONTACTLESS CARDS

Transit operators in several large U.S. cities are planning to accept contactless stored value fare cards in the future:

1. On the West Coast, planners in San Francisco and Seattle envision a universal transit card which could be used to pay fares on buses, subways, trolleys and ferry boats, and also pay for commuter parking. Contactless cards have been demonstrated in actual service in Ventura County, California and Washington, D.C. Transit operators have chosen contactless cards because of perceived advantages in passenger throughput and equipment maintenance. With contactless cards passengers can enter stations and vehicles without stopping, and there are no moving parts or mechanical connections to wear out.

2. In San Francisco, the Translink card will be accepted by over 20 different transit operators in the Bay Area. The regional planning authority, the Metropolitan Transportation Commission, tested a magnetic

too infrequently to buy a transit-only fare card would be more likely to use an open system card in place of cash or tokens. Applications of smart cards for taxi cab fare payments are also underway in Vienna, Dubai, and other cities. Parking meter applications of open system cards are also emerging.

U.S. TRANSIT OPERATORS MOVING TO CONTACTLESS CARDS (Continued)

stripe Translink card on the Bay Area Rapid Transit (BART) subways and the Contra Costa County bus lines, but decided they needed the flexibility of smart card technology if they were going to expand the project throughout the area. The MTC formed a Clearinghouse Committee to think through how the various agencies would implement the new card. Banks have expressed interest in participating in the venture to provide payment settlement and other services. Russell Driver, MTC Translink Project Manager, reports that transit agencies are enthusiastic about the program, and several have volunteered to participate in a pilot demonstration.

3. In Seattle, a half dozen different transportation providers have joined the King County Metro to develop a fare card valid throughout the region. Planners want to provide customers with a contactless smart card for buses, the state ferry, parking, and possibly intercity commuter rail. The Regional Fare Coordination Project team feels that a smart

---

PLAYERS AND MOTIVATIONS

Transit system operators are under increasing pressure to streamline operations, reduce costs, and provide "seamless" public transit service to consumers. Smart cards will reduce the costs of producing, distributing, collecting, and managing fare media. Contactless smart card technology promises high reliability and lower maintenance costs than some existing magnetic stripe card systems. In addition, smart cards will provide better security and reduce the workload of vehicle operators. Many transit operators are replacing older fare collection equipment and would like to realize the benefits of a smart card based system.

Operators also want to provide convenience to their customers and increase ridership and revenue. Customers could use the same card for any transit service, without worrying about exact change or tokens. Rechargeable smart cards would be easier to replenish with value, thus eliminating the need to stand in line at a limited number of fare media outlets. Value could be added anywhere a card is used, even possibly from screen phones at home or by computer over the Internet. The Ventura County Transportation Commission is demonstrating a system in which the customer authorizes an increase in value by telephone, and the card is recharged the next time it is used. Customers surveyed by transit operators in

Chicago said they expected to increase their ridership by two to five percent if an electronic fare card were available.

Transit operators see many other opportunities to increase revenue with smart cards. Those who are co-issuers of a smart card hope to earn a share of the float, or interest, earned on the cash collected, as well as a portion of the transaction fees. In addition, there is evidence that a percentage of the stored value on cards is never used, although some transit managers are concerned about their liability for this outstanding value and the implications of "escheat" (abandoned money) laws.

Smart cards will enable transit agencies to expand promotional programs, such as employer transit pass programs. Many employers are hesitant to participate in current fare programs because of the large cost of handling monthly paper passes. A rechargeable smart card would be much cheaper to administer, and would result in increased transit ridership and revenue through employer pass programs.

Other potential revenue sources with smart card fare systems may include purchases of illustrated cards by collectors, and advertising sales on these "pocket billboards." In Atlanta, the transit authority and banks targeted the collectors market with Olympic themes illustrated on their cards. In New York, the Metropolitan Transportation Authority (MTA) has issued a series of collectors fare cards, illustrated with different scenes of the Big Apple.

The New York MTA Metro Card Company has attempted to take the revenue generation concept one step further. The Card Company explored a business venture to issue their own stored value card, and sell the card service to other entities such as schools or other transit agencies.

U.S. TRANSIT OPERATORS MOVING TO CONTACTLESS CARDS (Continued)

card system will reduce the costs of distributing and collecting paper tickets, transfers, and passes. They expect that once smart cards streamline the process of distributing passes, many more large employers in the region will join their Employer Pass Program, generating new ridership and revenue. Like her counterparts in San Francisco, Project Manager Candace Carlson envisions a multi-modal, multi-use card in the future, with potential involvement by a financial institution.

4. In the nation's capital, the Washington Metropolitan Area Transit Authority (WMATA) has been demonstrating contactless smart cards since 1995. The Go Card has been used successfully by over 1000 riders in buses and Metro subway stations. In addition, the card can be used to pay for parking at suburban commuter lots on the rail transit lines. One objective in Washington was to make fare payment easier for the physically challenged rider, and Go Card readers have been installed on the fare gates so that

Transit officials in most cities agree that they forgo thousands of dollars of revenue each year because of fare evasion, theft, counterfeiting, incorrect payments, and other forms of fare abuse associated with existing fare collection systems. Smart cards will ensure that the correct fare is paid for the trip taken. Smart cards should also significantly reduce fraud and theft and increase passenger safety by eliminating cash. To achieve maximum results, however, other security-related improvements must accompany smart card implementation. For example, New York officials estimate that implementation of a combination of magnetic stripe cards, new turnstile designs, and increased police presence will reduce fare evasion losses by 50 percent. Some operators have expressed concern about the susceptibility of paper and magnetic strip fare media to counterfeiting. Smart card standards and designs are being developed for data encryption and embedded sensors which will greatly increase their resistance to counterfeiting or tampering. Stored value cards issued with a unique identification number have the added advantage that they can be invalidated if lost or stolen, and the passenger reimbursed.

A smart card system, in conjunction with other ITS technologies such as automatic vehicle location and passenger counting systems, could produce extensive ridership data that some planners call "more valuable than the fare revenue itself." This information is highly useful to planners and management in forecasting travel demand, designing new services, evaluating alternative fare structures, marketing, and compiling annual statistics required by the Federal Transit Administration. Accurate ridership data will become even more important in the future as operators attempt to optimize service in the face of declining budgets.

U.S. TRANSIT OPERATORS MOVING TO CONTACTLESS CARDS (Concluded)

passengers in wheel chairs can easily pass their card by the reader. The Go Card, like contactless cards tried in Hong Kong and Manchester, has proven very reliable. Peter Benjamin, WMATA's Chief Financial Officer, envisions expansion of the Go Card Program throughout the system, including commuter rail and other transportation services.

5. Contactless smart cards have also been demonstrated by the Ventura County Transportation Commission (VCTC) north of Los Angeles. Their Smart Passport card has been used on the buses and para-transit vans of six transit operators in two large counties. In addition to the smart card payment system, the VCTC has implemented other "Smart Bus" technology, including automatic vehicle location and automated passenger counting systems. Linking smart cards with these technologies will produce a wealth of data on ridership patterns which transit planners can use to optimize routes and schedules.

Smart cards ensure that accurate records of payment transactions are generated. This is particularly important on para-transit or contracted taxi services. A smart card system would greatly simplify the process for auditing service provided by contract carriers and discourage fraud. With an electronic record of service provided, operators, employers, human service agencies, and other third parties are more inclined to engage in "purchase of service contracts" and other agreements to transport their employees or clients.

Transit agencies would like to partner with banks or other financial institutions to take advantage of the established and growing infrastructure for producing and distributing smart cards, and the financial world's experience in operating and managing the payment settlement process. Several transit chief financial officers have expressed a desire to "get out of the fare collection business," and focus on their primary business of providing transportation.

Transit operators would also like to allow infrequent riders to use an "open" system payment card instead of using cash or tokens, which are the most costly types of fare media to handle. Infrequent riders are unlikely to want to purchase transit-only smart cards which would require a minimum balance worth more than one ride, but may have a bank card in their wallets.

Other transit operators are adopting a bank card for fare payment because it is the dominant payment instrument in the area. In towns where a smart card issued by a university and bank is used extensively by a large portion of the population, the transit authority may allow its use for transit fares. The transit authority takes advantage of the entire card management process, in exchange for paying the university and bank a percentage of their fare revenue.

For example, transit operators in the college town of Ann Arbor are now accepting the *Mcard* issued by the University of Michigan for payment of fares on buses. The University rolled out their smart card in late 1995, and it's now accepted for purchases and services throughout Ann Arbor. The University has implemented the card as a closed system, and exercises control over what types of merchants can accept its card. The card also serves as a picture ID and access control card for university students and faculty.

The University has partnered with First of America Bank to issue the card, and both share the revenues produced by fees and float. The Ann Arbor Transportation Authority (AATA) acts like another merchant, and pays a transaction fee when the card is used on a bus.

The *Mcard* is a contact smart card, so a contact card reader has been added to the bus fare collection equipment. Like other transit operators, the AATA would prefer contactless cards for the bus environment, but were compelled to accept the *Mcard* because it dominates the market in Ann Arbor. AATA planners say that a combination card, with both contact and contactless capabilities, would be their first choice.

If it can be economically produced, the ideal technology for transit operators may be the dual mode combi-card. This card can be used in the contactless mode for transit and the contact mode for retail and telephone applications. Many banks are also interested in the combi-card because it would position them with a product for the transit market.

The transit market is extremely attractive to financial organizations and other card issuers because of the large ridership population and product exposure which transit offers. A public transit system is one of the largest single users of smart cards in a region. The transit market is enhanced still further when several operators in a region decide to use the same smart card. In large urban areas a significant portion of the transit ridership may not have a bank account, and thus is a target market for disposable stored value cards. In addition, many banks are already providing cash management services to transit authorities, and may be willing to create attractive partnership agreements to reinforce existing, as well as future, business relationships.

ELECTRONIC TOLL APPLICATIONS

Dozens of agencies operating toll roads, bridges, and tunnels are implementing electronic toll and traffic management systems (ETTM). These systems allow the facility to collect tolls without stopping traffic. The first generation of electronic toll systems were mostly systems in which a transponder in the car or truck is interrogated as it approaches the toll booth. The transponder transmits a simple account number to the toll station, and the appropriate toll is deducted from the driver's account which is administered from a central accounting system and database. In many regions, the various toll authorities are coordinating their programs so that a driver's transponder will work at any facility.

Many electronic toll system operators plan to evolve to equipment that accepts smart cards. The smart card would be inserted into an ETTM transponder unit positioned on the car's dashboard. Value would be deducted from the card when it passes through a toll collection area, and no central accounting system would be needed for these transactions.

Players and Motivations Like transit system operators, toll facility managers are driven by two primary factors: a need to reduce costs, and a desire to provide customer convenience. Electronic toll systems will reduce the labor associated with toll collection considerably. Opportunities for theft, pilferage and fraud are also reduced. In addition, commuters no longer have to wait in line, but proceed without stopping through the toll facility, so more travelers may use the toll road. Private toll road operators see electronic toll systems as essential to attracting customers and providing value-added service efficiently.

Interoperability is essential for customer participation and satisfaction in regions with several toll facilities. In large metropolitan areas, such as New York and Boston, toll facility operators are collaborating to accept the same card. These operators are also attempting to benefit from joint procurements and, where feasible, combined marketing or administrative operations.

A smart card-based toll system may have cost advantages over the centrally administered toll systems. Administrative and back-end processing costs may be reduced if only smart cards were accepted for payment. More compelling, however, is the large potential market of customers who will likely have stored value smart cards for other purposes.

Both public and private toll roads may want branded cards of their own to reinforce their customer relationships and control revenues, but will certainly be interested in an open system card which increases business. The open system card is particularly important for toll roads which are used only occasionally by vacationers or travelers passing through an area.

Smart card-based toll systems would also work in several special circumstances where transponder systems with a single account number are problematic. A smart card system would work easily in rental cars operating through highway, bridge, or airport toll systems. Smart cards would also be ideal for taxi cabs, or other vehicles which are part of a fleet where several drivers use the same vehicle.

Another much valued benefit of smart card-based toll systems is the anonymity of transactions. Centrally administered toll systems usually create a record of usage by location, which some drivers find objectionable.

Many toll system developers and systems integrators are developing systems which accept smart cards so that they can capture the future market of stored value card users. Card vendors who are not involved in the back-end processing of centrally administered toll systems obviously favor the card based toll technology.

COMMERCIAL VEHICLE OPERATIONS

Smart cards will be used by commercial vehicles, such as trucks carrying freight, not only for paying tolls, but also for storing information about drivers, vehicles, and cargo. Commercial drivers' licenses will likely migrate to smart card technology. Other information about the driver, including time logs and safety records, may also be stored on smart cards. Vehicle records, such as size and weight data, proof of payment for taxes and insurance, and hazardous cargos may also be stored on them. Vehicle maintenance and fueling records, some linked to real-time equipment sensors on the truck or gas pump, will be used by commercial fleets. National networks are being developed to exchange the electronic documentation required for commercial truck operations, but some of this data could be carried on smart cards.

Truck, railroad, and marine freight carriers are implementing automated equipment identification (AEI) systems to maintain visibility of vehicles, containers, and cargo. First generation AEI systems employed passive, read only tags. These have been installed on every U.S. railcar, and on some multimodal containers and trucks. These systems were originally driven by the railroads' need to keep track of railcars traveling on the various companies' property, for payment purposes. AEI is now becoming critical to providing the in-transit visibility of shipments required for advanced logistics operations. Vehicle identification systems have been linked, by land line or satellite, to corporate logistics management systems. By linking vehicle locations with customer shipment data, carriers can provide the real time, in-transit visibility of shipments now essential to just-in-time manufacturing and retail systems.

The military, which often operates in remote locations out of reach of communications systems and logistics databases, has tried a more distributed approach, testing several types of electronic tags to provide visibility of shipping containers and equipment in transit. The destination and contents of containers are written on the tag, and attached to the container or pallet. The manifest can be read off the tag in the remote location, thus eliminating the need to query a central database. These systems are often linked to satellite global positioning and communications systems so shipments could be tracked anywhere in the world. If the shipment needs to be diverted to a different location, the satellite communications system could query the tag while it was in transit and write a new destination onto it. The tag would be read when the shipment reached the distribution point. The military has prototyped several types of smart tags, including those with integrated circuits and laser tags. Both commercial and military applications could migrate to smart cards. Special cargo information, such as whether hazardous materials are on board, could also be included on a smart card or tag.

Players and Motivations Government agencies which regulate commercial transportation are very interested in using smart card technology to streamline their operations and reduce administrative costs. Driver and vehicle licensing and taxation will be much more efficient if nationally coordinated with digitized information storage and dissemination. Because the drivers license has become the *de facto* national ID card, there is a large market for stolen and phony licenses. A smart card-based system, with digital photography or biometric information to identify the driver, could reduce fraud and counterfeiting. In addition, regulatory and law enforcement agencies want to share information on drivers' records among jurisdictions, and this will be facilitated by a national system with verifiable identification of the license holders.

Agencies involved in taxing and inspecting vehicles are also interested in electronic media to store driver and vehicle information. State agencies which assess fees, and national agencies responsible for immigration, customs, and agriculture inspections could all benefit from a common way to store and query driver, vehicle, or shipment information. This information could be queried just as in electronic toll collection systems. Highway inspections could be streamlined, and international border crossings expedited. State and local agencies are under increasing pressure to reduce costs, and automated payment and monitoring of vehicle fees could help do this. Border inspection agencies face similar budget constraints. More important, open trade agreements have increased the volume of border crossings of commercial vehicles. Both commercial carriers and inspection agencies want to increase throughout at border crossings, without large expenditures for new facilities or staff. While current systems are using networks and centralized databases to exchange information, a smart card-based system may help meet this growing international challenge.

Commercial carriers also want to reduce the paperwork and administrative costs associated with manifests, licenses, and vehicle registration and taxes. Electronic identification of shipments will be a critical part of an integrated logistics management system in the future. Shippers and carriers of commercial goods would like a seamless channel for shipment and exchange of goods to and through any location. Finally, cargo theft is a widespread problem, and a secure method of storing shipment data and verifying the identities of drivers and freight handlers can help reduce this threat.

TRAVELER IDENTIFICATION

Smart cards may also be used to identify travelers at international borders. Immigration agencies are implementing automated inspection systems to expedite the movement of travelers across borders and at international airports. The INSPASS system, fielded by the Immigration and Naturalization Service (INS), has issued over 60,000 cards to frequent international travelers. These cards can be used in automated INSPASS kiosks at several international airport terminals, enabling the traveler to bypass long lines. Data were stored on the initial INSPASS card using the optically read character format used on passports. Biometric data characterizing the traveler's hand geometry was written on the card, and hand geometry readers verify the person's identity at the INSPASS kiosk. INSPASS inspection stations have also been demonstrated at pedestrian border crossings. Based on the success of the INSPASS demonstration in the United States, other countries may initiate similar programs, and evolution to smart card technology is likely.

Automated border crossings for travelers in private vehicles are also being demonstrated by the INS. The Automated Permit Port enables travelers to pass through remote border crossings which are either not staffed, or are closed for the night. The Automated Permit Port uses remote video surveillance, and has tested voice verification to confirm travelers' identities. In addition, a Dedicated Commuter Lane (DCL) is being demonstrated at the U.S./Mexican border. The DCL will enable thousands of regular commuters to cross the border without waiting in long lines. The DCL will identify the commuter's car with a system similar to that used on electronic toll roads. In addition, a voice verification system may be used to verify the identity of vehicle occupants. INS may migrate all these traveler identification applications to smart cards, and coordinate them with similar international initiatives under consideration in Canada and other countries.

Players and Motivations An automated immigration inspection system would make border crossings much easier for travelers. Virtually non-stop travel is possible, as opposed to hour-long waits which travelers currently endure. Travelers who cross several different international borders would prefer to have one card which could be used everywhere. If the international crossing involves a toll facility, the traveler would prefer one card for both payment and immigration clearance.

Automated clearance systems will enable agencies which regulate international travel, such as the INS, to cut costs, improve traveler throughput, and reduce congestion at border and airport facilities. Security will be enhanced with the addition of biometric verification of travelers' identities. This issue of security and access will continue to plague transportation entities. Fortunately, smart cards provide greater security than existing systems.

Transportation carriers and the operators of transportation facilities, such as airports, view automated clearance facilities as a factor giving them competitive advantage. Travelers in the INSPASS and Dedicated Commuter Lane demonstrations have revealed strong preferences for travel through automated facilities.

TECHNOLOGY ISSUES

The transportation environment poses several difficult technological challenges for smart card systems which are not found in other applications, such as retail or banking. Smart card transactions for payment of transit fares or tolls must be carried out extremely quickly; in less than two seconds for transit fares, and in milliseconds for highway tolls. The operating environment is harsh, and equipment must be able to withstand abuse, grime, and rough cleaning and maintenance procedures. For the most part, smart card equipment in transportation will be unattended so it must be extremely reliable and user-friendly. Smart card readers, data storage devices, and communications systems must be integrated with other vehicle and facility systems. Finally, transportation systems typically have frugal capital and operating budgets so equipment must be reasonably priced, and is expected to last longer than in other applications.

A major technology issue for public transit applications is the type of smart card which operators require. Virtually all transit managers are asking for contactless smart cards for buses and subway stations, rather than contact cards. Contactless cards are perceived to provide higher throughput, ease of handling by users, durability, and lower maintenance costs. Transit systems would also like to be able to accept contact cards, however, for use by infrequent riders. In addition, many transit systems are planning to issue multi-use cards for purchases outside the transit system which could involve contact card readers.

As mentioned earlier, the variety of necessary requirements combined with the large potential transit market for smart cards has led the card industry to develop a dual mode or combi-card. The combi-card could be used in the contactless mode for payment of transit fares or the contact mode for retail or telephone applications. Ideally, the card would have a single memory and electronic processor shared by both modes. Since contactless cards require circuitry for transmitting and receiving information they cost more than contact cards. Card developers are introducing new design features, such as foil antennae, to reduce the cost of contactless and combi-cards.

Standardization and interoperability are still other transportation environment challenges. The first generation of contactless cards was primarily for access to facilities. Access control systems were proprietary and cards were generally not interoperable. Transportation system designers would like cards and card readers to be compatible and interoperable. They would like to be able to choose from many suppliers of contactless card systems and combine different system components over time. Standards for contactless smart cards are being developed by the International Organization for Standards (ISO), but are several years behind contact cards in the standardization process. ISO standards will probably not address all the interoperability requirements for transportation applications. Similarly, contact cards, even those adhering to ISO and financial industry standards, will not necessarily meet some of transportation's unique needs. Transaction times for contact card applications are often much longer than a transportation system could tolerate because of the "electronic handshake" required to ensure financial system security. Software and card firmware must be designed and tuned to meet transit's short transaction times. This may require different security checks which could affect electronic purse security. Separate purses may be required for retail/banking and transportation applications.

The durability of contact card equipment in transportation environments is a concern to many system operators. The vibration, grime, and potential vandalism in buses and other transit vehicles make operators wary about using equipment with a mechanical interface between the card and the reader.

Customers and operators have also expressed concern about the security of contactless cards. Systems must be designed to assure customers that their card could not be read inappropriately when passing near a card reader. Customers must also be assured that the value of their card cannot be stolen by "electronic pickpockets." Encryption and verification software should be able to provide adequate security, but consumers must be informed of these features as part of product introduction and marketing.

Another important technical issue is the ability to integrate smart card equipment into the overall vehicle or transportation facility design. Mass transit and toll highway operators have invested substantially in automatic revenue collection equipment, and in many cases, would like to be able to interface with this equipment rather than replace it. Some suppliers of legacy systems are hesitant to "open up" their system to other vendors because of data and revenue security concerns. In transit stations and highway toll facilities, smart card systems may require additional space, power system upgrades, and secure communications networks.

The bus environment presents additional difficulties. The smart card system must be integrated into the system which the driver uses to control other bus systems so that it does not add to driver workload. Smart card systems should be designed as part of the "smart bus" concept envisioned in the Intelligent Transportation System. Smart card equipment must be able to plug into the bus local area network and must be compatible with other systems, including: automatic passenger counters, automatic vehicle location systems, and data communications systems. The data from all these systems must be integrated to provide the information on ridership that transit operators desire. Transit operators also want to enter data on routes and passengers into all systems and be able to extract that data in one operation, if possible.

Integration problems also exist in other transportation applications. If smart cards are used in automated toll collection systems, cards and the transponders in vehicles must be compatible. There are no standards for toll systems or their components. The smart card market may drive the toll industry to develop interoperable transponders which would accept commonly used cards. And in some early testing of contactless cards in toll transponders, the transponder battery life was reduced to unacceptable levels.

Similarly, standards for the technology for automated border inspection services, electronic licenses, and identification have not been agreed upon. The initiatives of customs, immigration, and transportation licensing agencies of many countries need to be coordinated to ensure interoperability. Features like biometric verification are emerging, but no standards exist for the technology or the biometric data which will be captured.

LEGAL, REGULATORY, AND PUBLIC POLICY ISSUES

As discussed earlier, consumer demands are driving transportation planners to develop coordinated programs so that travelers will be able to use the same payment card for all transit fares and highway tolls in a region. To accomplish this requires the various operating agencies to agree on how revenue collection systems will be designed and managed. The degree of standardization and integration is often difficult to determine. Most individual transportation system operators want to maintain control over their fare or toll policy. Many want to have their own branded card to maintain market identity. The existing base of equipment on each system may be different, requiring somewhat different, but interoperable, technical solutions.

To realize the potential benefits of a regional transportation smart card program however, many aspects of the revenue collection process must be integrated, or at least coordinated. Combining the card production, distribution, and marketing of several agencies may produce significant cost savings. The clearinghouse, or payment settlement process, must be developed. Participating agencies will need to agree on revenue management policies and procedures. In some cases, agencies may have conflicting charters or legislation controlling revenue management. Partnership agreements will need to be developed specifying each party's position with regard to responsibilities, ownership, costs and revenues. When several public agencies coordinate their operations they will need to agree on how the process will be governed and who will perform each function.

The degree to which a transportation agency can collect and manage revenues and act like a bank has been questioned. Many agencies feel that these revenue processing functions are inappropriate for a transportation agency, and that financial institution partners are more appropriate and can perform these activities more cost-effectively. Even though many transit systems have used stored value tickets for decades, some operators are concerned about their responsibility for the unused value on smart cards under escheat laws.

Privacy is also a concern of many potential users of transportation smart cards. Smart card payment systems on transit or toll roads could produce a record of when travelers are using the system. Many public agencies feel that it is their right to collect this information because the traveler is using a public facility. Most agencies agree, however, that consumers must be assured that the information will only be used for planning or system management purposes. For example, cars with electronic toll transponders can be tracked along a highway, giving traffic management centers an indication of traffic flow or congestion. When this is done, the data from an individual's car are encrypted to ensure anonymity.

Some consumers have also worried about whether the energy generated by contactless card systems could be harmful. International standards have been developed to ensure that the power levels of these systems do not produce harmful levels of electromagnetic radiation, and consumers must be assured that this is the case.

Many government agencies or quasi-government agencies are under increasing criticism by the private sector for competing in their marketplace. If transit authorities issue cards usable in nontransit applications, there will be a greater likelihood for criticism.

BUSINESS ISSUES

Transportation system operators considering smart card applications must develop a positive business case for the initiative. Traditionally this type of initiative has been viewed as a technology upgrade, with the primary concerns being the capital and operating costs of equipment. The business case for transportation smart card initiatives must also consider many other factors, including: revenue generation opportunities, process reengineering, consolidation among agencies and partnerships with other public or private organizations.

A key issue for transportation smart card programs is deciding who a transportation operator should partner or contract with to implement and operate the system. Does the transportation system operator want to develop a closed system or accept cards used elsewhere? Transportation operators must decide if they are going to be an issuer of the payment card or a user of a card issued by a bank, university, or other organization. Public agencies may have different financial, operating, and political objectives, making coordination difficult. Joint procurements of equipment by several agencies may be desirable, but the concept is new to most agencies. Exhibit 11–2 lists the advantages and disadvantages of open and closed systems.

Public/private partnerships are also novel to most transportation agencies. Many public transit operators would like to partner with financial

EXHIBIT 11-2

Relative Advantages of Open and Closed Systems

	Closed System	Open System
Advantages	■ Program can be tailored to specific needs ■ Receive all financial benefits ■ Greater simplicity and flexibility—clearinghouse required ■ Less fraud risk ■ Complete authority over program	■ Share program operation risk and expense ■ More widespread card distribution ■ More appealing to consumers ■ Interoperability standards established ■ Larger terminal base
Disadvantages	■ Assume total financial risk ■ Single application may limit appeal ■ Incur all expenses and capital investment ■ Continue establishing card distribution network	■ Cooperation—need to share financial rewards among different parties ■ Lower flexibility ■ Added complexity ■ Greater fraud risk ■ Limited authority

Source: SCF Working Group on Transportation

institutions to leverage the vast infrastructure in place for transaction management and payment settlement. Other agencies would like an experienced third party to install and operate their system to reduce risk. Financial organizations see transit as a huge market which could provide widespread visibility for their stored value products. Issues about ownership of equipment, cost sharing, risk, and revenue sharing all need to be resolved.

CONCLUSION

Transportation applications of smart card technology are expected to grow rapidly over the next decade. Smart cards promise to provide convenience to travelers, and significant benefits to transportation system operators. The market for transportation cards is so large that many card issuers are seeking to form partnerships with transportation system operators. Smart cards are being used on dozens of bus and subway systems around the world, and are being demonstrated in several metropolitan areas in the United States. In addition, electronic toll collection, parking meters, automated border inspections, electronic driver's licenses, and electronic identification of commercial drivers and their cargo are all potential smart card applications. The transit market is the compelling force behind development of *contactless* smart cards, and a *dual mode technology* card is emerging, targeted at multi-use transportation applications. Smart cards will certainly be a key part of the evolving Intelligent Transportation System.

CHAPTER 12

Travel and Entertainment

Robert Wesley
MasterCard International

Cliff Wilke
Mobil Oil Credit Corporation

Smart Card products and services are currently being tested throughout the travel and entertainment sector. These early trials are igniting a tremendous amount of interest and speculation by industry participants. These players represent a rapidly growing segment of the world population that wants to utilize new technology to gain an advantage over their competitors. This use of smart cards may become a catalyst and a reinforcement for the rapid deployment of smart card technology by other industries.

The travel and entertainment industry has experienced explosive growth over the past decade. This expansion has been fueled by a rapid rise in per capita income and the increase in vacation and holiday time. Global consumer T&E demand has increased from $1.2 trillion in 1992 to $1.9 trillion in 1995, representing a real increase of over 20 percent. The industry is expected to continue growing rapdily, reaching over $3.9 trillion in 2002. The key players range from transportation, accommodation, catering, retail, recreation companies, to travel-related services. Governments also play a key role in facilitating tourism and benefit from the rewards of increased taxes and fees. In some countries, tourism is the leading source of employment.

The companies that make up T&E range dramatically in terms of size and economic might. There are the large airlines, hotel chains, car rental firms, and credit card companies which market to consumer constituencies. There are also smaller businesses such as travel agents, tour operators, restaurant, and lodging facilities. Regardless of size, all are striving to meet the ever evolving needs of customers as they travel the globe on vacation. While this is a fiercely competitive industry, there is a great deal of cooperation between participants to add value to the consumer's travel experience. By forging alliances, participants strive to create unique, value added services and products to build their market share and revenues. One of the major challenges these alliances face is to provide service in a seamless and convenient manner for the customer. Unfortunately, the execution of these programs relies heavily upon paper-based transaction technology or, at best, multiple magnetic stripe plastic cards.

EMPHASIS ON PAPER TRANSACTIONS

Paper-based travel transactions, today, are one of travel's dominant necessities. The airline industry relies upon the paper ticket throughout the world. Any seasoned traveler will openly decry the inconvenience related to the documentation and steps that must be accomplished prior to a trip. Today's traveler needs to carry at least four to five major documents to make a domestic trip and more for an international trip. These documents include a travel itinerary, passports—if international—credit cards, frequent flyer cards, cash, travelers cheques, and travel coupons. During the consumer's travels, he or she will collect hotel receipts, car rental forms, plastic room keys, restaurant charges, and other receipts. These paper-based systems are costly to process, and highly subject to fraud. This situation provides an opportunity for future applications that maximize productivity and streamline cash flow.

Recently airlines started to migrate to paper tickets with magnetic stripes. But the process remains cumbersome, labor intensive, and expensive to administer. Paper travel discount coupons are also used extensively. These coupons are used to record reservations, itineraries, discounts, prepaid arrangements, and much more. They are subject to loss and fraud, not to mention their inconvenience to the traveler. For international travelers, a paper-based passport is a must to gain access to another country. Paper receipts for hotel, car rentals, and restaurants are collected as one travels. These paper receipts become the basis the business travelers dreaded expense reports.

PLASTIC CARDS

Plastic cards, some with magnetic stripes, also have become one of the mainstays for the traveler. Most of the airlines, hotels, and car rental companies issue plastic loyalty cards in various colors denoting the customer's usage. These cards merely carry a unique customer number often embossed on the card, but sometimes also store encoded information on a magnetic stripe. These plastic cards facilitate, to a limited extent, loyalty programs with travel partners within the industry. For example, an airline may award frequent flyer points for staying at a travel partner hotel. These loyalty programs generally only facilitate point accumulation. Point redemption and reconciliation of points generally require human intervention, paper coupons, and statements. The administration associated with these programs is time consuming and costly.

CO-BRANDED CARDS

Co-branded plastic credit cards have also become popular travel-related service industry products. Examples are the American Advantage Citicorp Card, the Delta American Express Optima Cards, and the Hilton Optima Card. These programs offer frequent reward points to their customers every time the card is used to pay for products and services. However, the cards use magnetic stripes, and depend heavily upon on-line authorization systems. As consumer expectations evolve, the existing programs are becoming more generic and require greater differentiation. Further, the consumer would prefer a more flexible and convenient loyalty program which allows immediate redemption of mileage rewards and easier statement reconciliation. Airlines, hotels, and card companies find the cost of these programs extremely high.

To sum up, today's travelers leave on trips with wallets bulging with plastic cards and pockets full of paper airline tickets. While traveling, the consumer accumulates more documents and receipts which are paper based. The current process is inconvenient for the consumer, costly for the travel company to administer, and a nightmare for corporate travel and finance departments to manage. Smart cards have the potential to greatly improve the overall travel process.

APPLICATIONS WITHIN THE INDUSTRY

Airlines seem to be one of the early adopter groups to introduce smart cards in travel and entertainment. Resorts, the gaming industry, and interactive television are investigating or prototyping smart card technology solutions to gain a competitive edge. However, over the long term, multiapplication or multifunction smart cards will be issued to combine the services and product offerings of multiple travel and entertainment companies.

Airlines are leading the way in smart card enabled products, designing and piloting such services as smart card enabled ticketing. The objective is to use smart cards to replace the current paper-based ticketing process. This should reduce operating costs and improve customer service associated with the entire ticketing function. Some smart card ticketless travel cards also include other functions such as frequent flyer numbers and telephone prepayment. In addition, plans are underway to incorporate a credit card payment option within the card. The current airline ticketing pilot programs are operating on intercountry shuttle routes, but will expand rapidly. International Airline and Transportation Association (IATA) has formed a task force to develop interoperability standards for smart card ticketless travel. Its mission is to ensure easy and convenient negotiation of electronic airline tickets with a target date to release guidelines in late 1996. Credit card companies such as American Express, MasterCard, and industry groups including the Smart Card Forum are providing leadership to facilitate the interoperability with other companies in the travel industry.

T&E: PLAYERS AND MOTIVATIONS

The goals of entertainment and travel-related companies are quite simple: meet the consumers' needs, build market share, increase revenue, reduce expenses, and maximize profits in an extremely competitive environment. The major challenge: how can this be achieved in a fiercely competitive industry with a broad variety of players all attempting to gain an edge on their competitors? Tremendous pressure is on each company to differentiate themselves from the competition and to gain additional market share as well as maximize revenue. The major challenge for the industry players is to provide convenient, value added travel to its customers by forging alliances with key providers in the industry, while at the same time creating a unique competitive advantage. For example airlines, hotels, car rental companies, and credit card companies using paper and magnetic stripe technology developed unique product offerings to their joint customer constituencies. With smart card technology, the possibility of providing a more cohesive marketing offering that can be more easily accessed and tailored to the customer needs, becomes stronger.

Airlines There are three major global travel and entertainment card projects conducted by Lufthansa, Delta, and American Airlines and closely followed by the industry.

Lufthansa is currently testing chip technology integration in Germany. Launched in May of 1995, this project covers flights between Frankfurt and Berlin. Six hundred participants received multiapplication chip cards. The card was a standard magnetic stripe card with two chips, both contact and contactless technologies. The card allows the customer to automatically download an airline ticket on the card, access credit, prepay telephone tolls, and automatically stores the frequent flyer number. The contactless chip feature allows the passenger to board the plane by passing within ten centimeters of the reader. The benefits of the card are reduced lines at check in counters, faster boarding, paper elimination, issuance of tickets on short notice, automatic crediting of frequent flyer points, reduced processing costs, and less expensive hardware that is more reliable than ATB (paper mag stripe) hardware. Based on preliminary customer studies, 85 percent of the participants prefer the card to a regular paper ticket.

Delta Airlines is also piloting ticketless travel enabled by chip cards in the United States. The test market is the shuttle between New York and Boston. More than 600 customers have been enrolled in the program. Although exact details on customer satisfaction are not available, indicators reveal that consumers find this product extremely convenient. Industry sources state the program may expand depending on its results.

Targeted for September 1996, American Airlines has announced its intention to pilot a smart card enabled ticketless travel program. Unlike the Lufthansa pilot, the card will use a contact microprocessor chip. The intention is to have the file structure and data format in compliance with IATA specifications. The test is planned for frequent flyers residing in the Albuquerque, New Mexico, area. Albuquerque, Dallas, and New York airports will have interoperable readers and systems for smart cards. While not formally announced, it is expected that American will explore incorporating credit card functionality and a stored value function into the chip.

Hotels The hotel industry has tested smart card technology to facilitate check-in, payment for resort services, and check-out processes. At its VIP conference in 1995, Verifone demonstrated a stored value chip card that can be utilized at various concessions to complete low value transactions.

Smart cards have been fully implemented at a major resort in Posuadado-Rio Quente, Brazil. This hotel resort is found in the country's northern interior, is serviced by charter flights, and is spread out over several square miles. The challenge its management faced was how to process many customers all arriving and departing on charter flights at one time. In addition, the hotel was challenged to obtain all portfolio charges immediately upon check out. But due to the size of the resort, all charges are not always posted to the main computer account on a timely basis. The smart card is given to the client at check in and captures all portfolio charges as they are made. Of course the hotel's system also captures the same portfolio information. Moreover, the guest's smart card becomes the basis for the final charge information. The primary card holder (guest) has an option to receive additional cards for members of his or her party. The customers have found these cards, which have spending limits, to be very convenient. The smart card is durable enough to be immersed in the resort's hot springs without damage. The hotel has also issued employee identification smart cards, used by employees in providing restaurant and bar services. The cards are inserted into the point of sale (POS) devices and capture the guest's service transactions. The employee is able to provide a full accounting of the products and services sold using this card, thus providing greater fraud prevention, and security measures.

An all-inclusive resort in Jamaica is exploring smart card technology. You could download every aspect of your trip prior to leaving home, including meals and activity preferences. When you check in, everything from the bottle of Chardonnay you want waiting in your room, to the color of the toga you want to wear to the evening party will be communicated to the hotel staff. Truly, a way to have a totally carefree vacation.

Corporate Travel An employee utilizing a corporate smart card would be able to have his profile, payment method, and necessary information encoded in the card, allowing more efficient business traveling. In addition, the cardholder's company would be able to track and monitor expenses for each employee more effectively. Today, monitoring and processing expense accounts is a task no one ever looks forward to. In the future, utilizing smart card technology, the entire process will be used for travel, including an electronic purse to allow cash purchases to be captured and monitored.

Entertainment The potential for smart card applications within the entertainment industry is limitless. Applications utilizing smart card technology can and will be developed for the leading edge companies that strategically integrate smart cards in their business. Opportunities exist within this industry, ranging from a theater allowing you to purchase a ticket and participate in a frequent movie goers program, to a casino frequent players rewards program, to season tickets to a sports arena, the ballet, symphony, or theater ensemble. Companies like Blockbuster Video, Bally Entertainment, and Sony Theaters are exploring these applications. Many of these applications have the advantage of creating collectible card series featuring, for instance, a movie promotion, Academy Awards, or famous sports figures.

Consumer Information Smart card technology also allows the industry leaders to learn more about their customers. They will be able to determine and predict buying patterns and take that information to the next level to understand what motivates the customer to make the buying decision. In addition, rewards and recognition programs can be tailored to each customer. As the industry learns more about consumer needs and demands, its members will have the ability to further refine their messages utilizing smart card technology. Data mining techniques, as discussed previously, will be used to determine and segment markets and allow all industry players to target specific customer segments to maximize profits. This ability will be key for many businesses in the next decade.

TECHNOLOGICAL ISSUES

As in other industries, one challenge that T&E will face in making the change to smart card technology will be upgrading the existing infrastructure to accept smart cards. The current infrastructure allows a company to accept numerous payment types including cash, checks, and credit cards. In the airline industry, a paper-based ticket is used to document the sale. Credit cards are accepted through point-of-sale devices that are connected via telecommunication lines to an authorization host. The host checks the validity of the card and approves the sale amount up to the credit limit of the consumer. The system cannot verify who is using the card, or exactly what the customer's real desires are. Some systems available today provide additional purchase level detail, but the majority of systems provide only a sales total, date, transaction number, and merchant name.

For some companies the migration to smart cards will be quite painless. However, for others it will be a challenging undertaking that may delay the decision to accept smart cards. For smart cards to gain hold, new POS equipment will be necessary to accept them. This may be as simple as an inexpensive retrofit to accept cards for payment, or an entirely new system that will have the ability to capture consumer data and information.

The cards also present new opportunities. For instance, one day a consumer may be able to review his or her frequent flyer program information via the Internet, thus reducing the costs associated with mailing statements. Or they may be able to see the rewards live via the Internet and make immediate award selections. Both Intuit and Microsoft are reportedly working on software to manage loyalty programs.

LEGAL, REGULATORY, AND PUBLIC POLICY ISSUES

Consumer privacy is a paramount consideration. Today, mailing lists are purchased and sold to promote sales, however the advent of smart cards and the volume of information they make available could create a backlash against vendors who try to sell this detailed information.

IATA STANDARDS

In late 1995, IATA formed a special task force to address the use of smart cards in delivering ticketless travel. The task force is expected to release its specifications in late 1996, and its major thrust was to explore the interoperability of a smart card delivered ticketless travel system. The task force identified two prime areas of focus:

- Defining the data elements and file structure. The committee initially felt the file structures would have to comply with the credit card industry interoperability specifications, EMV. Further, it appeared that there would be several different file structures to which the industry players could migrate over the course of time. The following data elements would be required on each card:
  - Name
  - Language preference
  - Issuing bank card number
  - Card version number (operating system)
  - Sex
  - Airline code
  - Customer ID (16 Characters)

- Defining the functionality and interface (on terminal hardware and software) was the second area of focus. One of the key issues in this area, the use of contact and contactless technology, raised special concern. An important benefit of adopting contactless technology is to speed processing passengers at the boarding gate. Contact technology will probably prevail for the interim because the credit card industry prefers its security and because contactless technology requires a more sophisticated (microprocessor) chip. The ultimate solution will be a next generation chip which has both contactless and contact capabilities incorporated in one design. This new chip development should be available very shortly.

BUSINESS ISSUES

The industry will need to evaluate the potential benefits of smart card technology and its associated costs to create a business case. To find a profitable niche, it will need to evaluate all of the current expenses for the various tasks to be assumed by smart cards and smart card technology.

AIRLINES

The key business drivers for the airline industry are as follows:
- Cost of issuing the ticket. Depending on the complexity of the ticket, the actual cost can range between $15 to $50. The cost of issuance includes the labor required to prepare the ticket and to deliver the ticket to the customer.
- Airport processing costs. The airline industry currently incurs administrative charges in processing the ticket at the airport, issuing the boarding pass, and collection of the boarding pass at the gate.

- Backend processing costs. Currently all tickets collected at the airports are batched and sent to a central processing center. This labor-intensive capture function is not only costly, but also results in delays and potential errors in developing critical revenue accounting and necessary management information. The introduction of electronic ticketing is not only focused on reducing costs, but also on improving the airlines' ability to respond to changes in consumers' travel patterns.
- Fraudulent tickets. The current paper based airline tickets can be easily replicated, utilizing sophisticated techniques. In addition, the airlines find it difficult to prevent the fraudulent use of lost or stolen airline tickets. Smart cards can be designed to greatly reduce fraud overall.

In addition to the current business drivers, airlines are being required to meet increased security needs. For example, most airports around the world require passengers to show identification, but passengers use various forms of identity and there is little standardization. Since some drivers' licenses do not have photos, they cannot be used as a positive identification.

Also, consumers are searching for more convenient travel. For example, they look for easy redemption of frequent flyer points and better management of rewards programs. Some customers prefer having some points retained on their frequent flyer card for redemption, or upgrades at the ticket counter, or discounts for purchasing duty free items on board the aircraft.

CONCLUSION

Tomorrow's T&E industry will be dramatically different. Today's dreams are becoming tomorrow's reality. You may be able to carry one card that potentially will have everything you need for an entire vacation or business trip. This card may carry your airline ticket, hold all personal information including passport and positive identification for security screening, and identify all of your preferences including seat choices, automobile type, hotel room, and even what you want for breakfast and the type of newspaper you read. The card can also carry a prepaid electronic purse, and contain your credit card numbers to enable you to make purchases on the road. It could also track your frequent loyalty programs for you and allow you to get instant gratification in receiving the award of your choice on the spot. The idea of one card that does it all really gains focus utilizing smart card technology.

As we look to the future, travel and entertainment will continue to lead the way in exploring new opportunities utilizing technology to achieve its goals. The future for smart card applications within T&E is limitless. There will be numerous applications and possibilities for this technology to gain competitive advantages while gaining a larger share of the discretionary dollar.

The major players are actively testing and conducting trials with this new technology—learning and developing applications that will allow them to widen the gap between themselves and the competition.

CHAPTER 13

Retailing and Electronic Coupons

Cliff Wilke
Mobil Oil Credit Corporation

Beverly Matson
VeriFone

The retail industry is evolving at a rapid pace. The companies that were the players of the 70's and 80's are struggling to keep up with the emerging leaders of the 90's. The new leaders are using technology and information as their sword to attack the competition. As market leaders position themselves for the next decade, they will have another weapon at their disposal to further differentiate themselves from the competition—smart card technology, which has the ability and functionality to allow them to break away from competition.

Retailing in the United States includes the marketing, sales, and service of merchandise to consumers who visit a storefront location, or purchase goods and services via a remote server, through the mail, telephone, or Internet. The industry covers a broad range of categories including:

- Chain/general merchandise
- Department stores
- Petroleum/convenience stores
- Specialty retailing
  - Apparel and other soft goods
  - Hard goods
  - Entertainment
- Supermarkets—national and regional
- Small and medium size groceries
- Mom and pop—family-owned business
- Cash only—small business (newsstands, coffee shops)

When compared to other U.S. vertical markets addressed in this book, retailing represents one of the biggest challenges. The good news is, as a group, they embrace emerging technologies at the point of service. This includes such new introductions as electronic cash register (ECR) systems, in-store controllers, in-store management systems, in-lane customer-activated electronic payment systems, gas pumps, fully-integrated payment systems, and very sophisticated networking infrastructures.

Retailers have also been early adapters of an expanding range of POS payment options that include acceptance of charge cards—both third party and proprietary—debit cards, checks, and other noncash payment types, as well as cash. In many cases, the major retailers issue their own cards, which they also authorize via their own proprietary credit networks.

Here lies the challenge for the U.S. business case within this segment: With a telecommunications infrastructure that has proven both reliable and cost effective, how do retailers justify the introduction of smart card technology? With the ability to issue and authorize their own private label cards, and often to manage their own loyalty and frequency programs and accept a variety of payment types, do they need new card technology? With consumers increasingly looking for convenience, what new applications can be introduced to retain an existing customer base while attracting new customers? Can the introduction of a new enabling technology be evolutionary as opposed to revolutionary? These are some of the important questions we'll address throughout this chapter.

RETAILING TODAY

In order to identify the valuable opportunities available to a retailer interested in introducing smart card technology, we need to review where retailers are today, By understanding their goals, their knowledge of their customers, the information that is available to them based on their current transaction sets, and the current processing infrastructure, we can draw a clear picture of smart card potential.

Retailers that make up this industry range dramatically in size and economic power. Some have the ability to vertically control the sale, from the commercial ad that sparks the sale, through the settlement via their proprietary credit card processing network, to a small merchant who waits for the next person to walk through the door. Some merchants have the ability to conduct focus groups to determine customers' needs, while smaller retailers gain this information through personal contact.

RETAILING GOALS

From the retailer's perspective the major objectives are simple: increase revenue, reduce expenses, and maximize profits. The major question: how to achieve this in a new world where the marketplace is changing faster than ever before, with new products and services being introduced at an exponential rate? A retailer needs to be positioned to meet the needs of existing customers and to attract new customers or face the possibility of losing them all to competition. In addition, retailers are under tremendous pressure to differentiate themselves from the competition, to gain additional market share, improve customer service, and maintain customer loyalty while maximizing revenue. While these are goals, their competitors are also continuing to evolve and raising the ante to remain in the high-stake marketplace.

DOES THE RETAILER *REALLY* KNOW THE CUSTOMER?

Many retailers think they know their customers, but do they? Savvy retailers will utilize all available marketing tools to learn more about their customers and how to satisfy customer needs. However, no tools and extrapolations can definitively predict a clear buying pattern. Unless retailers actually track what an individual consumer purchases, they really do not effectively know the consumer's buying patterns. More important, what stimuli got the customer to make the purchase. Was the TV commercial last night, a recommendation from a friend, or the mail coupon, the catalyst for the sale?

RETAILERS' OPPORTUNITIES

A major opportunity exists on the horizon for the key players in tomorrow's market that have the ability to target the right message to the right customer to get the sale in the most cost effective manner. Utilizing data mining techniques to determine and segment markets will allow a retailer to target specific customers to maximize profits. Capturing sales data at the customer and transaction level will allow a retailer to determine potentials for increasing sales. Data mining will be the cornerstone for the new emerging leaders in the retailing field. This can be seen in many advertising campaigns today. For example, it is no secret that the breweries are major sponsors for many sporting events, matching the demographic profiles of the viewers and targeting customers for their products. We probably won't see a Laura Ashley or Donna Karan commercial on Monday Night Football or a Cadillac ad on MTV anytime soon. Another data mining operation is to match customers to specific commercials viewed or coupons received at home or at the point of purchase. Once this excavation has been dug, retail marketing, as we know it, will never be the same.

A second significant opportunity is the ability to reduce fraud and cash handling costs by reducing the amount of cash in store. Smart Card Forum research on merchant interest in smart cards found two leading reasons merchants were interested in this technology: Reduced cash and coupons at point of sale.

A third opportunity is for merchants to be able to sell goods and services through on-line environments like the Internet, in which payment can be enabled via stored value or electronic cash cards. This is especially attractive in instances in which no previous billing arrangement has been established, as with Pay TV, information on the Internet, and small-value items.

CURRENT INFRASTRUCTURE

The current infrastructure facilitates acceptance of numerous payment methods including cash, checks, charge cards, debit cards, credit cards, and other noncash tender such as paper coupons, gift certificates, and food stamps, depending on the type of retailer. Most credit, debit, charge cards, and checks are authorized at the point of sale/service (POS) by devices which are connected via telecommunications lines to an authorization host. In the case of credit and charge cards, the host checks the validity of the card account and grants approval for the sale up to the credit limit of the consumer. Debit (ATM) cards and checks may be either authorized electronically, directly from the bank or service center, or may be authorized off line.

Noncash payment tenders can create a cumbersome and costly reconciliation and management challenge. Coupons are a good example. There are thousands of vendor and promotional coupon types which the merchant normally accepts in lieu of cash. The coupons must then be counted and forwarded to a clearinghouse for remuneration. The merchant rarely determines the source or age of the coupon to assist in marketing efforts.

Food stamps are another balancing nightmare. They are counted and treated as cash, complete with deposit into the supermarket's and grocer's bank accounts. These balancing and accounting activities are timely and costly. Exhibit 13–1 highlights the typical payment types today by retail segment.

The current infrastructure and data capabilities capture a limited amount of sales information. Beyond payment data, the level of information available depends on the level of sophistication in the retailer's system. Most systems do not verify who is actually using the card. And with the exception of department stores, specialty shops, and some general merchandise retailers, most sellers have no exact way of tracking what the consumer is purchasing. They

EXHIBIT 13-1

Payment Type by Retail Segment

Market Segment	Payment Type						Typical Network Environment		
	Cash	Check	Debit	Credit Card 3rd Party	Credit Card Private	ECR's Smart Card Capable	On-Line	Dial	Private
Supermarkets	x	x	x	x		Yes		x	
Small/Medium-Size Grocer	x	x		x	x	Evolving		x	
Petroleum	x	x	x	x	x	Yes	x		x
Convenience Store	x	x	x	x	x	Yes	x	x	
Chain/General Merchandiser	x	x	x	x	x	Yes	x	x	x
Specialty									
Apparel	x	x		x	x	Yes	x	x	x
Entertainment	x	x		x	x	Yes		x	
Hard Goods	x	x		x	x	Yes		x	
Mom and Pop	x	x		x		Depends		x	

"x" indicates usage.

only capture limited data such as date/time, transaction number, basic merchandise category (such as department code) dollar amount, and customer account number.

The benefits enjoyed by those retailers investing in their telecommunications and processing systems include:

- Two- to ten-second response time for authorization
- Improved customer service at the point of sale
- Improved customer convenience in terms of:
  - Payment options
  - Efficient transaction times
  - Merchandise selection
  - Targeted marketing programs
- Reduced fraud risk
- Improved cash management systems
- Sophisticated merchandise systems
- Complete or selective data capture
- Improved inventory management systems, especially including:
  - Just-in-time
  - Promotional merchandise
  - Staple stock replenishment
- Electronic Data Exchange

LOYALTY SYSTEMS

Loyalty Systems are becoming more prevalent in retailing, based on the astounding success of frequency programs in the travel and entertainment industry. Once again, we see them being implemented by those retailers with the more sophisticated information processing systems, such as department stores, service stations, and aggressive specialty retailers. Since the systems of these retailers are predominantly built on magnetic stripe cards, the loyalty programs use technology to leverage the existing infrastructure. It exists, it works, and has the capacity to meet the business requirements. The cards are typically the current private label issued by the retailer, but may also be issued for loyalty programs. In the United States, examples include the Blockbuster Video Card and the Saks First Card. Blockbuster's card was part of a test which included such incentives as free videos based on attaining certain usage levels. The Saks First Card yields purchasing power based on annual card dollar volume. These programs reflect a growing trend that has proven effective in attracting and retaining important customers.

With this as background, we will move into the opportunities available to introduce smart card technology within retailing, looking at some of the possible applications, the players, and their motivations.

APPLICATIONS WITHIN THE INDUSTRY

Currently, there are applications underway utilizing smart card technology to differentiate a retailer from the competition. In the United Kingdom, Shell has introduced a smart card-based loyalty program at their gasoline stations to attract, motivate, and reward loyalty. Although the chip-based card is not currently used as a charge card for purchases, the potential and platform is there for future applications utilizing the technology. There are also many other mag-stripe and manual based motivation and recognition programs around the world to reward loyalty, and reward the customer for purchases made.

The Olympic Games program in Atlanta, with hundreds of merchants participating, allowed both consumers and merchants to use the new technology and utilize the electronic purse function when making purchases at participating locations. Involved merchants included transportation, oil and gas, fast food, vending machines, and retailers.

SMART TV–THE ELECTRONIC COUPON

One of the newest and most exciting developments on the horizon is downloading electronic coupons directly from a television. Smart TV has developed a beeper-sized device, that when coupled with a smart card, has the potential to change what a coupon will look like in the future. The consumer can point the device toward a conventional television set whenever an electronic coupon symbol appears and capture coupons from the advertisement. Then, the coupon can be redeemed through the existing scanner system at a local grocery store. One of the most promising aspects of this new product is that it utilizes the existing infrastructure and requires no equipment but the device and smart card. In addition, since the coupon is received by the customer by pointing the device at the television screen, the merchant can track what coupons are taken, and more powerfully, where and when they are redeemed. This is a tremendous opportunity for supermarkets and product marketers to work together to revolutionize and automate couponing.

Similar access to electronic coupons from home or car radios is being evaluated. Here we expect to see innovative start-ups, such as CouponRadio, working with the automotive industry, radio manufacturers, radio stations, and product marketing groups. Much like Smart TV, CouponRadio is in a position to leverage a conventional broadcast medium, with an existing broadcasting environment, to move into the smart card age. The smart card can be programmed to accept electronic coupon data via the broadcast, selected by the consumer. Once captured on the chip, the coupon detail can be read at the point of sale by the electronic cash register system or other device with the following benefits:

- Convenience for the consumer—no coupons to cut or manage
- The merchant captures and reconciles coupon data electronically, which represents a huge labor and cost savings
- Faster remittance to the merchant
- The merchant and product market groups gain valuable demographic data quickly allowing them to be more effective when targeting marketing consumers
- The system has the potential to build loyalty for all involved, through its efficiencies, creating a WIN-WIN-WIN for everyone involved

HOW WILL THE ELECTRONIC COUPON MOVEMENT START?

What are the components necessary to move into this new and efficient environment? Where can we experience this type of flexibility, convenience, savings, and incentives? The smart cards and reader/writer technology exist today, and the infrastructure is partially there, but changes and integration are a key to success:

- The bandwidth for Smart TV and CouponRadio exist today
- The devices to interface with the TV and radio need to gain acceptance and refinement to price points acceptable within the marketplace
- Smart cards are here, distribution channels must be established to gain critical mass numbers required for success

Clearly, electronic distribution of coupons in any medium offers excellent data collection and marketing potential. It also represents an exciting opportunity for partnership or alliance groups. The challenge will be to achieve critical mass on a regionalized or local basis to gain marketing advantage.

Another point of convenience and attraction for electronic couponing will be the PC in the home or office, which offers similiar electronic coupon promotions based on Internet advertising to a captive audience of one. Redemption may be electronic or via a physical location. The PC represents one of the most attractive and cost-effective prospects for smart card interaction, as there are peripherals available now to connect the computer to the card. New hardware offerings, including keyboards with integrated smart card readers, are in progress. The ability to leverage the masses and entice new users are clearly on the horizon.

APPLICATIONS GOING FORWARD

What are the sure-fire applications that will drive smart card technology into the broader retail market in the United States? We see several areas of potential that appeal to different segments of this market group:

- Identification of the consumer:
  - When present in a retailer's store location
  - Over the telephone
  - Via the Internet
- Electronic access to certain information (credit and loyalty accounts)
  - In-store kiosk
  - Via the Internet
- Data/information warehousing
- Electronic couponing
- Loyalty programs—information and point balance
- Stored value or electronic purse
- Credit/charge card processing
- Bank account (ATM card and check processing)
- Cash management

A VISION OF THE FUTURE

Imagine a future in which a merchant would know precisely where to focus an advertising budget to maximize sales. Applications such as the ones we have discussed provide a gateway for these developments. Imagine a time when retailers could team up in alliances to maximize advertising and reach more customers than they ever believed possible. Smart card applications allow retailers to know their customers better and to know which partners will maximize revenue.

PLAYERS AND MOTIVATIONS

Smart card technology can provide a retailer with information essential to determining goals and strategies. Retailers will be able to get detailed customer information at a level never before been available at reasonable cost.

This will allow retailers to reinforce, modify or even change their strategic direction. In addition, they will be able to measure performance versus projections to determine if the actions taken to grow sales were effective and profitable. Also, retailers will be able to ascertain the buying patterns of their consumers and determine and analyze what stimuli effect a sale. They will have the ability to reward and induce consumers to remain loyal to the merchant. Over the past decade, the airline industry utilized frequent flyer programs to reward travelers for remaining loyal to their airline. Certainly, these programs will become more prevalent in other industries over the next few years.

CUSTOMER SERVICE

An added smart card benefit for retailers will be the ability to determine why, and more important how, they gain or lose customers. The customer information that will be available will allow them to utilize new technology, coupled with existing methodologies such as focus groups, to learn more about what the customer wants. Conversely, they will have the ability to learn more about their noncustomers to determine what it takes to gain new customers. As an outgrowth, customer service will improve, because the retailer will learn more about what the customer really wants, as opposed to today's market in which the retailer can only broadly assume what the customer wants.

CASH CONTROL AND FRAUD REDUCTION

One of the greatest opportunities for smart card technology in retailing will be in improving cash control and reducing fraud losses. Within the credit card industry, fraud is a $1.5–2 billion yearly expense. Smart card technology will create more sophisticated ways of reducing fraud. Currently there are numerous tests in place pairing smart card technology with biometrics to ensure that the user is authorized to use the card. Some of the technologies to reduce fraud from the retailers' perspective include a simple Personal Identification Code (PIN) to more sophisticated technologies such as retina and iris scan and fingerprints.

This is just the starting point. Down the road, numerous new ways to positively affirm identity will be possible. For example, someday a consumer might drag a finger across a rough pad that will scrape off a single cell of dead skin and then match it to a DNA map contained on a smart card. Or a camera will detect an identity based on a digitally encrypted map of the consumer's face and match it to the identity contained on the smart card. These examples may sound far-fetched, but as technology improves, the mechanics to improve security will also improve.

CASH MANAGEMENT

Cash handling will also be an important benefit to the retailer utilizing smart card technology. Today the estimated price of handling cash is between five and eight percent of total transaction amounts. This includes counting, safeguarding, banking, and the security aspects of handling cash. Utilizing smart card technology, a merchant will have the ability to transfer money electronically from the store to the bank in one simple process through existing telecommunications technology.

Leveraging stored value cards is an opportunity to significantly reduce the utilization and handling of coins. One potential driver for change could be the total amount of money that currently exists in corporate allocations for a change till in each register and the potential to speed transactions. By accepting a stored value card, a retailer can realize an offset in expenses for coin handling, coin inventory, and reduce the potential for internal theft.

DRIVING FORCES

As time passes, technologies improve, and more retailers realize the potential of smart cards, the individual merchant will need to make a decision. They can either view smart card opportunities as a strategic advantage to separate them from the competition, or they can struggle with the decision to use the new tools and be left in a defensive position as they try to survive tomorrow.

The retailers that lead the way will use market segmentation and proactive target marketing to leverage their resources and maximize their return on investment. Smart card technology will assist the retailer in achieving this objective. As mentioned previously, retailers will be able to measure the buying patterns of their most important customers and refine the advertising message accordingly. In addition, smart card technology will provide many retailers unable to afford the above mentioned tools the ability to measure their customers' sales and buying patterns.

TECHNOLOGICAL ISSUES

One of the most important aspects of the successful implementation and integration of smart card technology into today's retail marketplace is the early involvement of retailers in the process. Every company has its own rationale for making a move to new technology, but the bottom line is that the retailer is the key to the overall acceptance of smart cards at the point of sale. One challenge that retailers will have to face in making the shift to smart card technology will be changing the existing infrastructure to accept smart cards. For some retailers it will be as easy as exchanging their existing terminal for a new point of sale device. Larger merchants will face the challenge of retrofitting all of their existing registers and terminals to accept this new payment system. Currently, most of the major point of sale equipment manufacturers are planning to have retrofit kits available to upgrade existing infrastructures. Funding and justifying the costs associated with upgrading to smart card technology.

While retrofitting and upgrading will be the course of action for the retailer with a fully integrated POS system, other factors may motivate retailers preparing to overhaul an information system. For them, smart card technology may offer the opportunity to "leap frog" into a whole new area of the information business. This approach to system architecture may be more closely oriented to a client/server-based processing with access to portable and distributed data coming from the chip embedded in the card.

As the Internet grows and becomes more a part of daily life, more retailers will find ways to access this technology to maximize sales and revenue potential and smart cards will be integral to this new buying world. A customer will be able to insert a smart card into a computer via a PCMCIA-compatible holder and complete purchases via the computer. The funds would be transferred directly to the merchant.

The Internet may also be another avenue for facilitating electronic couponing. While customers are browsing on a web site, they may be attracted to an electronic advertisement and want to take advantage of a specific promotion. The instructions will prompt the consumers to insert their smart card and accept the coupon electronically when shopping at their local merchant. The expiration and dollar amount can be processed electronically at the point of sale, with the added benefit of tracking the success of the targeted promotion.

Some key thoughts for consideration:

- As with the introduction of ATM cards into the petroleum and supermarket segments, training and marketing are extremely important.
- Each retailer's existing infrastructure is unique. This warrants close planning and cooperation by the players.
- The industry has evolved to the point at which the electronic payment and critical merchandise flow is a by-product of the transaction from the POS terminal. Merchants will demand a single multifunctional unit from the hardware providers. Once again, careful planning and cooperation can allow this to occur.
- Retailers will need to analyze how they can use their existing infrastructure. In many cases the additional data processed can be addressed and integrated through a front-end processor designed to strip off needed data and store extra data that can be used later.

EXHIBIT 13-2

Consumers' Smart Cards Usage Concerns

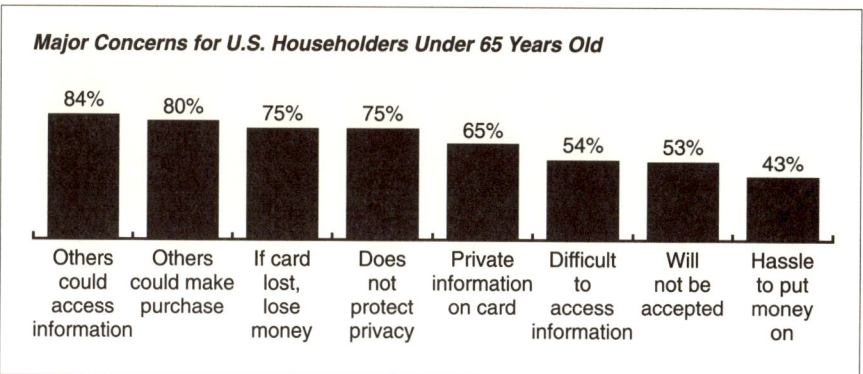

Source: Smart Card Forum, 1994

- An opportunity to look at the advantages of partnering and forming alliances to introduce this new technology definitely exists. Potential partners may include banks, the RBOC's, telecommunications companies, card associations, and systems vendors. The benefits are varied, but would include sharing the expense, risk, and market growth opportunities.

LEGAL, REGULATORY, AND PUBLIC POLICY ISSUES

Privacy concerns loom as one of the critical gating factors on consumer and market acceptance of smart cards. Recent Smart Card Forum research shows privacy as the number one concern of consumers. (See Exhibit 13-2.)

One potential question that will need to be addressed is how will consumers feel about retailers' knowing their buying habits. Today, a good retailer knows his loyal customers well because of their personal relationship. Tomorrow, the retailer will have vastly more information on existing and potential customers. Determining how consumer will react to retailers' knowing their buying habits is critical. Some people may not wish to have their buying habits known. For instance, some purchasers still do not use credit cards or checks, paying entirely by cash, to avoid anyone knowing what goods or services they purchase, or where.

Will some groups take action to protect their privacy? Will the customer have the ability to only let information go to selected retailers and remain anonymous to others? These and other questions will be addressed over time.

BUSINESS ISSUES

A retailer will need to develop a business case, as outlined in Chapter 2, to justify the migration to smart cards. With this business case, retailers can analyze many aspects of their business to evaluate the potential for implementing smart card technology. For example, the ability to recognize a customer may have great value to one company. Another firm may see the real benefit in fraud reduction. If the advantages are great, a particular retailer may migrate to smart card technology early on in the process. Other companies will wait until the last minute, and make the change in an effort to keep up with the competition. If retailers use technology to examine all aspects of potential rewards, decisions will be much easier. Coming to grips with this timing issue is a serious factor in any business proposition.

CONCLUSION

Tomorrow will be a truly exiting place to be a leader in the retail industry. Imagine a shopper entering a retail clothing store. For this example, let's call her Karen. As she enters the store, the contactless smart card reader advises the in-store computer that Karen is a frequent customer who is a size seven and has purchased four black outfits in the past two years. As Karen walks through the store, she selects items that interest her by pressing a button near a display that is linked to the backroom inventory system. When she enters the dressing room, the items she selected are waiting for her. She tries on the outfits while a video touch screen in the changing room makes other suggestions, including new outfits in black. Still in the changing room, the dress store's computer links to the local music store where Karen shops. The music store is in alliance with the dress store, and lets her know that the new Celine Dion CD is now available, and a teaser of the CD plays for her. The music store's computer knew she would be interested in that CD since she purchased other recordings by the same artist. She then confirms her selections while still in the dressing room, her credit card is charged, and determines if she wants to take the purchases with her, or if she wants them delivered. The changing room, as we know it, will never be the same. In addition, the in-store security system has verified her identity through biometrics prior to the sale, and the store has minimized any potential fraud loss.

The future for smart card applications within the retail industry is limitless. There will be numerous applications and possibilities for utilizing this technology to gain competitive advantages over the competition. Today's dreams will be tomorrow's reality in the retail arena. Currently, many companies are sitting on the sidelines analyzing the potential of smart card technology, while closely watching the latest developments around the world. Major players are conducting trials with this new technology, learning and developing applications that will allow them to widen the gap between themselves and competition. The future in which a retailer will be able to target resources to attract new customers, while at the same time totally satisfying and retaining existing customers, is quickly becoming reality. The retailers that master this technology will be the players of tomorrow.

CHAPTER 14

Education

Michael Smith
Schlumberger

Danyl and Dan Cunningham
Potomac Technology Systems

While the clear mission of a university or college is education, there is no escaping the fact that they are also very large businesses, entailing enormous administrative activity. Over the last several years, the United States educational market has improved the delivery of campus services by consolidating access from many separate cards to a single magnetic stripe card, which also serves as the student identity card. These services range from food service to paying for copies without coins. Now, driven by the dual desires of improving the quality of student life and reengineering the delivery of education for the Information Age, campus administrators are turning toward the smart card as the enabling card technology for the future.

The college and university campus market offers one of the best opportunities for early adoption of smart card technology in the United States. Several factors combine to make this true. First, the educational campus and its environs define a community for which there is effectively a single decision maker. Secondly, there is a clearer business case based on existing campus card applications and the desire for future applications. Thirdly, in many cases there is no existing infrastructure, or there is a need to replace it. Fourth, students and faculty are generally early adopters of new technologies and innovations, minimizing widespread customer acceptance as a problem. And finally, it is helpful that educational institutions have a natural capacity to play a leading role with new technology that promises to have a major impact on the world around us.

After several years of pilot installations in the United States, successful smart card installations were made at several universities in 1995. There is a particular focus on stored value, because applications such as replacing coins in a copier with value stored on magnetic stripe cards have long been used on the campus. In addition, there is an immediate need for multiple applications and a demand to address other emerging applications like network access. As a result, the higher education market will serve as a microcosm for the rest of the United States market, allowing for the evaluation of everything from customer reactions to new services to the issues surrounding multiple application card distribution and personalization.

CARD APPLICATIONS ON THE EDUCATIONAL CAMPUS

The common ground of smart card technology and university administrative systems is the many card activated services found on a campus, known as "campus card systems." These applications are accessed by students, faculty, and administrators with magnetic stripe cards or smart cards, and delivered by on-line or off-line systems in any combination.

An entire book could be written about campus card systems, but this chapter focuses on what is being done with smart cards and why this is proving to be the appropriate technology. In order to better understand the "why," some background information is provided. We will first discuss the major applications typically found in a campus card system, then present the reasons that smart cards are being used.

The major card uses on campus are:

- Access to services and security
  - Meal plan
  - Physical access (rooms, laboratories, buildings)
  - Computer access (printers, equipment, administration systems)
  - Library book lending
  - Event admission
  - Photo ID
  - PIN
- Information
  - Administrative self-service access
  - Prepaid or other long distance phone
- Financial and stored value
  - Copiers
  - Vending
  - Laundry
  - Merchants
  - Parking
  - Proprietary debit (bookstore, other food service like fast food)

Automation of these applications or services was implemented piecemeal in the campus environment. Individual departments, each with their own priorities, timing, and budgets, did as they saw fit. Soon, the universities found themselves with many different systems, each with a separate card. Each student required several cards to use all the services. What had seemed like a practical approach to decentralization suddenly looked disorganized.

College administrators were quick to react to the need to use one card to access all the systems. This need became a driving force from 1990 to 1994, creating a trend that is known in the industry as "one card systems."

In the mid to late 1980's, applications for each department were typically implemented using PC based standalone systems. In most cases the card had only an identity number, and any information required for the application was held in a database accessed locally or over a network. The card was magnetic stripe, bar code, or OCR. The readers were read only devices on-line to a PC, mainframe, or workstation.

In the late 1980's, stored value applications started to appear in copier machines. In this case a dedicated card with a thin magnetic "value stripe" stored a value that was debited by the copier machine. (This stripe, located near the bottom of a card, was sometimes referred to as the "junk stripe," rumored to be named for its use in purchasing "junk food.") The card readers were read/write magnetic stripe. A card value station was added to allow cash-to-card value loading. These stored value systems were off-line and isolated from the other applications, and are in widespread use today in copiers, vending, and laundry machines.

In the first half of the 1990's, a trend emerged to consolidate these different cards onto a single card. From a card standpoint, this was easily achieved by putting a combination of magnetic stripe, value stripes, OCR or bar code as needed on the student ID card. This enabled the typical campus environment to continue to use previously installed "legacy" systems.

As the single card trend began, it was most common and simplest to tie all the devices on campus on-line to a central computer. The advantage of this approach was that a read-only magnetic stripe reader was easier to develop and support for the vendor. The disadvantages for the school were that every copier, doorway, vending machine, or other card accepting device on campus had to be connected by wire to the central computer, a problem when buildings are 70 years old on a campus covering several square miles.

While this worked well enough for many applications like accessing administrative services and meal plans, the on-line centralized data approach broke down in stored value applications. For example, installed in copiers, each device had to be connected to a server for every five cent copy transaction. And if the server went down or critical interconnections failed everything went down, and response times could stretch out at peak periods. Requests for enhancements went to the central system provider, who controlled the prioritization. If you remember the "old days" of central computers before the minicomputer and PC revolutions, you can immediately appreciate the problems of doing stored value on-line.

Into this world came the integrated circuit card. The driving force at first was the stored value application. Given that off-line value stripes were read/write magnetic stripe devices, the same operational advantages that helped smart cards win over the card payphone market gave it superiority in stored value. Since there are no moving parts, the smart card reader is much more reliable than a magnetic stripe read/write reader. This maintenance savings, which can be significant, helps to offset the higher card costs. Also, security is upgraded to world class bank card standards, versus the easily defrauded magnetic stripe cards. Some universities have already had problems with card alteration and duplication.

Another very important smart card advantage is that the infrastructure has a future. Smart card technology is at the beginning of its life cycle, and provides the possibilities to migrate to other existing applications and to develop entirely new applications over the years. As the technology in the chip advances, system functionality will continue to grow.

Another important aspect of campus card systems is maintaining compatibility with emerging bank card technology. As it is becoming clearer that bank cards will evolve to smart cards, campus card systems users want to follow a path that provides for compatibility, especially in urban communities. This has the added advantage of simplifying the expansion of stored value services off-campus at college oriented community merchants when a banking partner is used. Other applications, such as library services and security are also being implemented. As legacy systems are increasingly replaced, the applications can be concentrated on the smart card. Exhibit 14–1 (following page) indicates some of applications currently used on the hybrid campus cards that could be accessed via smart cards.

INDUSTRY TRENDS

From the starting point of stored value, several forces are now shaping the campus card market of the future:

- The success of one card systems has stimulated the demand for more services on the card. University and college administrators nationwide are sharing information on cost savings and technology implementations
- College administrators continue to look for operational cost reductions and new revenue sources

EXHIBIT 14-1
Campus Card Applications

University Business Systems	Laundry Services
■ Photocopiers ■ Laser printers ■ Facsimile ■ Microfiche ■ CD-ROM ■ PC	■ Washers ■ Dryers ■ Soap dispensers
	Miscellaneous
	■ Fees and fines ■ Pay parking ■ Cashless POS
Vending Services	
■ Snack machines ■ Beverages ■ Miscellaneous	**Small Retail**
	■ Athletic events ■ Supplies ■ Food stand

- The impact of networking and other information age technology is causing educators to look at new ways of delivering higher education

The result of these forces is an emerging shift to smart card technology in campus card systems. By using smart cards, administrators can achieve immediate benefits and at the same time position a card platform and an infrastructure of card accepting devices that can carry forward into applications like remote learning and network access control.

As early as 1989, college administrators saw the potential for Integrated cirucit (IC) card technology on campus when Murray State University in Murray, Kentucky, issued 8,000 smart cards with photographs as student IDs. Not surprisingly, this installation along with other early installations at Loyola College and elsewhere experienced many difficulties. These less successful pioneering efforts, however, did pave the way for a second wave of clearly successful installations in 1995, led by the University of Michigan, Western Michigan University, and Washington University in St. Louis among others.

UNIVERSITY OF MICHIGAN

One of the country's premier educational institutions, the University of Michigan also determined to be a leader in the United States implementation of smart cards. Finding themselves at the point of making a significant investment in equipment to provide one-card services in 1995, administrators responsible for implementation recognized that the future of campus card systems and financial card systems was the smart card.

The situation at the university was typical. They had several "legacy" or existing systems using different card technologies such as bar code and magnetic stripe. Their approach was to use existing systems when feasible, and to implement new services with smart cards. This was achieved by including OCR, bar code, and magnetic stripe on the student identity card as well as the integrated circuit chip. Over time, all services are likely to be migrated to the chip.

Two factors distinguish this implementation—the expansion of the stored value card into area merchants and the cooperative relationship with a banking partner. Historically, student cards that had a stored value or on-line value feature were limited to use only on campus. The student desire to use the cards off-campus was blocked by the limitations of magnetic stripe implementations. By using a smart card based stored value system and a banking partner, the new system is useable at off-campus merchants.

There is also a parallel trend emerging for banks and universities to partner the implementation of financial services on campus card systems. The University of Michigan worked very closely with their chosen bank partner, First of America Bank of Kalamazoo, Michigan. This model of university/bank cooperation is attractive to the institution because it is more efficient for a bank to administer the accounts, merchants, transaction collection, the funds pool and settlement, and the regulatory requirements, than it is for the school to do so. In addition, fees generated by the system help the university to provide a higher level of student service at the same or lower cost. Many universities are enlarging partnerships with banks to include general cash management, treasury, student loan, and credit functions.

The University of Michigan chose to use a smart card for their system for three main reasons. First, they preferred an off-line approach for unattended POS devices like copiers and vending machines, and recognized the operational efficiencies of smart card reader technology in handling this. Second, they wanted a platform that would position the university to add new applications and services in the future. Third, they wanted to implement stored value in off-campus merchants, and recognized that smart cards are the most secure and cost-effective way to do so.

The University of Michigan issued over 40,000 cards in 1995, making it one of the largest smart card installations in the United States. First of America Bank has been very successful in taking their smart card system to several other midwest universities.

WASHINGTON UNIVERSITY, ST. LOUIS, MISSOURI

Washington University in St. Louis made another important early smart card installation. By 1996, more than 8,000 cards had been issued to students and faculty. The cards contained two magnetic stripes to support legacy systems, a microprocessor chip, and a student photo. One of the magnetic stripes is a standard banking stripe, while the other specialized stripe is used for existing on-line systems (residence hall access, library book lending, event access, and meal plan). The chip contains the stored value application and student information.

One feature of this installation provides an interesting example of how the university systems will help banks to determine the best ways to position stored value card services. The Washington University card chip contains two electronic cash accounts. One account is PIN protected, and acts as a "safe." This primary account is refunded if lost. The second stored value account is not PIN protected and acts as the "cash" account for low value purchases. The second cash account, like cash, is lost if the card is lost. Money can be transferred from the safe account to the cash account.

The decision to put two accounts in the chip is an important one, and is typical of the questions operators ask themselves when they position a stored value product. Will it confuse consumers? Will it be convenient or a nuisance? Will merchants understand the difference? By testing these concepts and others, the campus systems will provide very valuable insights into the future of stored value and multiplication smart cards.

PLAYERS AND MOTIVATIONS

There are many different players involved in a campus card system, but generally they can be classified as one of the following:

- Educational institution
- Service providers (telecom, vending, copiers, banking)
- Equipment and system suppliers (card reading devices, applications, integrators)

The motivations of the educational institution are to enhance the quality of the education and campus life experience of the student, while minimizing operational expenses. Economic self-benefit motivates the service and equipment providers.

Two industries—financial services and telecommunications companies—have a mutually beneficial relationship with educational institutions. For these industries, there is the opportunity to earn income by providing services to the students and faculty, and to develop interesting long term relations with potentially higher income consumers. For the university, there is the potential to share some of the service income generated from the campus population, thereby reducing the overall expenses of educational services for the institutions' students. This practice can be referred to as revenue sharing.

Increasingly, the campus card industry is affected by revenue sharing, as the service providers find formulas to share their income streams with the university. For example, long distance providers generate significant revenues at high margins from the students. In order to become a preferred provider (an exclusive provider is not practical), the long distance provider subsidizes other services, such as identity card issuance. This lowers the costs for the university and hence the students. They may also share service revenue with the school.

A second example found on is on the campus of the University of Southern California where the university and 3M partnered a business center for copying, word processing, and graphic design.

These win-win approaches have been rapidly understood by bankers. The potential role of banks as partners is to provide services including card issuing and banking services such as checking, debit, and stored value. The revenue streams from account balances, float, and merchant fees can then be shared with the university.

Credit card companies, specifically American Express, now seem to be developing the same logic. In 1995, American Express acquired one of the leading meal plan providers to universities. Since meal plan providers are one of the primary incumbent systems suppliers on a campus and have been very active in single card applications, this positions them well for an expanded role with the universities.

Phone companies have an even better motivation for working with higher education institutions. The high rate of phone usage by students calling home combined with the high margins of long distance service create an ideal opportunity for revenue sharing with the university. Both MCI and AT&T have active university programs, and have developed a variety of carding programs that share revenue and defer expenses.

As a result of this mutual interest, financial institutions, phone companies, and universities work together in many different formulas to provide identity card and financial services. This dynamic impacts the university market significantly.

LEGAL AND REGULATORY ISSUES

Regulatory issues are one of the factors motivating universities to partner with banks for financial services. The more financial features are added to campus card systems, the more carefully regulators examine universities. For example, a regulator sees a student declining balance account as very similar to a checking account. This leads to requirements such as PIN protection, and compliance with consumer protection laws such as Regulation E. These complications become strong motivators for the campus card administrator to partner with a bank which already understands and is prepared to deal with compliance issues.

Of course, the banks are just as interested in this arrangement as the schools are. When stored value and banks come together, security advantages and easier expansion of the off-campus merchant program become stronger arguments to use the smart card. For these reasons, some banks are particularly motivated to expand into stored value using smart cards, as First of America Bank has done.

General financial industry regulatory requirements for smart card stored value are likely to apply to university stored value systems.

CONCLUSION

The educational arena has been a prime proving ground for multiple application smart cards working in an open system. These sites have demonstrated the effectiveness of the technology and the demand from both consumer and merchant to provide broad accessibility and combined usage. The campus setting is an ideal location for this technology. Not only is it a community open to new technology, but it is a ready environment in which the conditions are excellent for successful adoption.

Many of the same obstacles that must be overcome in broader applications are already being done in campus systems. For example, one key to success is training participating merchants; another is appropriate marketing to student and faculty users of the new service of stored value. More mundane but critical issues such as installing equipment in older, remote buildings and collecting information on vending routes must be addressed. All of these experiences and lessons are directly transferable to the broader, open market.

As we move forward, it is likely that universities will shift rapidly into smart cards. By 1999, over half of all new single card systems are projected to be smart cards. Applications will be implemented as needed, with legacy systems continuing to use magnetic stripe until they become uneconomic.

The important features of portability and security (using the active cryptography capabilities of smart cards) present many interesting future possibilities. Students remote from the campus, can be identified securely using a smart card, and documents signed or encrypted with personal keys if needed. Network access to Internet, administrative, and other systems can be secured

EXHIBIT 14-2

Smart Cards in Higher Education—Advanced Functions

Financial	Data Storage	Gain access
■ Stored value	■ Student records	■ Door access
■ Multiple purses	■ Health data	■ Parking gates
■ Loyalty programs	■ Security "keys"	■ Secure e-mail
■ ATM access	■ PIN	■ Internet
■ Transit and parking	■ Digital signature	■ Ticketless event entry
■ PIN on card	■ Privilege codes	■ Distance learning
■ Portable POS	■ Inventory tracking	■ Demand publishing
■ Integrated bank debit, credit, and stored value	■ Biometrics data	■ Electronic validation sticker

Source: Smart Card Forum, Education Workgroup, 1996

and controlled more completely. Distribution of documents and payment over networks are also possible uses. Exhibit 14–2 shows advanced applications for the education market.

Clearly educational institutions will innovate and change, increasingly finding new ways to deliver learning with technology. As that unfolds, the smart card will play an important role in securely identifying students and delivering access to institutional services.

PART THREE
Technology Issues

This book has a strategic focus but we would be remiss if the technology itself were not defined in more detail. The two chapters in Part Three will provide you with the terminology, the basics of the technology, and related standards and specifications. It will also demonstrate why privacy and security issues are at the forefront of industry and consumer concerns and how smart card technology enables an entirely new solution or approach to these concerns.

The experts on technology from the Technology Committee of the Forum have written this section. They represent a group of executives who know state-of-the-art technical as well as implementation issues. They come from the applications provider as well as vendor communities.

More detailed discussions of technology issues will be referenced in this section from Forum and other documents if you choose to immerse yourself in the technical aspects. We have tried to make the chapters as "reader friendly to nontechnical people" as possible.

CHAPTER 15

A Smart Card Primer

Smart Card Forum Technology Committee

Edited by Judy D. Tarbox
Thornebrook Associates

Starting about 5,000 years ago with the abacus, we have been on a lengthy path to make "computing" easier, more reliable, and more secure. We have come a long way from the 1600's when Pascal invented his adding machine, to the 1800's when Charles Babbage invented the *punchcard* system of programming (which some of us used well into this century), to the 1940's when the transistor was invented and started to miniaturize and speed up transaction time. In fact, if we look at the first *electric circuit* Tabulating Machine used to calculate the census of *1890*, we would probably find it amusing that the government was thrilled it would calculate the whole census in only two years! The first simple count was done in *only* six months. Thanks to the smart card technology capabilities of the *1990's*, a big city mass transit system can calculate the number of riders passing through their gates at approximately the rate of one transaction every 300 milliseconds!

This chapter provides a brief background of smart card terminology and the basics of the technology. Chapter 16 goes into greater depth on the security and privacy aspects of this emerging technology.

SMART CARD TERMINOLOGY

Since smart cards are a fairly new technology in the United States, some of the terms used in the industry may also be new or unfamiliar. In order to address this situation, the Smart Card Forum has compiled an official glossary of terms used in the industry. This glossary lists the terminology and definitions used in conjunction with smart cards and their uses. It can be found on page 279 of this book.

The term *smart card* itself is loosely applied to a class of cards that contains electronics. These cards are the same physical size and have the same flexible characteristics as existing credit cards, which are based on ISO 7810. The official definition of a smart card in the Smart Card Forum Glossary is "An integrated circuit card with memory capable of making decisions." There are, however, two main types of cards—memory cards and IC (integrated circuit) cards.

CARD TYPES

The *memory card* can only *store data,* similar to the magnetic stripe card. The major difference between the two is that the memory card can reuse its memory capacity by rewriting data over existing data whereas the mag stripe card is typically a *WORM* (Write Once Read Many) memory technology. Another significant difference is the memory card can store up to 2 Kbytes of information and a mag stripe card can only store .2 Kbytes. The memory card also requires power to operate whereas a mag stripe card does not.

The *IC (Integrated Circuit) chip card* is what we refer to as a smart card. This type of card includes a small microcomputer that is capable of performing calculations, processing data, executing encryption algorithms, and managing data files. It is really a small computer that requires all aspects of software development. It comes with a Card Operating System (COS) and various card vendors offer Application Programming Interface (API) tools. There is a wide and ever increasing range of capabilities available on these IC smart cards. They can have memory capacities in the range of 1–16 Kbytes while clock rates range from 4–16 MHz. Most IC cards have 1–4 Kbytes of memory and operate at 4 MHz forming a *defacto* standard for electrical interoperability. As mentioned earlier, a 64-Kbyte prototype card is available now. The key capacity (memory and processing) issues are miniaturization and cost.

There are also *Hybrid* cards that include some form of electronic capability plus other technologies such as magnetic stripe, optical memory, and bar code for use in a broader spectrum of terminals equipment or applications.

Card Memory The amount of memory on a card is important because it dictates how much information can be stored. The more memory, the more sophisticated the application can be, and the more data that can be kept on the card. The clock speed is important because it determines how fast data calculations are made within the card.

For example, to store a cardholder portrait requires approximately 50 to 300 bytes. Retrieval time takes only a fraction of a second.

There are four types of memory that enable smart cards to store data and programs. Random Access Memory (RAM) is the fastest and can be accessed in billionths of a second. It is also the most volatile and can lose its information immediately if power is cut. Therefore, it is most often used for buffer or temporary storage.

Read Only Memory (ROM) is permanent semiconductor memory. It is used to store the basic operating system programs (such as the program needed to start the smart card when power is turned on). For this reason it is usually designed so that it cannot be read or altered by the user.

Erasable Programmable Read Only Memory (EPROM) is a nonvolatile memory technology that can be written to only once before being erased using ultraviolet light—after which it may be written to again. Most smart cards that use EPROM, however, store information so that it is permanently erasure proof. This is done to increase security so the data can neither be altered nor erased.

Electrically Erasable Programmable Read Only Memory (EEPROM) is a nonvolatile memory technology where data can be electrically erased and rewritten on a reader/writer device. It is the basis for stored value and information management applications.

CONTACT VERSUS CONTACTLESS CARDS

A major distinguishing feature of smart cards is the way in which they interact with corresponding terminal equipment. This divides them into two main IC card classifications: contact and contactless. The differences between the two types are illustrated in Exhibit 15-1.

Contact cards have gold plated metallic contacts on the surface of the card which physically touch corresponding contacts in the terminal equipment itself. These cards must be precisely positioned in the terminal and their contacts must be free from non-conducting contaminants such as oil. The power that runs the card is generated by the Card Acceptance Device or Card Reader.

Contactless cards do not have surface contacts, but rather interact with the terminal via electromagnetic coupling. Low frequency coupling is used for a close proximity connection where the card is placed on or in a terminal device. Higher frequency coupling is used for remote connections where the card is farther away from the terminal device. There are actually two types of contactless cards—passive and active. The passive card derives its power from a frequency generated by the reader. The active card actually has a battery imbedded within it. For more detailed information see the Smart Card Forum document "Contactless Smart Cards—An Overview."

Card Life Cycle Understanding the differences between smart card types is only the first step in the process of utilizing smart card technology to its fullest potential. The use of IC technology brings with it many issues related

FIGURE 15-1

The Differences between Contact and Contactless Smart Cards

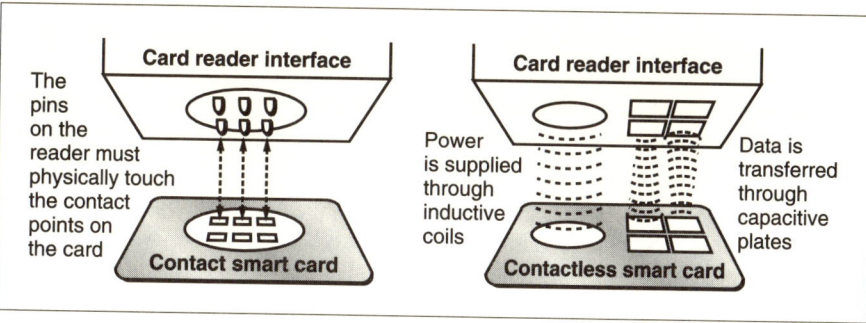

Source: Adapted from National Institute of Standards and Technology (NIST) Special Publication 500-157: *Smart Card Technology: New Methods for Computer Access Control,* September 1988.

EXHIBIT 15-2

Lifecycle Phases of a Smart Card

Card Manufacturing Stage
- IC's are produced
- A serial number or other unique information is placed on each IC
- General smart card control program is burned in ROM
- The IC module is fabricated
- The IC module is embedded in the smart card

Application Development Stage
- Application is developed and written
- Memory zones alloted
- Cryptographic keys are written to memory
- Issuer password(s) are written to memory
- Application data is written to memory
- Card is personalized and issued

Card Active Use Stage
- Card is fully functional, in possession of user
- Information can be read from and/or written to the card, as required in the application design
- Security functions such as cryptographic algorithms can be performed by card

Card Termination Stage
- Card is no longer useable/its application has expired
- Card is recovered and returned to the issuer
- The card is erased and reused or destroyed

Source: Adapted from National Institute of Standards and Technology (NIST) Special Publication 500-157: *Smart Card Technology: New Methods for Computer Access Control,* September 1988.

to the production of the IC's and the loading of data into them to create applications. Exhibit 15–2 (preceding page) presents the four main stages in the life of a smart card and explains what happens during each stage.

When examining this lifecycle, it is important to recognize the key groups that are involved. These include the IC manufacturer, the module manufacturers, the software developer, the card manufacturer, the systems integrators, the card acceptance device manufacturer, the issuer, and finally, the end user and merchant acceptor. They are the stakeholders of the card and application and can be described as follows in Exhibit 15–3.

Smart Card IC Criteria Smart card IC's are generally put through an extensive qualification process before being imbedded into the card material. Several factors are tested including: environment (temperature changes), mechanics (how the card will 'flex'), physicality (how many bond layers), and the actual composition of the chip.

The chip manufacturer's reliability is of primary importance and is determined by rejection rate, tools provided (emulator, simulator), the product (single chip versus module tape), and finally, overall quality and price.

Functionality is as important in purchasing chips as in purchasing cards since the chips are the most important element of the card itself. Things like internal security, supported algorithms (RSA, DES), memory, and operating systems are all key considerations.

Card manufacturers should be especially concerened about chip standards and specifications. In financial applications, for instance, most card manufacturers are including EMV compatibility.

EXHIBIT 15–3

Stakeholders in a Smart Card Lifecycle

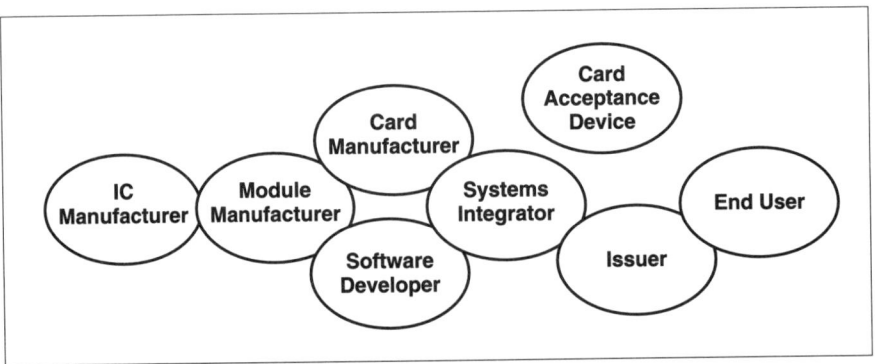

Smart Card Criteria Card functionality is directly related to application complexity. Do you need a simple ID card or is the application more complex—including stored value for example? Also, you need to consider your long range plans. How will the application, and card, evolve—will it be more cost-effective to have a card that can be updated or to have a simpler card that may have to be replaced?

From a consumer acceptance perspective, it is important to consider the existing infrastructure and "market share" of the card manufacturer. It is also necessary to consider multiple applications on a single card since this may be more cost-effective for the issuers, merchants, and consumers. Interoperability issues are similarly significant.

Card operating systems (COS), like any computer operating system, generally offer commands allowing file management, password management, security functions, and application functions. Some COS allow multiple applications to reside on the same card. Some allow multiple services on the same card (multiple files or multiple purses with different protection schemes). It's important to examine this feature when selecting the best card for a particular application.

Card Reader Device Criteria How the information is displayed to users and how users interact with the information are two keys to selecting a card acceptance device (CAD). Devices can be as simple as a "green light—OK, red light—error" to *whole screens* of information. User interaction varies from simple push buttons with one choice to extensive menu-based interfaces. The application developer needs to consider the scope of the application—what meets minimum functional needs, as well as marketing needs —what is easiest for the consumer and attractive as well.

System security is another important consideration in CAD selection. Security modules may be used for storing secret cryptographic keys and encryption algorithms. SAM (Security Access Modules) contain secret file protection keys that protect transactions containing value (i.e., electronic purse). The SAM may also possess the computational power to initiate and follow through an authentication protocol. On the other hand, debit applications may require security modules to hold working keys used to encrypt PINs.

Where the CAD will be used is as important as how it will be used. For example, few—if any—CADs are designed for outdoor use. Restaurant applications, especially fast food outlets, may require semi-washable terminals with protected displays and key pads. A good example of a potentially hostile environment for CADs would be a gas pump application where fumes may react negatively with plastics and glues.

CADs that support both mag stripe and smart card technology allow the system designer to support current applications and introduce smart card applications at the same time. This allows a smoother transition for users and may reduce system cost and system footprint for those applications utilizing many card technologies. MasterCard, VISA, Citibank, and Chase are testing devices in New York City that transparently accept alternate stored value applications. More and more devices will have to house co-resident applications.

Those wishing to develop their own applications must carefully consider the CAD's operating system and associated development tools. They should examine documentation, looking for coding examples and a good set of operating system commands. Sample applications can also be of great value along with development tools such as compilers and cross-compilers, and the supporting documentation.

To promote interoperability and to minimize maintenance difficulties attributable to nonstandard software languages, data structures, and protocols, the application should comply with existing standards and specifications. For example, in a contact card application, ISO 7816-3 provides for three different communication methods: T=0, T=1, and T=14. Two methods, T=0 and T=1 are standard. T=14 is actually proprietary. This means that a company can develop their own method that may or may not be compatible with the other two. In addition, not all smart card readers are currently capable of reading all three methods.

Finally, it is important to identify the major players in the various phases of manufacturing and integration of smart cards. These can be grouped into eight main areas as in Exhibit 15–4.

It is also important to note the key groups exerting a major influence on the development of smart cards and related applications. These include large corporations like AT&T, American Express, IBM, Microsoft, and Motorola; organizations like VISA, MasterCard, Europay, the Smart Card Forum, government agencies, and various other service providers as mentioned in this book.

STANDARDS AND SPECIFICATIONS

No discussion of smart card technology terminology would be complete without addressing the various relevant standards and specifications surrounding them.

International Organization for Standardization

The International Organization for Standardization (ISO), is a worldwide federation of national standards bodies. The work of preparing international standards is normally carried out through ISO technical committees. Each member body interested in a subject covered by a technical committee has the right to

EXHIBIT 15-4
Major Smart Card Players

Card Manufacturers	Gemplus, Schlumberger, Orga, US3, Bull CP8, Solaic, G&D, Toshiba
RF-ID System Manufacturers	Motorola Indala, Intellitag, Cubic, Cotag, Destron, Idesco, Hughes, Mikron, Racom/Bull
Terminal Manufacturers	G&D, IBM, US3, NCR, Interbold/Diebold, Danyl, Schlumberger, Bull/MCTI, Gemplus
Card Operating Systems	Gemplus, Bull/MCTI, Orga, G&D, Schlumberger, SGS Thomson
Systems Integrators	IBM, ASI, Amtech, Motorola, EPS, EDS, Honeywell, Innovatron, Schlumberger
IC (Chip) Suppliers	Motorola, SGS Thomson, Oki, TI, Siemens, Atmel, Hitachi, Raycon
Micromodule Suppliers	Siemens, SGS Thomson, IBM, Hitachi, Orga, Bull/MCTI, Schlumberger, Gemplus
Tag and RF-ID Circuit Suppliers	Mikron, Micron, Atmel, Nedap

be represented on that committee. International organizations, governmental and non-governmental, in liaison with ISO also take part in the work. ISO collaborates closely with the International Electrotechnical Commission (IEC) on all matters of electrotechnical standardization.

Draft international standards adopted by the technical committees are circulated to the member bodies for voting. Publication as an International Standard requires approval by at least 75 percent of voting members. Following are the three main standards pertaining to smart cards:

ISO 7816: Identification cards—Integrated circuit(s) cards with contacts addresses the following six areas:

- *ISO 7816-1 (1987): Physical characteristics*—specifies the physical characteristics of integrated circuit(s) cards with contacts. It applies to identification cards of the ID-1 card type which may include embossing and/or a magnetic stripe as specified in ISO 7811 parts 1 to 5. It applies to cards which have a physical interface with electrical contacts. It does not, however, define the nature, number, and position of the integrated circuits in the cards.
- *ISO 7816-2 (1988): Dimensions and location of the contacts*—specifies the dimensions, locations, and alignment for each of the contacts on integrated circuits(s) card of an ID-1 card type. This part of ISO 7816 is to be used in conjunction with ISO 7816-1.

- *ISO 7816-3 (1989): Electronic signals and transmission protocols*—specifies the power and signal structures, and information exchange between an integrated circuit(s) card and an interface device such as a terminal. It also covers signal rates, voltage levels, current values, parity conventions, operation procedures, transmission mechanisms and communication with the integrated circuit(s) card. It does not cover information and instruction content, such as identification of issues, services and limits, security features, journaling, and instruction definitions.
- *ISO 7816-4 (1995): Interindustry commands for interchange*—specifies the content of the messages, commands, and responses transmitted by the interface device to the card and conversely,
  1. The content of the historical bytes sent by the card during the answer to reset
  2. The structure of files and data, as seen at the interface when processing interindustry commands for interchange
  3. Access methods to files and data in the card
  4. A security architecture defining access rights to files and data in the card
  5. Methods for secure messaging
  6. Access methods to the algorithms processed by the card. (It does not describe these algorithms.)

  It does not cover the internal implementation within the cards and/or the outside world. It allows further standardization of additional interindustry commands and security architecture.
- *ISO 7816-5 (1994): Numbering system and registration procedure for application identifiers*—specifies a numbering system for applications and a registration procedure for application provider identifiers. The numbering system described in this standard provides a means for an application and related services offered by a provider to identify if a given card contains the elements required by its application and related services. An application identifier (AID) is used to address an application in the card. This part of ISO 7816 specifies the coding of application identifiers together with means and mechanisms for addressing application parts in cards. It also establishes the authorities and procedures to ensure and optimize the reliability of the corresponding registration.
- *CD 7816-6: Interindustry data elements for interchange*—specifies directly or by reference the Data Elements (DE), including composite DE, used in interindustry interchange, based on

integrated circuit cards (ICCs). It identifies the following characteristics of each DE:
1. Identifier.
2. Name.
3. Description and ISO reference.
4. Format and coding (if not available in other ISO standards or parts of ISO 7816).
5. The layout of each DE is described as seen at the interface between the interface device (IFD) and the ICC. This part of ISO 7816 defines the means of retrieval of the DE in the card (historical bytes, reset, commands(s) to perform, and commands defined in this international standard).
6. This part also provides the definition of DE without consideration of any restrictions on the usage of the DE. It is intended that new interindustry data objects be incorporated into this standard.

Two ISO standards are being developed for contactless technology—*ISO 10536: Close Coupling Cards (<1mm)* and *ISO 14443: Remote Coupling Cards (~10 cm)*. Each contactless standard has four defined parts.

ISO 10536: Identification cards—Contactless Integrated Circuit(s) Cards (CICC). *ISO 10536:* parts 1–3 are complete and part 4 is in the final sign-off phase.

- *ISO 10536-1 (1992): Physical characteristics*—this part applies to integrated circuit(s) cards that have a physical interface for transmitting power, clock signal, and data signals into the CICC and receiving data signals from the CICC without the use of conductive contacts. This part does not define the nature, number, and position of the contactless interfaces.
- *ISO 10536-2: Dimensions and location of coupling areas*—this specifies the dimensions, location, nature, and assignment of each of the coupling areas to be provided for interfacing slot or surface card coupling devices (CCDs) with contactless integrated circuit(s) cards (CICCs) of the ID-1 card type.
- *ISO 10536-3: Electronic Signals and Mode Switching*—this specifies the nature and characteristics of the fields to be provided for power and bi-directional communications between card coupling devices (CCDs) and the contactless integrated circuit(s) cards (CICCs) of the ID-1 card type in slot or surface operation.
- *WD 10536-4* concerns the answer-to-reset and transmission protocols. The answer-to-reset and character and half-duplex block

protocols are compatible with contact cards. In addition, part 4 contains a full-duplex block transmission protocol (T=2) for contactless cards. The same protocol could be used for contact cards as well.

ISO 14443: Remote Coupling Cards was started in 1994 and a draft of part 2 is planned for a late 1996 release. This is the most difficult part because of the selection of the Interface Frequency. Part 1 is planned to be the same as ISO 10536 and parts 3 and 4 should develop very quickly.

American National Standards Institute In the United States, The American National Standards Institute (ANSI) develops standards, recommendations specific to the needs of this country, and supervises standards making activities. It does not write or develop standards itself. Anyone who participates in the work of the ISO/IEC must first participate in a national organization like ANSI. The working groups within ANSI of most importance to the smart card marketplace are:

- ANSI Accredited Standard Committee (ASC) X3: Information Processing Systems
- B10: Credit/Identification Cards
  - X3B10.1: Integrated Circuit Cards with Contacts
  - X3B10.5: Integrated Circuit Cards without Contacts

These groups contribute directly to the ISO/TEC 7816 standards development via ISO/IEC JTC1/SC17/WG4 & WG7 respectively, and:

- X3T6: Noncontact Information System Interface

This is an important standardization effort in the use of contactless Radio Frequency Tags. It is essentially a selection process based on the prevalent existing technologies.

Other Standards and Specifications There are many additional standards and specifications developed in relation to smart cards. Most notable are the Integrated Circuit Card Terminal and Application Specifications for Payment Systems that have been developed jointly by Europay, MasterCard, and Visa. The International Association of Travel Agents is also developing a specification for the travel and entertainment industry. There are also some specifications developed using a combination of technologies in the healthcare industry. More information on any of these can be received by contacting the companies or agencies directly. The Smart Card Forum also has a document *Standards and Specifications of Smart Cards—An Overview* that covers these and additional standards related to the smart card industry.

CHAPTER 15   A Smart Card Primer

The Technology Committee of the Smart Card Forum serves as the basic conduit to the industry on technology related issues. This provides support for each of the application Working Groups. The Committee has some of the leading smart card technologists as members.

CHAPTER 16

Security, Privacy, and Smart Cards

Andy Tarbox
MasterCard International

Gilles Lisimaque
GemPlus

Bryan Icihikawa
MCI Communications

Issues surrounding the privacy rights of individuals and the security of cards and systems continue to draw interest and spur action by the various industries discussed in this book. This chapter explores these sets of issues in depth and provides a context for smart card technology's imminent explosion in applications and acceptance.

THE NATURE OF SECURITY

Security consists of three important components. First, the confidentiality of the information—ensuring that whatever information is exchanged between two or more parties remains private to the authorized entities.

Second is the integrity of the information, important because exchanged information can be changed in several ways: by entering or editing errors, faulty data transmission, and finally, unauthorized modifications. Guaranteeing information integrity allows for detection and correction of all these possibilities.

The third important aspect of security is to make sure the information is available for those allowed to access it. If data are not accessible, they are very secure, but not very useful. Generally, this is the most problematic security issue.

Exhibit 16–1, extracted from, *Information Security Handbook*, shows the possible impacts of security breaches.

In the center of the chart is the information to protect: the data (i.e., the transaction). Around the data are the three basic elements of security as we have just defined them: confidentiality, integrity, and availability. How these elements are implemented and enforced is a business decision. How to protect

CHAPTER 16 Security, Privacy, and Smart Cards

EXHIBIT 16–1

Data Security Breaches and Impacts

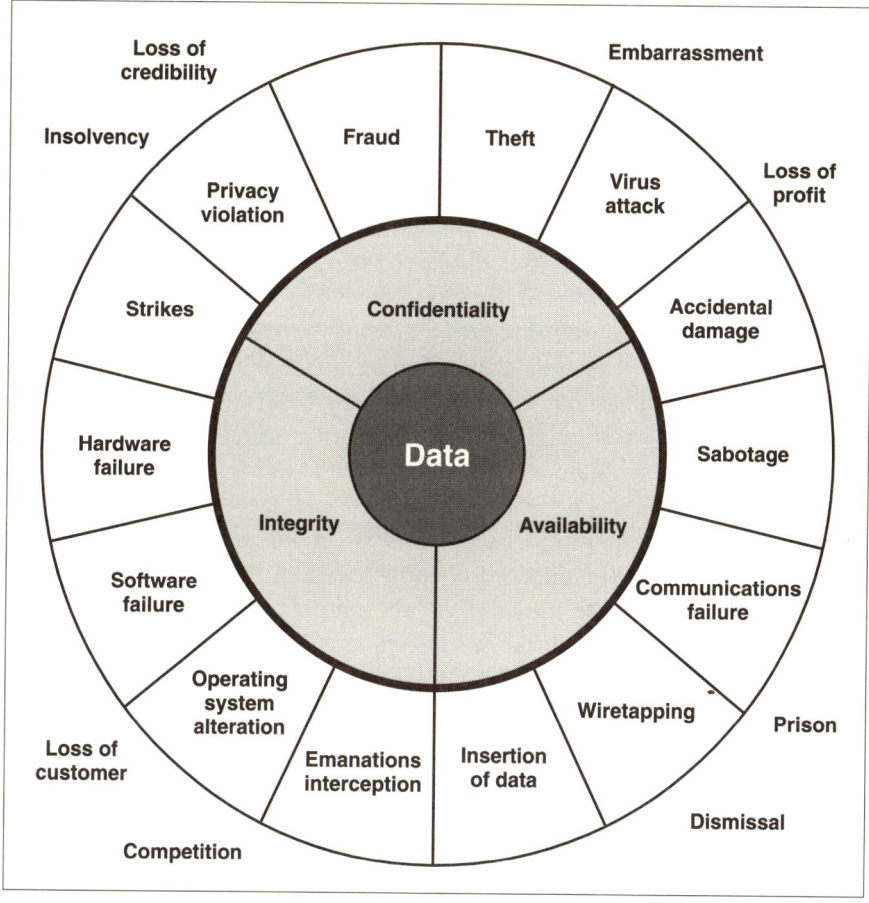

Source: *Information Security Handbook*

the information, how to detect misuse when it happens, how to ensure the originators are correctly authenticated, and how fast data are accessible, is a matter of policy.

Each business, and, in fact, each application, will have to define how individuals, computers, and networks are going to deal with the data; how confidential and how available they are going to be.

Each business has to define for itself the policy which protects its information. The result can differ from one company to the next, even in the same business, depending on the financial risk and the context in which the business operates. It is not a decision one can find in a book and just apply. Security experts are there to help determine the risks and threats. They can also propose actions and tools or corrections. The final decision driving the cost of the application has to be made by the business.

Around this Security Policy, represented as a thick line on Exhibit 16–1, are the results of a security breach. Fraud, theft, as well as hardware failures imperil the information. For example, a bit of information modified by a hardware memory failure will modify the total information and may give the same result as a willful attack on the system. If the information on a pay check goes from $5,000 to $1,000, (only one bit modified would create such a problem), the person receiving the check would not be happy even if the "computer" is to blame. This same modification could very well be an intentional modification of the amount to misappropriate the missing $4,000 into another account.

Some consequences of data alteration cannot be measured directly, even in terms of money. These include the loss of customers, or the loss of credibility of the business indicated outside the security circle. On the other hand, this does not mean absolute security is required to run a profitable business. Millions of magnetic stripe credit cards are in use today even though it is very simple to attack the system and fraud does exist. People still use cards because they believe in them. But someone is going to take responsibility for the liability in the end, because globally we all appreciate the convenience and receive value by using them. This is the nature of business.

SECURITY: A HISTORICAL PERSPECTIVE

Early Security Issues of security and privacy are obviously not new. They have been around for thousands of years, at least. One of the earliest security systems, for example, dates back to Julius Caesar. During the Gallic War, in what is now France, when Caesar was sending information from Rome to his generals, he would cipher it using a very simple system of transposition or substitution. This worked by taking the alphabet and transposing it. For example, the "A" becomes the letter "B", and so on. This can be done with one or two or three letters. Then the whole message becomes re-coded.

Today, this code can be cracked by computers in a matter of milliseconds, but at that time not everyone could read. Therefore, it was a good information protection system.

Throughout the centuries, cryptology was tied to wars and took many forms from the Cipher Wheel described by Sir Francis Bacon as early as 1605 to the Signal Flag System (forerunner of the U.S. Signal Core) developed during the U.S. Civil War.

There are a few examples, however, closer to what we have today. The first was called the Codetalkers. It was developed by the Army during World War I using Choctaw Indians. The Choctaws were employed to encrypt voice communications, using their native language, itself encoded. Even before we entered World War II in 1941, the Army expanded the program to employ Commanches, Choctaws, Kiowas, Winnebagos, Seminoles, Navajos, Hopis, Inuits, and Cherokees. The Marine Corps then took the Army work and codified and perfected it using the Navajo' language. During the war, the enemy never broke this system.

Another system developed during World War II was the German Enigma Machine, a forerunner of one of today's cryptographic processes. When a letter was typed, it would create another letter at the end depending on how the machine was set.

World War II added other cryptology machines including the Tunney and Sturgeon machines used by the Allies. These developed the concept of on-line communications by being able to encipher and transmit data simultaneously. They became the forerunners of the computer era, and have opened the door to the more complex types of security systems that we have today.

THE BASICS OF SECURITY: DEFINITIONS AND PRINCIPLES

While the techniques and methods of security have become more sophisticated, the basic concepts and principles have remained the same. There are the basic elements of encryption, authentication, and nonrepudiation. In order to make these elements work, various techniques have been developed, including algorithms and keys. Let's examine security's basic elements.

Encryption   The first element in the process is encryption (and its reverse, decryption). Encryption is the transformation of data into a form unreadable by anyone without a secret key.

The mathematical functions used in this process can be represented by two boxes, one for encryption and one for decryption. The one for encryption denotes the plain text message in which the encryption key is used to encrypt the information. The decryption box reverses the process, using the decryption key that matches the encryption key. When the encrypted text is processed by the decryption box with the appropriate key, the plain text is recovered. The two functions (encryption and decryption) are required for confidentiality, but not all mathematical functions have this reverse process. Even mathematical functions with a reverse function may not have the same level of complexity. In some cases, for example, decryption may be much more difficult than encryption or vice versa. A good example of such a two-way function can be taken from the physical world. It is quite easy to take a watch apart with the appropriate tools. However, it is much more difficult to put it back together without knowledge of the product and how it works.

Authentication The second, and very important, element in the security system is authentication—the process that guarantees the message received is the correct message issued by the correct person. It also guarantees that the text of the message has not been altered. Today, this is often called the electronic signature of a message. It prevents modification of the message and can be used to guarantee its origin.

Nonrepudiation The final element in the security system is nonrepudiation, which is the process whereby the receiver of a given message can be confident the sender of the message will not be able to deny sending it. Nonrepudiation is related to the element of authentication, to a large extent, because once the message and sender have been guaranteed, the sender cannot deny sending it—thereby allowing for nonrepudiation.

Take our example of Julius Caesar. As stated previously, it was important that he protect his messages from being accessed by unauthorized readers. He would write a text and encrypt or cipher it, (those two words have basically the same meaning), using a secret process (or a secret number and a known process). This would then prevent anyone not sharing his secret from being able to decipher the text of the message. Caesar also added his seal to the message in order to identify himself as the originator of the message. The text was authenticated by this seal that only he had. Since the message and the seal could not be copied (by the technology existing at that time), the possession of the document was a means of nonrepudiation regarding the order received from Caesar. In turn, Caesar could not later deny giving the order without destroying the physical evidence.

Algorithms The very simple example of Caesar illustrates a major concern in cryptographic techniques still in use today. The key that Julius Caesar was using indicated the number of letters of the alphabet which had to be skipped to find the correct letter from the letter found in the document (encrypted text). As the decryption process was the reverse function of the encryption process, the same key was used on both ends. The whole security would reside in the knowledge of this *shared* secret key. Knowing this key allowed encryption of messages as well as decryption of messages. Symmetric algorithms, which are widely used today, have to share the same key on both sides (encryption and decryption).

This imposes a secure communication means to transfer this key from one correspondent to the other. A key dedicated to transfer other keys is used in most systems but this does not solve the transfer of the initial key. Smart cards are a very good answer to this dilemma. They can protect a secret key and use it without exposing it.

Data Encryption Standard (DES) One of the most used symmetric algorithms within the industry today is DES (Data Encryption Standard). This algorithm, invented by IBM in the 1970s, is based on bit manipulation and was designed to be efficiently implemented in hardwired devices in order to encrypt large amounts of information very quickly. This information was to be transmitted on hostile or unprotected networks. DES is used by most smart cards today and is relatively easy to implement in software with acceptable performances (typically between 5 and 10 milliseconds to encrypt a bloc of eight information bytes). The size of the keys used by the DES algorithm consist of 56 bits stored on eight bytes. One bit per byte is used for parity checking.

When DES is used, both parties have the same capabilities. That is, they can encrypt as well as decrypt unless they do not have access to the full functions of the algorithm. In order to provide authentication between two parties using DES, it is necessary to guarantee a key per pair of entities exchanging messages.

With the power of computers increasing every day, algorithms are not secure for ever. The techniques used by Caesar would not resist a simple PC today. Similarly, it has been estimated in 1994 that a dedicated machine built to break DES by brute force (trying all the possible keys) would cost around a half million dollars for half a day according to Sandia National Laboratories. The response to such a machine is to either move to more sophisticated algorithms (triple DES, for example) or to limit the incentive for the attacker under the "economic level."

Public Key Cryptography Within ten years after DES, (in the beginning of the 1980's), different algorithms were developed that addressed the issue of authentication and nonrepudiation as well as key sharing. One such idea was developed by Rivest, Shamir, and Adelman (RSA) who were working at MIT. Rivest, Shamir, and Adelman developed an algorithm to find mathematical functions that allowed two parties to encrypt and decrypt information without sharing the same secret. An encryption key would allow for protection (or concealment) of the information. A related, but different, decryption key would allow for decryption of the information. Along with this, the knowledge of one key would not allow for deduction (or calculation) of the other key in order not to fall back into a shared key system. Their work gave birth to the modern public key cryptography in which RSA is still the most commonly used algorithm.

Public key cryptography allows any member of a given group to sign and cipher messages by using a pair of related keys per member. One is called the *private key* and is kept secret by its owner. The other is called the *public key* because its owner can put this key in the public domain. For example, if a person wants to send information, he will use his private key to encrypt the message. Anybody in the group, knowing his public key, is able to verify that he signed it, but nobody can sign in his place, because his private key is secret and not shared. If he now wants to send a confidential message to someone else, he will use that person's public key to encipher the information, just as anybody else in the group could do. He can then send the ciphered text to this person. That person will be the only one able to decipher the information with his private key. This is a very simple example of Public Key Cryptography. The complete application protocol, when confidentiality and signature are required at the same time, is a actually more complex.

Other public key algorithms that are used include the DSS (Digital Signature Standard), developed by the National Institute of Standards and Technology and the National Secutiry Agency. DSS cannot be used for confidentiality, but only signature.

Confidentiality versus Authentication The difference between confidentiality and authentication (signatures) is not always obvious. Even though they may both use the same cryptographic engine, they do not address the same issue.

Encryption is a process whereby the receiver of a ciphered message can get back to the original message using either the same key or a related key. When a message is signed, it is first compressed to get a smaller string of information, and the resulting digest is ciphered. The ciphered digest is then sent along with the message, just as a signature is attached to a document. If a bit of the text is changed, the signature is no longer valid. When the receiver of the document attempts to verify the signature, it will not match. The verifier can check the signature either by performing the same operation in a shared key system that was done when the signature was created or by using the related public key of the sender to verify the match.

A simple analogy, using a paper check helps explain the difference between confidentiality and authentication. When a check is written, the signature on the check seals the transaction. But with only a signature, it is not possible to do anything with the check. It is missing other vital information such as the amount, account number, or bank. In other words, the signature itself doesn't allow someone to get back to the whole message. It just seals the transaction and that's all it does. It is part of the message. Ciphering on the other hand is like putting the check in a sealed envelope. Looking at the envelope one knows a message is being exchanged, but cannot read the contents unless he knows how to open the envelope.

Some other algorithms are being used on smart cards. For example, one-way algorithms can be used for authentication in GSM. Both entities (the sender: the smart card in the GSM phone, and the receiver of the message: the network) share the same key and the same algorithm. In order to verify a signature created by the card, the network can do the same calculation. This type of authentication works because the network cannot sign in place of the real card. In this process, the message is in fact encrypted but is only used as a signature. This is because there is no known way to get back to the original message, even with the key that was used to do the original cipher.

These type of algorithms, those not being able to cipher information, are limited to authentication only and are not concerned with cryptography export regulations.

We have briefly explained the most commonly used algorithms. There are other types of algorithms used for specific purposes. Stream cipher algorithms are used for high speed encryption and smart cards are used as key generators for such algorithms. More recently, zero-knowledge algorithms were developed, allowing authentication of an entity without having knowledge of any key on the verifier side. Zero-knowledge algorithms are frequently used in Pay-TV boxes secured by removable tokens such as smart cards.

Key Management While having strong algorithms and powerful computers to execute them is important, it is still far from being enough security. It is also important to manage the keys used. A good analogy is that of keys to a person's house. A house may be very well protected by many locks and steel doors, but if a number of keys are made, and not managed or protected, the house may be broken into, anyway. Let's take this one step further. If a cleaning person comes when no one is home, he or she will need a key to enter. By the same token, if the house is being repaired, there may be a need to give keys to the people hired to do the work. Later on, if it is discovered that the house has been broken into, it may be difficult to find out who did it since many people had access to the keys. In order to prevent this from happening again, it would be possible to have doors with different locks in order to restrict access. This would demand many keys and would be very cumbersome to manage.

Symmetric algorithms that share secret keys have the same basic problems as the keys of the house in the previous example. Key management techniques, such as keys derived from a master key, are commonly used in the banking community to help address these issues. The bank (considered the trustworthy entity), owns a master key which is kept secret. Each card user will get a card from the bank with a unique card number as well as a unique secret key derived from the master key. This secret key uses the cardholder's number as a derivation parameter, allowing each cardholder to have his or her own unique key. The bank can then be sure of the authentication coming from the individual cardholder. However, in such a hierarchical system, two users cannot authenticate themselves without the bank being involved in the process.

Now that we have discussed the basic definitions and principles of a security system, the next step is to identify and discuss the various components that make up a security system.

PARTS OF A SECURITY SYSTEM

A security system contains many different parts or pieces and must be considered on an end-to-end basis. When designing a system, it is important to keep each piece in mind since each one contributes to the system's total success or lack of success. The pieces include the host computer, a network, the Point of Service or Point of Sale, the service provider, the card issuer, the cardholder, and a thief or hacker.

Host Computer Generally, only one host computer manages a central database. This could be the database of a clearing house, a financial institution, subscribers to a telephone network operator, the marketing database of a retailer, or even a mix of these databases. This host computer can generally be accessed through a network. Physical access as well as network access must be considered as occasion for security breaches.

Network A network can be designed in a number of ways depending on the type of system needed—a dedicated network, an open network, a SWIFT network, an Internet network, or a sneakernet network (paper mail). By definition, a network has to be considered hostile, because it is quite simple for an outsider to get into it. A hacker could be on the network, tinkering with it, and modifying it, or injecting wrong messages into it. As soon as there is a line or a connection between computers, there is a higher risk of attack.

A simple example of this unsecured communication involves car door openers and TV remote controls. Infrared remote car door openers are very convenient. Unfortunately the devices used to replace TV remote controls work on the exact same principles and are programmed to learn and repeat a signal just by watching it. It is very easy for a car thief to use such a device and copy the infrared garage key by "watching" its signals. A very similar technique is used to clone cellular phones on the existing analog network in the United States. Cryptographic techniques are now used to secure remote key openers for cars and smart cards are used to secure cellular phones in some implementations.

Point of Service or Point of Sale Another important part of the system is the point of service or point of sale (POS). This could be at the merchant location, but also could be a TV set, a phone, a PC, a terminal, an ATM, or at any kind of place where a transaction can be executed. This point of service is linked (physically or by contract) to a service provider.

Service Provider A service provider is the entity that actually performs the service for the customer. A phone, for example, is connected by a local telephone company, which might also have to connect to another service provider, such as a long distance company, to complete the transaction. In most applications, there will be multiple service providers for a given transaction. In the case of a vending machine, for example, someone has to provide the service of maintaining that machine—filling it, collecting money, and fixing it. In all cases, the service providers have to be paid for their work. This creates the need to keep track of the transactions to reward all these intermediary services on the basis of their contribution.

Naturally, card issuers and cardholders are prime system constituents. We define the issuer as the institution identified on the card that is issued to the cardholder.

The cardholder, simply, is the customer buying the product offered by the service provider or the merchant.

Thief or Hacker Finally, some uninvited players have to be taken into account during the design of the security system. Thieves and hackers will be tempted to attack the system sooner or later. How to detect them, measure the level of acceptable fraud, and then combat them is all part of the system design. The attack can come from an outsider, but can also come from one of the players mentioned earlier. It could be the cardholder or the merchant or somebody in the service chain exposed to secrets which enable them to attack the system.

SYSTEM SECURITY REQUIREMENTS AND ATTACK SCENARIOS

One of the keys to developing a secure system is to understand that an attack may occur at any point in the system. The system developer and security architect must identify each element in the system and then design appropriate safeguards around the entire system. Following are the areas that need to be incorporated into the overall design.

Authentication of User or Sender Most systems require a means of assuring that the users are who they say they are. Generally, systems either ask the user to give a piece of information that only he or she would know or to use physical information unique to the user. In financial systems today, a Personal Identification Number (PIN) is often used. PINs range from 4 to 12 digits and are memorized by the consumer. During the course of the transaction the PIN is entered on a keypad to authenticate the user. In other systems, a biometric method of identification may be used. Biometrics involve testing a unique physical feature of the user against a previous test of the same feature. Examples of biometrics include fingerprints, retina or iris scans, and voice or hand geometry.

The security advantage that smart cards bring to a system is that the data used to identify the user, whether PIN or biometric, are stored securely inside the chip. This means the data are not transmitted over a network and the transaction may take place off line. This results in less expensive, more secure, and faster transactions.

Authentication of the Transaction (Validation) In many systems, a method is required where the user validates that the event or transaction that takes place is authentic. In financial systems, for example, a transaction certificate serves to validate the transaction. This is a digital signature of all the relevant pieces of the transaction. This certificate may be used later by the card issuer to prove that the date, time, and amount were not altered, and that the user's card was present during the transaction.

The transaction certificate created by the smart card essentially signs the entire transaction, like a signature on a check. If any element of the transaction is altered, then the transaction certificate will not match the test signature of the transmitted data. For example, if someone attempts to alter the retailer's terminal data or the information on the receipt, the transaction certificate will not match. This calls into question the possibility of fraud.

Message Authentication A system must be able to prove that the message is authentic. Again, the concept is to use a secret key known to both ends (the secret may be in a public key system) to sign a message so that only the sender could have known the secret key and so that the receiver may prove it (nonrepudiation).

A simple method of ensuring that the message has not been altered in transmission is a Cyclic Redundancy Check or CRC. In a CRC, the bytes of a message are logically added together and the resulting byte is added to the message. If the message itself must be confidential, the sender will use an algorithm to encrypt the information such that only the receiver can decrypt it.

For example, when writing a check, the writer makes sure that there are no blanks between the name and the numbers. In fact, people often put a straight line before and after a written amount so that nobody can change the value.

Program Validity In developing a system a significant amount of time should be invested in determining the type of algorithms it requires. As we mentioned earlier, there are a number of algorithms available including: symmetric, asymmetric, zero-knowledge, and elliptical. Each type of algorithm has its own inherent benefits and problems. A competent cryptographer should be employed to determine the effective alternatives based on the overall system needs. Things to be considered in that evaluation include: speed, key size, usage (e.g., digital signature, encryption), intellectual property rights, cost, and export regulations.

Viruses Recently, computer hackers have developed viruses that attack computer systems often in strange ways. While most viruses are spread via contact with public networks like the Internet, even closed loop systems should develop programs to monitor activity and prevent the spread of viruses.

Multiapplications Smart cards are often considered for use in multiple applications. For example, a smart card containing medical information could also be used for financial payment. The security designer must also consider the security between applications on the smart card. When the consumer is using the card for payment they would not want the merchant to have access to the medical information and vice-versa.

ATTACK SCENARIOS

While we have just reviewed elements of a system that must be secured, we must also understand how a typical system can be attacked by a fraudster. The following chart illustrates some of the common attacks and possible counter measures.

Common Security Attacks and How to Protect against Them
This list is not exhaustive and must be considered within the context of each application.

Attack	Description	Counter-Attack(s)
False identity	The number or name used to identify the user is not valid and has been invented by the attacker	■ Maintain active lists ■ Cryptographic signature of user identities (Passive authentication)
Copied identity	The number or name used to identify the user is copied from an existing valid user	■ Check physical transaction location ■ Velocity and Coherence Check
Message alteration	Modification of the information contained in the message	■ Cryptographic signatures ■ Cyclic Redundancy Codes
Message duplication	A genuine message is sent twice to the same recipient	■ Random numbers ■ Time stamps ■ Transaction counters
Message suppression	A genuine message is not delivered to its recipient	■ Acknowledgment, counters ■ Non-repudiation signatures
Message injection	A false message is created (invented) by an attacker	■ Cryptographic signatures generated by senders
Message interception	A genuine message is read by an outsider and used fraudulently	■ Ciphering of information
Message delayed	A genuine message is suppressed from the network and reinjected later	■ Time-based acknowledgment

Attacks of this type are not new. Photocopy machines were used for fraud as soon as they appeared. So manufacturers have to be very creative to limit the standard capabilities of their equipment. With computer data, cryptography is the solution of choice and, when used appropriately can supply powerful counters to most known attacks.

SMART CARD SECURITY FEATURES

The security advantages that a smart card offers are significant, and we've already mentioned several. These advantages, along with good application design, make them very appealing to many types of systems.

An important security feature smart cards bring to a system is an evolution path. The same hardware can be used for all smart cards. Only software will have to be upgraded to move from one type of card to a more secure one. If the software is correctly layered and designed to cope with security changes, the impact could be minimized and the system could be easily improved. This allows upgrading to the next level of security when required without having to change all the applications and all the hardware.

Another security feature of smart cards is that they each have a unique serial number, similar to existing bank notes. Therefore, smart cards can be identified by this number. This means that a system can test for fraud by checking for consistent behavior with the number's use. Credit cards are doing this with very sophisticated risk management systems that use velocity check as well as spending patterns. Very similar tests can be done with smart cards, detecting fraud as soon as it appears.

One of the most interesting security features of smart cards is their ability to execute algorithms with keys securely stored in their memory. This allows systems to have a different digital signature for each transaction (the card will increment its internal transaction counter after each transaction) and allows active authentication which cannot be replayed.

A smart card's security edge over software is obvious. With some basic knowledge and a little time, it is quite easy to read the machine code that software comprises. Most of the security features embedded into computer games can be cracked in a matter of hours. The first level of security smart cards provide is based on the difficulty of reading the information physically stored in their memory. The memory and its associated computer are combined on the same chip (this is a basic patent owned by BULL S.A.) and no secret stored in the memory ever leaves this unique secure component inside the chip. Data residing in the host or terminal are sent to the card. This information is then combined with the information in the card and the secret keys in the chip are applied to algorithms. During this process, no secret ever leaves the chip. The results are then sent back to the host or terminal. No indication of the value of the key the smart card has used is given to the outside world.

Using very sophisticated techniques accessible to most semiconductor manufacturers, it is possible, though not easy, to get back to the memory of a given component and then access the secrets stored in it. If the component's architecture is not known, the integrated circuit and the software embedded in the component must be reverse engineered. With a lot of time, a lot of identical components, a lot of specialists and a lot of money, it is possible (in theory) to access the information on a given chip. Semiconductor manufacturers also add various features to their components to make this as difficult as possible. Even though it is very difficult to put a price tag on such a brute force attack, it is estimated by industry experts that it would take a couple of million dollars to crack one unique chip.

Another point to keep in mind is that access to a single chip does not give access to any other part of the system. Cracking a card just gives access to that card—and no more—since each smart card has a unique identifier and unique secrets attached to it. The architecture of a smart card system should take into account such a possible card clone and limit the rights granted to one card to limit the risk of attack.

One big difference between smart card components and other integrated circuits is that an IC for smart cards must work not only within the limits of its specification but must also not work outside of them. What this means is that if someone tries to get around the security system by modifying or changing one of the specifications, they can't. The system won't work. For example, the system may be designed to work at 2.5 volts and 0.5 megahertz. If a hacker tries to use a smart card with 3 volts, it won't work.

SMART CARDS AND PRIVACY

Whenever a consumer is giving out confidential information, the issue of the privacy and ownership of that information surfaces. With smart card technology, the consumer can literally carry around a great deal of sensitive information on one card. How that information is accessed, who accesses it, and how it is disseminated and used, is of great importance and concern not only to the consumer, but to the issuer of the card and the application developer.

Smart cards can be programmed to be very secure with several levels of passwords and other protection devices such as biometric information. The key is to develop security features early in the process to raise the confidence of the card issuers and card holders. More background information on this can be obtained in the Smart Card Forum document, *The Lifecycle of A Smart Card Application.*

It is also important to note that the United States has no comprehensive, integrated structure of privacy laws and regulations, and that there is no central authority to enforce privacy laws, regulations, controls, or policies. Rather, the laws and regulations that deal with privacy protection come from a variety of sources including the U.S. Constitution, state constitutions, and various statutes with regulations. This means the laws can vary greatly from one area to another which poses difficult questions with respect to global privacy issues that surface from technology like smart cards.

Constitutional Rights In general, Constitutional rights are good only against action by the government. Therefore, the Constitutional connection with smart card use focuses on government's use of records stored on, or transmitted via, smart cards. This represents informational privacy rights, as opposed to other types of privacy rights such as privacy of person or privacy of place. These informational privacy rights are proected under the First, Fourth, Fifth, and Fourteenth Amendments.

Legislative Rights While constitutional issues touch a wide range of data that might be stored on or transmitted through smart cards, this is not true for legislative efforts to protect informational privacy. In general, at both the federal and state levels, legislation covers categories of information by various segments or industries. Following is a list of areas where privacy legislation might prove relevant to smart card uses:

- Credit records
- Banking and financial records
- Labor-related records
- Benefits-related records
- Cable television records
- Medical information and records
- Social Security numbers
- Tax information
- Electronic communications
- Employer inquiries
- Video rental or sale records
- Family and educational records
- Telephone toll records

Privacy Torts Privacy torts may also evolve to cover various aspects of smart card activity. These torts include intrusion upon seclusion, publicity of private matters, appropriation of a person's name or likeness for commercial use, and placing a person in a false light. They have been recognized in almost every state.

The Smart Card Forum has created a legal and Public Policy Committee with a subcommittee on privacy. The general committee comprises attorneys and business executives from major organization members. The Privacy Subcommittee is in the process of developing recommended industry privacy guidelines. For more information on privacy, see the Smart Card Forum white paper, *Smart Card Privacy Issues—An Overview.*

THE FUTURE

As the use of smart card technology increases, there are many additional areas that could fall under the banner of "protected" information that are not currently there. These include passports and customs data, supermarket transaction records, travel information, such as airline ticket purchases, hotel records, auto rental transactions, medical records, drivers' license records, and highway toll-collection records, to name a few. It would be prudent for smart card application developers to remember this when designing and planning applications for these areas. One way to do this is to store similar areas of information on separate cards even though smart cards can handle a wide variety of information, one card for healthcare and a separate one for travel and entertainment, for example. In this way, it would be easy to perform a detailed legal and regulatory assessment on a specific card.

CONCLUSION—HOW SECURE ARE SMART CARDS?

Any security device invented by man can be broken with enough money and time.

Egyptians thought they would be able to protect their dead from the action of time and thieves. They did exceptional and clever work embalming the corpses of their dead and building sophisticated tombs protected by tunnels, traps, and even malediction. It took time and money to get to most of their treasures but the incentive was so high that most of their treasures disappeared soon after the tomb was sealed. If the incentive is high enough, no system can be protected against attacks.

In this context, smart cards are very secure devices but under no circumstances should an application rely soley on them for security. Techniques now unknown may be found to break into what was considered secure. Moreover, smart cards are only one element providing security in a system and there may be breaches in other system areas. Security is a never-ending battle in which the system that survives must be able to detect fraud and react when it reaches a level incompatible with application economics. Preventing fraud completely, even if it were possible, would be too expensive. Companies must access risk against economic benefit when determining the security required for a particular application.

APPENDIX

About the Smart Card Forum

The Smart Card Forum is the industry organization that has made smart cards happen in North America. This section gives you more information about the Forum, its Board of Directors, Committees, Working Group activities, membership, and the material it offers.

Of course, you can get even more up-to-date information by reaching us on the world wide web http://www.smartcrd.com, where details of upcoming meetings, white papers, research, worldwide pilots, and other industry information are available.

We hope you are interested in smart cards and will join the Forum as you explore the tremendous opportunities and challenges offered by this technology.

Thank you for buying and reading our book. Let us know what you would like to see from the Forum in the future.

SMART CARD FORUM BACKGROUND

WHAT IS THE SMART CARD FORUM?

The Forum is a nonprofit, multi-industry organization created to promote the widespread acceptance of multiple application smart card technology in North America. The Forum was established in September 1993 and currently has more than 230 corporate members—leading companies in the banking, financial services, telecommunications. computer, technology, healthcare, retail, entertainment industries—as well as a number of government agencies. The convergence of these major players is unprecedented and represents a shared vision and commitment to provide an interoperable platform for the delivery of a new generation of products and services based on smart card technology.

WHAT ARE THE FORUM'S GOALS?

The Smart Card Forum brings together both users and technologists from the public and private sectors to work on the following common goals:

- Promotion of the interoperability of cards, devices, and systems to assure an open market capable of rapid growth
- Facilitation of information exchange, communications, and relationship development across industries in order to stimulate market trials
- Service as a resource to policy makers, regulatory bodies, and consumer groups on issues impacting smart cards, especially in the areas of social responsibility and privacy

WHAT IS THE FORUM'S FOCUS?

True to its name, the Smart Card Forum focuses on information exchange, policy development, and member interaction. Actual implementation of smart card trials, development of standards, and other activities specific to members' business interests take place independently of their participation in the Forum.

Central to the Forum's mission is education in the marketplace, the development of business propositions and positions on public policy issues. Members recognize that for smart cards to succeed, there needs to be a critical mass of cards supporting applications of interest to consumers, merchants, and to those organizations wishing to issue and accept smart cards.

WHAT ARE THE FORUM'S PRIMARY ACTIVITIES?

To accomplish its goals, the Forum has organized Work Groups and Cross-Industry Committees to explore and define application requirements in key areas. Work Groups include: Financial Services; Telecommunications and Information Services; Healthcare; Travel and Entertainment; Retail;, Transportation; and Government and Education. Cross-industry Committees have been established as well for Technology and Legal and Public Policy.

Combined Work Groups and Cross-Industry Committees meet quarterly. A two-day annual meeting is held in September to showcase the year's activities and highlight industry progress. The Forum also hosts seminars and symposiums as well as industry roundtables.

The outcome of Forum activities is published research on consumer and merchant interest, public policy positions, industry white papers, and other deliverables that include documents such as a glossary of terms, business case models, smart card descriptions and comparisons, standards specifications, and industry status presentations.

WHAT IS THE MEMBERSHIP STRUCTURE?

There are three membership levels: Principal, Government, and Auditing. In general, large corporate organizations join at the Principal level for $15,000/year. Government membership is priced at $1,500. Auditing members, who pay $3,500, generally comprise small to medium-sized companies who have a specific interest in one of the industry segments. Benefits differ between classes and annual membership renewal is the first of September each year.

WHAT RESOURCES ARE AVAILABLE TO MEMBERS?

Published Forum documents are available to members along with access to a research library, on-line Internet access, a monthly abstracts report, a quarterly newsletter, and significant networking opportunities at each Work Group session.

1996-97 Partial Membership List*
Accomando Consulting, Inc.
AIB Group
Aladdin Knowledge Systems
Alexander Consulting, Inc.
American Bankers Association
American Express TRS
American General Life Insurance Company
American Magnetics Corporation
American Management Systems
Ameritech Cellular
Amphenol Corporation
Andersen Consulting
Applied Communications, Inc.
Associates Bankcorp
AT&T
BA Custom Cards
Bank of America
Bank of Boston
Bank of Montreal
Barclaycard
Battelle
BayBank Systems, Inc.
BB&T
BDM Technologies, Inc.
Beacon Financial Group
Bell Atlantic Corporation
Bell Canada
Bellcore
BellSouth Public Communications
BellSouth Wireless Inc.
Blue Cross/Blue Shield of Florida
Booz, Allen & Hamilton, Inc.
Bridgepoint Systems, Inc.

---

*Some members prefer not to be listed on the membership list.

Canadian Payment Association
CardTech/SecurTech
Cash Station, Inc.
Center of Financial Technologies, Inc.
CEP Exposium/Cartes
Chase
Checkmate Electronics
Citibank
Comdata Corporation
Comerica, Inc.
Conavi
Connecticut Mutual Life Insurance
Copyright Clearance Center
CU Cooperative Systems, Inc.
CyberMark, Inc.
Dassault A.T.
DataCard Corporation
De La Rue Plc.
Diebold/Interbold
Digital Equipment
Dove Associates Inc.
Dreifus Associates
Duncan Industries
Eastman Kodak
EDS
Equifax Credit Information Services, Inc.
Ernst & Young
Faulkner & Gray, Inc.
FBS Software
Federal Reserve Bank of New York
Federal Reserve Bank of San Francisco
Fidelity Trust Company
First American National Bank
First Chicago NBD Bankcorp
First Data Corporation

First National Bank of Omaha
First Union National Bank
First USA Bank
Flatbush Federal Savings & Loan Association of Brooklyn
Fleet Services Corporation
Florida State University
Forrester Research
Framatome Connectors USA Inc.
Fujitsu—ICL Systems Inc.
Furash & Company
GE Capital
Gemplus Card International
G.I.C. Identicard, Ltd.
Giesecke & Devrient America, Inc.
Gilbarco, Inc.
GiroVend Holdings, Ltd.
Golden 1 Credit Union
Gould Electronics Inc.
Groupmark Canada Limited
GTE
Health Card Technologies, Inc.
Hewlett-Packard Company
Huntington Bancshares
Hypercom, Inc.
IBM
IC One
Identicator
Identix
Informix Software
Intel Corporation
Interac Association
International Game Technology
Internet, Inc.
Intuit
Iridium, Inc.

ITT Cannon
JCPenney Business Services
Kaiser Permanente
Kansas City Area Development Council
Keycorp Limited
Litle & Company
Los Alamos National Laboratory
Manufacturers & Traders Trust Company
Marsh Supermarkets
MasterCard International
MBNA America
MCI Telecommunications, Inc.
Mellon Bank
Meridian Bank
Michigan National Bank
Micro Card Technologies, Inc.
Microcell 1-2-1
Microsoft
Midwest Payment Systems
Mobil Oil
Mondex International
Motorola
MTA Card Company
Multisystems, Inc.
Mutronix, Inc.
National Association of Federal Credit Unions
National City Stored Value Systems
National Data Corporation
National Semiconductor
NationsBank
Nat West Bank
NBS Card Services
NEC Planning Research Ltd.
New York Times
NJ Transit Corporation

Nokia Mobile Phones
Northern Telecom, Inc.
Norwest Card Services
Nova Information Systems, Inc.
Novus Services
NYCE Corporation
Omron Electronics, Inc.
ORGA Card Systems
Pacific Bell Mobil Service
Pennsylvania Turnpike Commission
Perot Systems
PHH Vehicle Management Services
Phoenix Planning and Evaluation, Ltd.
Pitney Bowes
Polaroid
Product Technologies, Inc.
PSI
Racom Systems, Inc.
Reynolds & Associates
Rosenbluth International
Royal Bank of Canada
Royal Bank of Trinidad & Tobago, Ltd.
Sandia National Laboratory
Schlumberger-DANYL
SCM Microsystems
SEFCU
Sensar, Inc.
SGS-Thomson
Shell Oil Products Company
Siemens, Inc.
Smartcard International, Inc.
Solaic Smart Cards Inc.
Southeast Switch, Inc.
Speer & Associates, Inc.
SPS Payment Systems

Star System, Inc.
State of Ohio
State of Texas
Stentor Resource Centre Inc./MPR Teltech Ltd.
Superior Bankcard Service
Sweden Post
Synapsys, Inc.
Systems & Computer Technology
Tel-A-Tech Communications, Inc.
Telephonics Corporation
TelePlus Card Systems
Telequip Corporation
The Santa Fe Group
Thomson CSF
3-G International
Tokheim Corporation
Total System Services, Inc.
Transway Limited
UBIQ Incorporated
Unisys Corporation
U.S. Bank of Oregon
U.S. Department of Agriculture
U.S. Department of Defense
U.S. Department of Transportation
U.S. Department of Treasury (FinCEN)
U.S. Department of Treasury FMS
USE Credit Union
U.S. Mint
U.S. Postal Service
US WEST
UtiliCorp United, Inc.
VeriFone
Visa International
Wells Fargo Bank
Zions Bank

1996-97 Board of Directors

Catherine A. Allen (Ex-Officio)
President & CEO
The Santa Fe Group

William Barr (Vice President)
Executive Director
Bellcore

Ronald Braco (Executive Committee)
Senior Vice President & Director, Electronic Banking Services
Chase Manhattan

David Boyles
Senior Vice President
American Express

Frederick Honold
CIO
AT&T

Gerald Hubbard (Treasurer)
Vice-President, Marketing
Micro Card Technologies, Inc.

Bryan Ichikawa
Member of the Executive Staff
MCI Telecommunications

Julie Krueger
Product Marketing Manager
Siemens, Inc.

Dennis Lynch
Executive Vice President & COO
InfiNet

Beverly Matson
Director, Strategic Business Partners
VeriFone

Jean T. McKenna (President)
Vice President, Technology Development
Visa International

Mary Pat McMahon
Vice President
Cash Station, Inc.

Christine Nautiyal
Senior Vice President
NationsBank

Marth Rea
Executive Vice President
PSI

Rebekah Schloss
Senior Product Manager
Diebold

Michael H. Smith (Secretary)
General Manager, Operations
Schlumberger-DANYL

Andrew Tarbox
Vice President, Chip Card Technology
MasterCard International

Cliff Wilke
Vice President, Business Development
Mobil Oil Credit Corporation

Government Representative:
Doug McGovern
Manaager, Security Technology/Application
Sandia National Laboratories

Auditing Representative:
Dave Lott
Senior Associate
Dove Associates, Inc.

1996-97 Work Group Chairs and Descriptions
Financial Services Work Group
Co-Chairs: Ron Braco, Chase (212) 622-0097 & Martha Rea, PSI; (813) 287-2774

- Addresses initiatives & issues leading to active Smart Card Programs in the Financial Services Industry.

- Establishes "business elements" and methodology for successful programs.
- Conducts market research for value-added applications.
- Provides guideline direction and input to standards development entities.
- Addresses potential issues arising from regulatory or consumer interests.

Subgroups:
Prepaid: Chair: Mary Pat McMahon, Cash Station; (312) 977-1150
Focuses on development & prioritization of key components of an open system.
Security: Chair: Kathy Lawton, Chase; (212) 623-0959
Addresses points of risks, potential solutions, and recommends approaches based on business risks/rewards.
Multiapplications: Chair: Martha Rea, PSI: (813) 287-2774
Concentrates on consumer market research, leading to future applications.

Transportation Work Group

Co-Chairs: Hassan Tavassoli, G&D America, Inc.; (703) 709-2866 & Mike Dinning, U.S. Dept. of Transportation; (617) 494-2422

- Identifies the unique requirements of the transportation industry as it relates to smart cards.
- Explores the smart card as a single or multiapplication media for transportation use in either an open or closed system architecture.
- Establishes business cases and methodologies for smart card programs in a transportation environment.
- Promotes the adoption of smart card within the transportation industry.
- Sets smart card interface standards for equipment and software utilized in the transportation industry.

Telephony Work Group

Chair: Ken Lutz, Bellcore; (908) 758-2518

- Promotes the use of smart cards in wireline (e.g., public pay phones) and wireless (e.g., cellular and PCs) telephony.
- Identifies and defines telecommunications applications in areas such as prepaid telephony, mobile communications, personalized communications, and privacy and authentication.

- Addresses interoperability of smart cards among telecommunications applications and with nontelecommunications applications.
- Promotes the introduction of multiple application cards between telephony and nontelephony uses (e.g., home banking on a screen-based telephone).

Healthcare Work Group

Chair: Lorainne Brainerd, Kaiser Permanente; (510) 926-5051

- Focuses on understanding the healthcare market for smart card technology.
- Developing a white paper analysis of the smart card industry as it applies to healthcare.
- Demonstrates benefits of smart card to government, provider, and payors.

Retail Work Group

Co-Chairs: Bette Wasserman, Bank of America; (415) 241-3902 & Bev Matson, VeriFone; (770) 587-4757

- Mission is to advance the perspectives of the retailer in the widespread acceptance of smart card technology.
- Identify and articulate the issues and opportunities of retailers focusing on key market segments.
- Encourage collaborative effort among retailers, financial institutions, industry service providers, appropriate government agencies, and technology vendors to facilitate the development and deployment of smart card technology in the retail environment.
- Exchange ideas on the uses of smart card technology in the retail environment.
- Educate retail industry members on how smart card technology can be leveraged for a variety of new and existing applications.
- Educate the retail community through seminars, industry publications and attendance at trade shows.
- Explore the implications of roll-out of smart card applications.

Technology Work Group

Co-Chairs: Bryan Ichikawa, MCI; (719) 535-1905 & Gilles Lisimaque, Gemplus; (301) 990-8800

- Addresses technology issues.
- Publishes white papers regarding specific technology issues.

- Supports overall Forum in indentification of key technology issues that cross applications.
- Provides the Forum liaison to existing standards bodies and communicates standards developments to working groups.

Subgroups:

Retail, Transportation, Telecommunications, Financial Services, Healthcare, Education, and T&E

Governmental Services Work Group

Contact the Smart Card Forum Office: (813) 286-2339

- Focuses on improving the partnership toward smart card interoperability among government and private sectors, as well as federal and state programs.

Travel and Entertainment Work Group

Chair: Michael Chittaro, Citibank; (312) 380-5581

- Promotes smart card products and services within the T&E industry.
- Identifies specific T&E applications, enabled by smart card technology.
- Facilitates the development of T&E applications based on smart cards standards.
- Encourages broad participation of the T&E industry in smart card pilots and market trials.
- Acts as a liaison between the T&E industry and other industry efforts for smart card deployment.

Legal and Public Policy Work Group

Chair: John David Wright, Wells Fargo Bank; (415) 396-4226

- The mission of the Legal and Public Policy Committee of the Smart Card Forum is to provide advice and counsel to the Forum Board by identifying and analyzing legal and public policy issues relating to smart card applications. To develop proposals that remove legal barriers to the implementation of related public policies, and to act as a national and international legal information clearinghouse.

Education Work Group

Contact the Smart Card Forum Office: (813) 286-2339

- Focuses on smart card technology as it relates to colleges, universities, and other school systems.

GLOSSARY

abs Acrylonitrile butadiene styrene. Plastic material used to make integrated circuit cards. Unlike poly vinyl chloride, it is formed through injection molding which allows the dimensions of the card and the hole into which the chip module is inserted to be precisely controlled.

acceptor Party who accepts a payment card for provision of goods and services and presents transaction data to an acquirer.

access card A machine-readable card used to achieve computer access, physical entry, or passage.

account A relationship between a financial institution and a customer.

accumulators Healthcare: deductibles, caps, etc.

acquirer An institution (or its agent) that obtains card transaction information from the card acceptor.

adjudicate The administrative review process conducted by a plan administrator to determine the amount to be paid for a particular claim.

Administrative Services Only (ASO) An arrangement where an organization will perform specific administrative functions relating to healthcare programs such as claims processing for self-insured groups or third party providers/payers for a fee.

algorithm A set of rules specifying the procedures to perform a specific computation.

ambulatory care All types of healthcare services that are provided to an outpatient, i.e., a patient who is not treated in the home or not confined to a hospital or nursing facility.

American National Standards Institute (ANSI) The national standards setting body in the United States.

American Standards Committee (ASC) A committee of the American National Standards Institute (ANSI).

anticrime features Features or functions intended to inhibit criminal misuse or modification of payment media and systems.

application A commercial use or purpose for using a device, e.g., an integrated circuit card used for transfers, inquiries, credits, etc.

Application Specific Integrated Circuit (ASIC) A computer chip designed with special features to satisfy particular requirements. In the integrated circuit card context, an ASIC generally refers to chips with special "cells" for functions such as security (exponentiation used in public key cryptography) or communications (radio frequency).

ASC X12 Accredited Standards Committee X12 for Electronic Data Interchange (part of ANSI).

ASO Healthcare: See Administrative Services Only.

assignment Healthcare: The transfer of payments under an insurance policy by a beneficiary to a provider.

assured pay Healthcare: assured pay is the amount of a claim the carrier will stand behind based on estimates generated by the carrier payment estimate formula.

asymmetric key cryptography See public key cryptography and encryption.

asynchronous password generation A method of generating a unique one-time password for a computer user based on a challenge-response sequence between a host and a device possessed by the user.

Asynchronous Transfer Mode A very high speed fast-packet transmission protocol. It is capable of interface speeds from 50 Mbps to 24Gbps.

ATM See automatic teller machine or Asynchronous Transfer Mode.

audit An examination of records or accounts to verify their accuracy and status.

audit trail Financial data to facilitate a security autdit.

authentication routine See Handshake.

authorization The approval or guarantee given by an Issuer to an Acquirer and/or Acceptor to honor a transaction.

authorization code A specific value issued and stored with the transaction data to allow confirmation that a valid authorization occurred.

automated clearing house An organization that handles automated payments, e.g., direct debits, standing order payments, direct payroll deposits and other electronic credit transfers, and to consolidate provider billings for healthcare claims across multiple payers.

automatic teller machine A self-service unit that allows, with a suitable identification and account relationship, financial transactions, e.g., a cash withdrawal.

beneficiary Healthcare: The person designated or provided by the contract to receive the insurance benefits as they become available.

benefits consultant Healthcare: A person or agency which performs in-depth plan analyses, designs plans, and/or produces reports for corporations, that are usually larger than 500 employees.

billing Healthcare: The process of submitting a claim to a payer or to multiple payers for reimbursement. Payers include insurance companies, fiscal intermediaries, government agencies, and individual patients.

biometrics Method of validating the user by electronically measuring a unique characteristic such as fingerprint, voice print, retina scan, or signature dynamics.

bit Derived from the words Binary digit. A bit is the basic element of electronic information.

black list See hot list.

BPI Bits per inch, as on a magnetic stripe card.

broker Healthcare: A person or agency which handles the health care benefits analysis and plan/carrier selection for smaller organizations.

budget account card A retailer credit card.

bundled rate Healthcare: The total charge for a series of office visits or treatment related to a single diagnosis; e.g., maternity benefits are usually paid as a bundled rate. In other words, a single claim includes prenatal care and the delivery. Separate claims are not submitted for each office visit.

byte A group of 8 bits.

CAD See card accepting device.

CAM Card Authentication Method.

GLOSSARY

cap Healthcare: The upper limit on a payment, e.g., the maximum amount that a provider can charge for a specific procedure.

capitation Healthcare: A system of payment which stipulates maximum fees allowable for levels of care between a PIAs provider and insured individuals.

card A rectangular paper or plastic medium used to carry information relating to its issuer and user.

Card Accepting Device (CAD) Device which is used to communicate with the ICC during a transaction. It may also provide power and timing to the ICC.

card acceptor See acceptor.

card authentication method Process used to verify authenticity of a card.

cardholder The person or entity with whom an account relationship is established and to whom a card is issued. May not be cardholder, see "company card," "holder," and "user." Customer associated with PAN.

card life cycle The stages for a card from initial manufacturing to usage completion and destruction.

card number For credit cards this is the same as the primary account number. In other applications this may only be a card retailer.

card reader See card acceptor device

card read-writer Equipment that can electronically read the information on one or many types of cards and modify specific data fields.

card supplier A manufacturer of cards.

carrier Healthcare: An indemnity insurance company.

cash Currency. This may take many forms including, but not limited to, currency carried or prepaid cards.

cash card See prepayment card.

cash dispenser A self-service unit that dispenses cash. See also automated teller machine.

cash management system System which allows customers to obtain information about their accounts, access databases, and obtain forecasts using appropriate terminals such as television sets or personal computers.

CAT See "credit authorization terminal"

CEN European Committee for Standardization.

CEPT Council of European Post and Telecommunications.

challenge-response See asynchronous password generation.

charge-back Issuer generated reversal of all or a portion of an amount previously posted to a cardholder account..

charge card A payment card that does not provide automatic credit beyond the invoice date (usually monthly).

check/cheque Paper payment instruction drawn by the holder on his/her bank concerning his/her bank account.

check digit Suffix used to test the validity of a number.

chip A small square of thin, semiconductor material, such as silicon, that has been chemically processed to have a specific set of electrical characteristics such as circuits, storage, and/or logic elements. Also known as an Integrated Circuit (IC).

chip card See integrated circuit card.

ciphertext Encrypted output of a cryptographic algorithm.

claim A request for payment under an insurance contract for services rendered.

claim adjudication The process involving the examination of a claim for eligibility and coverage resulting in payment, denial, or suspension.

claim form The form used to describe the services rendered by a provider requesting reimbursement from the payer.

claim preparation The process of assembling information needed to develop a healthcare claim and preparing the bill for services rendered. This includes, but is not limited to, data entry, data collection, conversion, editing, formatting, and related coordination processes.

Claim Transmittal Form (CTF) The record of charges form which the employees or patient will sign to acknowledge receipt of treatment.

claims control The system of batching, numbering, and archiving claims to protect from loss or misplacement and to facilitate tracking of individual claim status.

clean claim A healthcare claim which is complete and accurate in content and form, i.e. meeting all the specifications required by the relevant payer.

clearing The processing of financial transactions between the Acquirer and Issuer for reconciliation, billing, and statement use.

clear text Data in its original, unencrypted form (same as plaintext).

closed environment management system See closed prepaid system.

closed prepaid system A system where the Issuer and Acquirer of the card are the same party. The card is issued by the party that provides those services that can be accessed by the card.

CMOS Complementary Metal Oxide Semi-conductor. A chip fabrication technology requiring lower performance and moderate power.

COB Chip On Board. Frequently referred to as the integrated chip module.

COB (Healthcare) Coordination of benefits. A method by which an insurer coordinates the responsible carrier both primarily and secondarily liable for the payment of a specific medical claim. The term is used to designate the anti-duplication provision limiting benefits when more than one group insurance policy covers a beneficiary, to 100 percent of the expenses covered and designating the order in which the insurers are to pay benefits.

coercive force The strengths of the reverse magnetic field required to demagnetize a given piece of magnetic material, expressed in "oersteds."

coercivity The magnetic "retention value" of different ferromagnetic materials. For example, a high coercivity magnetic stripe will be less vulnerable to degaussing or erasure than a low coercivity magnetic stripe.

coins Metal token cash issued by national authorities and universally used for cash transactions.

company card A card issued to or by a company for use by an employee for business related transactions. (e.g., purchases, logical access, physical access).

Competitive Medical Plan (CMP) A healthcare program with characteristics that are very similar to a Health Maintenance Organization (HMO), but subject to less extensive federal requirements under the Tax Equity and Fiscal Responsibility Act (TEFRA) of 1982. Unlike certain HMOs, CMPs do no have to be separate entities.

contact An electrical connecting surface on an integrated circuit card and/or interfacing device that permits a flow of energy current between the two.

GLOSSARY

contactless card An integrated circuit card that enables energy to flow between the card and the interfacing device without the use of contact. Instead, induction or high-frequency transmission techniques are used through a radio frequency (RF) interface.

contributory Healthcare: An arrangement between employer and employee under which both parties share the cost of the employees healthcare coverage.

co-pay (co-insurance) Healthcare: A patient's out-of-pocket expense for each healthcare claim. This amount is paid to the provider and typically a percentage of the total claim amount.

corporate card See company card.

COS Card (Chip) Operating System.

coverage verification Healthcare: Confirmation of a patient's coverage for specific services proposed by the provider.

CPE Healthcare: Carrier Payment Estimate of the carrier's portion of a claim.

CPT Healthcare: Current Procedure Terminology Service codes are used by physicians and other providers to identify services or procedures rendered for the purpose of billing insurers.

Credit Authorization Terminal (CAT) A device placed in a merchant location which is designed to authorize, record and forward data by electronic means for each transaction.

credit card A card that enables the cardholder to make transactions against a credit account established with the Issuer, whereby the Issuer has agreed to make available a specified amount of funds to the cardholder.

credit limit Maximum amount that can be borrowed by a cardholder at any one time on an account.

credit transfer A transfer initiated by the payer in which funds are sent directly to the payee's account through the banking system, without the payee's involvement.

cryptographic key Parameter used in conjunction with an algorithm for the purposes of validation, authentication, encipherment, or decipherment.

cryptoki Cryptographic Token Interface; RSA Data Security Inc. driven standard for Smart Cards, PCMCIA cards, and other hardware and software solutions.

custom chip A chip whose characteristics have been set for the handling of a specific set of application or job requirements.

data capture The electronic recording of information for subsequent use and information processing.

data encryption algorithm An ANSI Standard that describes a cryptographic algorithm for encrypting data The algorithm is private key driven. Also referred to as the Data Encryption Standard (DES). (See ANSI X3.92 and X9.23).

data tag A tag that contains a chip and functions as an identification device. (e.g., Military dog tag).

DEA See Data Encryption Algorithm.

debit card A card used to make transactions that is linked to the cardholder's direct deposit account.

decipherment See decryption.

decrementing value card See prepaid card.

decryption Converting encrypted information back into plain text (or clear text). Also known as Decipherment.

dedicated network A communications facility established for a specific purpose, such as servicing point-of-sale facilities.

deductible Healthcare: A patient's fixed out-of-pocket expense for healthcare claims exclusive of any co-payment amount. This amount is paid to the provider and can be an absolute dollar amount perineum, an absolute dollar amount for a specific period of time, or an absolute dollar amount for each healthcare claim.

degaussing Magnetic stripe data erasure.

DES Data Encryption Standard. See Data Encryption Algorithm.

device card An integrated circuit card that carries information (logic and data); used to configure, operate, and supervise a work station that accepts integrated circuit cards or contains integrated circuit card functions.

diagnosis code Healthcare: The code which providers enter on the claims forms so that adjudication can be based on services rendered.

Diagnosis-Related Groups (DRGs) Healthcare: These are standard diagnostic categories established as a basis for determining amount of prospective payment for treatment of specific illnesses. Today, DRGs are primarily adapted for the Medicare Program to prevent excessive charges on inpatient hospital services.

digit A symbol in a numeric system. (e.g. 0 and 1 are binary digits; 0 - 9 are decimal digits).

digital optical laser card A portable card that passively stores information in the form of high-density marks or bars.

digital signature A technique used to prevent denial of a transaction or message by the sender. A technique used to authenticate a transaction or message by the sender. The digital signature is generated using a cryptographic algorithm and information that identifies the user, including a cryptographic key. (FIPS 186 part 1 of ANSI X9.30).

Digital Signature Standard (DSS) A standard for generating a non-repudiatable electronic code linking the user to a specific transaction. The standard specifies an algorithm called the Digital Signature Algorithm (DSA). (FIPS 186 part 1 of ANSI X9.30).

discharge Healthcare: Formal release of a patient from a hospital or skilled nursing facility. This also applies to patients who died during confinement or were transferred to another healthcare facility.

discount fee See merchant service charge.

display telephone A telephone with a visual information presentation device for communicating with the user.

DRG See Diagnosis Related Group.

DSA Digital Signature Algorithm.

EBT Electronic Benefits Transfer.

EDI Electronic Data Interchange.

EDP Electronic Data Processing.

EEPROM Electrical Erasable Programmable Read-Only Memory. A non-volatile memory technology where data can be electrically erased and rewritten.

EFTPOS Electronic Funds Transfer at the Point of Sale. Any payment by a user at an Acceptor that is processed electronically.

electronic claim Healthcare: A digital representation of a healthcare claim generated by a provider or by a contractor for submission to a payer, such as tape, cassette or disk.

electronic credit transfer Paperless funds transfer, e.g., on magnetic tape, disk or cassette, or by telecommunication, initiated by the payer.

electronic directory On-line data base that cross-references one piece of information with other information. An example is an electronic version of the printed "white pages" telephone directory.

electronic funds transfer A funds transfer that is sent electronically, either by telecommunication or written on magnetic media such as tape, cassette or disk.

electronic purse An application in a card where value is stored for low-dollar transactions. A card may be dedicated to the purse function or contain memory and programs for other applications.

electronic submission Healthcare: The filing of claims electronically (tape, CPU-CPU, teletype) from a provider's office to the plan administrator.

electronic wallet Generally refers to integrated circuit card or super smart card capable of executing a variety of financial transactions and identification functions. More sophisticated than an electronic purse, a wallet may include debit, credit, cash card, and other functions

eligibility Healthcare: A patient's entitlement to payer coverage for healthcare.

eligibility file A file which contains pertinent data for each eligible individual enrolled in a healthcare program. The data elements include, but are not limited to, name, identification number, date of birth, sex, period of coverage, type of coverage, and dependents. Each payer should maintain such a file for each contract/employer.

eligibility verification Confirmation of a patient's enrollment and coverage in a healthcare program.

eligible employee An employee who is covered under a group health insurance plan.

eligible individual An individual certified by his/her payer to receive benefits under a selected healthcare program.

embossing Characters in relief (raised) from the front surface of the card.

emulator A program that allows one processor to simulate the instruction set of another processor or an electronic device that achieves this.

EMV Europay, Master Card and Visa joint project to define global specifications for Smart Cards.

encipherment See encryption.

encryption The use of cryptographic algorithms to encode clear text data (e.g., PINs) to ensure that the clear text data cannot be learned.

enrollment The certification of an individual in a healthcare program, e.g., healthcare.

EOB (Explanation of Benefits) Healthcare: An Explanation of Benefits provides the beneficiary details of payments/coverage for processed claims.

EPO Healthcare: Exclusive Provider Organization.

EPROM Electrically Programmable Read-Only Memory. A non-volatile memory technology that can be written to only once before being erased using ultraviolet light, after which it may be written to again.

ETSI European Telecommunications Standards Institute.

exception A transaction that is not processed by the accepted rules, procedures, and conditions.

expiration date The date after which a card, account, or application ceases to be valid for transaction use, unless an exception process is used to gain permission. Also known as expiry date.

expiry date See expiration date.

extended credit A formal borrowing facility for credit cardholders who choose not to pay off their accounts in full by the date due for settlement.

FIPS Federal Information Processing (standard).

float The value of funds tied up in the payment process, reflecting the value of payment processing time.

floor limit A transaction amount limit above which an Acceptor must obtain authorization from the Issuer.

front end The communications network interfacing equipment at a control point or central site.

FSTC Financial Services Technology Consortium.

general purpose chip A chip with electrical properties that are set for the handling of a common set of requirements, such as a microprocessor or storage unit.

Global System Mobile (GSM) A European Telecommunications Standards Institute (ETSI) standard for digital cellular telephones that employ integrated cards for identification and security.

government directed issuer. The commercial provider of a service as in the issuer of Smart Cards for military use.

group insurance A contract of insurance between an insurer and plan sponsor to cover a group of people.

GSM See Global System Mobile.

handshake A process between two devices such as a card, terminal, or modem to establish a common dialog. Parameters of the dialog may include speed, parity, number of bits, stop bits, and other basic information.

HCFA Health Care Financing Administration

HCFA-1500 A claim form designed by the Health Care Financing Administration. This form is required for all physician visits for Medicare. Presenting a card to an Acceptor for a transaction, where the user may not be the cardholder. Note: This definition does not apply to users of access cards.

health insurance A method of protection that provides benefits to cover sickness or injury. Examples include payments made for loss of income due to long-term disability, and medical expenses.

Health Maintenance Organization (HMO) An organization which offers a healthcare program to a specified group for a fixed periodic payment. HMOs provide a wide range of comprehensive healthcare services and can be part of a larger organization such as the government, a hospital, or an insurance company.

GLOSSARY

healthcare agent A person who generally handles small health plan set-up.

healthcare provider A person, organization, or institution that provides medical services or services related to medical treatment.

HMO See Health Maintenance Organization

holder The individual or business in whose name a payment card is issued. (This may not be the card user.)

hologram Unique photographic printing that gives the image a three-dimensional effect.

home banking System that allows customers to access banking services from home, e.g., inquiries, transfers, via devices such as telephones, televisions, personal computers, screen phones.

hot list A compilation of lost, stolen, over limit, or counterfeit cards, which may be used to verify the legitimacy of the transaction during authorization.

IC See integrated circuit.

IC Card See Integrated Circuit Card.

ICC See Integrated Circuit Card.

ICD-CM International Classification of Diseases, Clinical Modification standard codes used to describe diagnoses.

IEC International Electrotechnical Commission.

IFDs Interface Devices.

Individual Practice Association (IPA) A physician organization which has a contractual agreement with an HMO to provide medical services to the HMO members. The medical services are provided in the private offices of the individual physicians who also continue to see patients other than the HMO members.

initialization Setting data fields on card.

insult rate Percentage of occasions a valid user is rejected for a service, e.g., alleged erroneous billings or erroneous rejections of valid users by biometrics.

integrated circuit Electronic components designed to perform processing and/or memory functions.

Integrated Circuit Card (ICC) A card into which one or more integrated circuits are inserted. Includes both memory cards and smart cards.

intermediary Healthcare: An organization contracted by healthcare providers to provide administrative services such as claims processing.

interchange Communication between a communicating pair in the form of the structured combinations of data elements.

International Organization for Standardization (ISO) An international standards-setting body.

ISO See International Organization for Standardization.

ISO 7810 Identification cards—physical characteristics. Specifies the nominal dimensions of identification cards.

ISO 7811 Identification cards—recording technique. Consists of several parts specifying the location of embossing areas as well as magnetic track locations.

ISO 7812 Identification cards—identification of issuers. Consists of two elements; numbering system and applications and registration procedures for card issuer identifiers.

ISO 7813 Identification cards—financial transaction cards. Specifies the dimensions of financial cards (specific option of 7810) as well as the structure of the data stored in magnetic tracks 1 and 2.

ISO 7816 Identification cards—Integrated circuit(s) cards with contacts. Consists of several parts dealing with the physical dimensions of the cards, the dimensions and the contacts location, the electronic signals and the transmission protocols, the interindustry commands and responses, a numbering system and registration procedure for application identifiers, Data for interchange and in the future the Advanced commands as well as the Security architecture.

ISO 9992 Financial transaction cards—messages between the integrated circuit card and the card accepting device. Specifies the functions, messages, data elements as well as the structures of a multi application financial cards built for interchange.

ISO 10202 Financial transaction cards—security architecture of financial transaction systems using integrated circuit cards. Consist of multiple parts dealing with the card life cycle, the transaction process, cryptographic key relationships, secure application modules, algorithms, and key management.

ISO 10373 Identification cards—test methods.

ISO 10536 Identification cards—contactless integrated circuit(s) cards. Consists of several parts dealing with the physical dimensions of the cards, the dimensions and location of the coupling areas, and electronic signals for closely coupled contactless cards.

ISO 11693 Optical cards - general characteristics.

ISO 11694 Optical cards - physical characteristics, dimensions, and location of accessible optical area, optical properties, logical data structure.

issuer The institution identified on the card issued to the cardholder.

journal A listing of all pertinent payment transactions and the account(s) to which they apply.

k Kilo, represents 1,024 units. Usually measuring number of bit or bytes available for use.

key A parameter used in conjunction with a cryptographic algorithm that is computationally infeasible to deduce from the input and output data. See also Public Key, Private Key, Symmetric Key, and Cryptographic Key.

key management The process by which cryptographic keys are provided for use between authorized communicating parties and whereby those keys are subject to secure procedures until they have been destroyed.

laser card See optical memory card.

line tapping A means of connecting to a communications line for listening to and possibly recording data being transferred.

liquid crystal An electrically driven display technology used for work stations that is small, lightweight, and with low power needs.

magnetic stripe Magnetic material in the shape of a stripe on which signals can be stored electromagnetically.

magnetic stripe card A card with a magnetic stripe.

major medical A type of health insurance which protects an individual against the cost of major illness or injury. It usually pays for most charges relating to hospital charges, physician fees, private nurses, medical appliances, prescribed out-of-hospital treatment, and prescribed medicines.

Medicaid A public assistance program offered by each state to its residents, regardless of age, who have insufficient financial resources to pay for healthcare expenses. This program is described in the Social Security Act under Title XIX.

Medicare A public health insurance program for the aged designed to provide for hospital expenses and supplement other existing healthcare coverage of qualified beneficiaries. This program is provided through the Social Security Administration under Title XVII.

memory card Integrated circuit card capable of storing information but not having calculating capability, i.e., no microprocessor.

merchant service charge The fee paid by an Acceptor to an Acquirer for transactions made by a payment card.

Message Authentication Code (MAC) Code in a message between the sender and the receiver used to validate the source and part or all of the text of the message. The code is the result of an agreed calculation (DEA).

microcircuit card See integrated circuit card.

microprocessor A microcomputer with all of its processing facilities on a single chip. Also called microprocessor-on-a-chip. A microprocessor is a computer processor on a chip including registers and possible cache memory. A microcomputer or microcontroller also has data and program memory on the same chip.

microcontroller See microprocessor.

Minimum Payment Plan (MPP) An arrangement where a self-insured group pays a fee to a carrier to provide claims administration services and insure against above a maximum limit.

money order A fixed-value, prepaid payment voucher which can be purchased at banks, post offices, or other retail outlets and used to give or send to a payee.

monthly account card A charge card with a monthly billing cycle.

multi-application card A card that can support more than one application, where the applications may be provided by different parties.

MVE See VME

negative file Selection of identifiers and conditions to be treated as exceptions.

NIST National Institute of Standards and Technologies.

NMOS N-channel metal oxide semiconductor. A chip fabrication technology requiring moderate performance and moderate power.

non-contributory Healthcare: A type of arrangement between employer and employee under which the employer pays for the full cost of the employee's healthcare coverage.

nonreplenishable card A prepayment card that cannot have value reinstated.

non-volatile memory A semiconductor memory that retains its content when power is removed.

OCR See Optical Character Recognition.

off-line Computer based data files and operations reside on the ICC.

off-us See Interchange.

on-line Direct access to computer-based data files and operations systems via computer terminals.

open system A card system that involves multiple issuers of cards that can be used to access services or purchase products at multiple service providers. An open system requires the processing of interchange transactions, usually by an independent 'system operator'.

optical character recognition (OCR) Electronic reading and digital conversion of numeric or alphabetic characters from printed documents.

optical memory card Also known as laser cards, because a low-intensity laser is used to burn holes of several microns in diameter into a reflective material exposing a substrata of lower reflectivity. The presence, or absence, or a burned hole represents bits. The areas of high and low reflectivity are read using a precision light source.

OTP One Time Programmable Memory.

package A physical container, case, or enclosure for the integrated circuit chip(s) in a Integrated Circuit Card.

PAN See Primary Account Number.

password generation A method of generating a unique one-time password for a computer user based on a challenge-response sequence between a host and a device possessed by the user, e.g., a smart card.

password tokens Portable devices that contain chips, batteries, LCD and sometimes keypads. The devices are designed to generate a unique password for users logging on to computer systems and employ techniques known as synchronous or asynchronous password generation.

payers Healthcare: Insurance companies, fiscal intermediaries, government agencies, or individuals responsible for the payment of healthcare claims.

payment hierarchy Healthcare: The appropriate sequence of billing and payment for claims with multiple payers.

payment transaction The exchange of funds for goods or services.

PCMCIA Personal Computer Memory Card International Association. Association founded to standardize PC cards.

PCS Personal Communication Systems.

PDA Personal Digital Assistant.

peer review Healthcare: A system of evaluation where physicians use established standards of medical practice to assess the performance of their colleagues.

periodic payment Healthcare: Payments made to providers at regular time intervals and in fixed amounts.

Personal Identification Number (PIN) Code the customer possesses for verification of identity when using a card.

Personal Identification Verification (PIV) Techniques used to test physical traits to validate an individual's unique characteristics. See also Biometric.

personalization The process of initializing a card with data that ties it uniquely to a given cardholder and account.

PIN See Personal Identification Number.

PIN Pad A keypad for entering PIN values.

PIV See Personal Identification Verification.

PKCS Public Key Cryptographic Standards

PKE Public Key Encryption

PKP Public Key Partners; private company holding RSA encryption patents.

plaintext See cleartext.

plasticizers Chemical used in the materials and fabrication of plastic cards.

Point of Sale (POS) The location at which electronic payment transactions occur for the exchange of value for goods or services. Many times used to reference the hardware and/or terminal used for the transaction.

point of service Location where a transaction is originated.

polyvinyl chloride PVC. Material used to make plastic cards, including Smart Cards.

POS See point of sale

positive file Record of activated cards used for monitoring and control purposes.

positive list A description of account numbers and pertinent data for all active and issued account numbers. Some of these may also appear on a hot list.

pre-authorized payment A payment for which the payer gives a mandate requesting or permitting the financial institution to debit his/her account with defined or variable amounts. Standing orders and direct debits are examples.

Preferred Provider Organization (PPO) Healthcare: A formal arrangement where a payer contracts the services of healthcare providers at lower than usual fees.

premium The fee charged by the payer to put healthcare coverage into effect. This fee reflects the payer's expected utilization of benefits.

prepaid card or prepayment card A card that is purchased with stored value for which the value is decremented when used.

Primary Account Number (PAN) Series of digits used to identify a customer account or relationship.

prior approval The evaluation of a provider request for specific service by a medical professional to determine the medical necessity and appropriateness of the care requested for an individual.

prior authorization The acceptance of financial liability for services to be rendered by a provider to an individual by the payer. This does not automatically ensure payment.

private key In asymmetric cryptography, the key which is held only by the user, either in hardware or software authentication and encryption.

private key system See secret key.

private label/proprietary card A card with the Issuer's identification that is intended for use to obtain only those services that are available from that Issuer.

Prospective Payment System (PPS) A system of payment established for Medicare program where hospitals are paid a predetermined amount for specific services. If the specified payment is above the actual cost, the hospital is allowed to keep the difference; the hospital is also at risk for assuming any costs above the specified payment.

provider Healthcare: A person, organization, or institution that provides medical services or services related to medical treatment.

provider information system The provider's system for collecting, generating, assembling, and transmitting information internally and externally.

public key cryptography See public key system

public key system Cryptographic method using pairs of cryptographic keys, one of which is secret and one is public. If encipherment is done using the public key, decipherment requires application of the corresponding secret key and vice versa.

published key In asymmetric cryptography, the key which is published by the user to others for their use in verifying signatures and encrypting messages.

PVC See polyvinyl chloride.

radio-frequency ID A class of methods for transmitting information from a card without physical contact between card and reader.

RAM See random access memory.

random access memory A volatile memory used in integrated circuit cards that requires power to maintain data.

read-only memory Non-volatile memory that is written once, usually during card production. It is used to store operating systems and algorithms employed by the microprocessor in an integrated circuit card during transactions.

reasonable and customary charge Healthcare: The fee payable for a particular medical service or supply consistent with the acceptable rate for a similar service or supply within a particular geographical area.

recipient Healthcare: An individual who receives medical treatment or related services from a provider.

Reg. "E" Registration Authority Regulation promulgated by the Federal Reserve Bank under the Electronic Funds Transfer Act establishing the rights and responsibilities of parties involved in electronic funds transfer transactions.

reloadable prepayment card See Replenishable Prepayment Card.

replenishable prepayment card A prepayment card where the cardholder can add value after the initial issuance of the card.

retailer card Proprietary card issued by a retailer or retailing group.

retinal scan A PIV technique based on an infrared scan of the eye retina.

RF Radio frequency.

ROM See read-only memory.

RSA A public key cryptographic algorithm developed by mathematicians Rivest, Shamir, and Adelman of MIT. See also public key cryptography.

screen-based phone See display phone.

secret key The key used in a symmetric cryptographic algorithm, where the same key is used for encryption and decryption.

security features Measures taken to achieve a reasonable freedom from accidental, criminal, fraudulent, and vandalizing actions while maintaining sensitivity to unexpected attacks or system failures that cannot be distinguished from attacks.

self-insurance A type of group insurance where the group uses internal means and assumes the financial risks involved in providing healthcare protection. This takes the place of obtaining coverage from commercial health insurance carriers.

signature dynamics A PIV technique based on measurements of pen position and pressure as a function of time during signature writing.

signature panel A space on a card bearing the cardholder's signature.

skimming Electronically copying the card data from one card to another.

smart card An integrated circuit card with memory capable of making decisions.

special purpose Chip See custom chip.

standard A voluntary agreement to a uniform and consistent methodology and/or specification to achieve a common action or result.

standardized processes and protocols Guidelines for common data requirements, utilization control requirements, and documentation requirements across all payers.

standing order A preauthorized payment in which a customer instructs his/her bank to pay fixed sums at regular intervals or on defined dates.

stop-loss plan Healthcare: An arrangement where a self-insured group pays a fee to a carrier to provide administrative services and indemnify the group on claims payments that are above the predetermined amount.

storage An electronic and/or mechanical-magnetic device that holds information for subsequent use or retrieval.

store card See retailer card.

stored-value card See Prepayment Card.

subscriber identity A device used in the GSM application to link a phone number to a specific person instead of linking the number to a specific phone set.

super smart card A card-shaped device that has an on-board keypad, LCDs, and batteries, as well as one or more integrated circuit chips capable of storing and processing data.

symmetric key cryptography Cryptographic processes in which encryption and decryption rely on the same secret key. See DEA.

synchronous password generation A method of generating a unique one-time password for computer users based on time or transaction synchronization between a host and a device at the point of transmission.

T&E Travel and Entertainment.

telephone card A card that can be utilized for the payment of telephone calls. This card maybe a prepaid card, a credit card, or one that adds the cost of the call to the standard telephone bill.

third-party administration Healthcare: Administration of a group plan by a person or organization other that the carrier or insured.

third-party payer The individual or organization that pays for healthcare claims other than the patient or provider.

transaction A business or payment event for the exchange of value for goods or services.

transistor A discrete electronic component whose use preceded chip-based devices.

Travel and Entertainment Card (T&E Card) A card issued primarily for use in the travel and entertainment sector.

underwriting Healthcare: The process of evaluating the risk involved in insuring an individual. This determines whether the application for insurance is accepted or rejected, and to determine the premium to be charged to the employer.

universal prepayment card See multiple application card.

user The person presenting a card to an Acceptor for a transaction, where the user may not be the cardholder. Note: This definition does not apply to users of access cards.

utilization controls Payer-specific methods and procedures related to the medical review of proposed services. Controls are aimed at ensuring the adequacy, appropriateness, and necessity of medical care. These include, but are not limited to, second surgical opinion, and pre-admission certification.

utilization review Payer-specific methods and procedures related to the medical review of proposed services. Reviews are conducted to determine coverage based on quality of care, necessity, and appropriateness.

VME See EMV.

voucher Any piece of paper that is used to carry a payment message, e.g., checks, credit transfers, and credit card vouchers.

work station A combination of input and output devices intended to provide transaction implementation.

write-once A storage medium in which data cannot be altered or erased once it has been written.

zones Areas of integrated circuit card storage designated for free access, specific applications that may each have a different level of access.

SMART CARD RESOURCE LIST

Books & Reports

Advanced Card and Identificaiton Sourcebook. Warfel & Miller, Inc. 1993.

1990 Biometric Industry. By Benjamin Miller. Warfel & Miller, Inc. 1990.

Applications of Computer Card Technology. U.S. Department of Labor. 1989.

CardTech/SecureTech Conference Proceedings. CardTech/SecureTech Inc. 1991.

CardTech/SecureTech Conference Proceedings. CardTech/SecureTech Inc. 1992.

CardTech/SecureTech Conference Proceedings. CardTech/SecureTech Inc. 1993.

CardTech/SecureTech Conference Proceedings. CardTech/SecureTech Inc. 1994.

Cryptology on Smart Cards. Ernie Bricknell. Sandia National Laboratories. 1994.

Future of Prepayment Cards: Market, Technologies and Opportunities. Retail Banking Research Ltd. July 1994.

Healthcare Card Systems International Conference: September 1993. Institut International de Robotique et d' Intelligence Artificielle de Marseille.

I/C Smart Card Industry Directory. Benjamin Miller. Warfel & Miller. 1989.

Memory Card Issues: Activities and Opportunities. Conference Proceedings. Battelle Columbus Laboratories. 1985.

Prepaid Cash Card System: Japanese Market Report. PSI. 1989.

Prepayment Cards. The Electronic Purse Becomes Big Business. Peter Harrop. Financial Times Business Information. 1991.

Report on the Integrated Circuit Card: A Joint Study. Groupement Carte Bleue, Bank of America, The Royal Bank and VISA. 1985.

Smart Cards: New Bank Cards. By Jerome Svigals. Macmillan Publishing Company. 1993.

Smart Cards: A Technology Impact Report. Frost & Sullivan Inc. 1990.

Smart Cards: The Ultimate Personal Computer. By Jerome Svigals. Macmillan. 1985.

1990 Biometric Industry. By Benjamin Miller. Warfel & Miller, Inc. 1990.

Credit Cards: Business Implications for the 70's. Business Communicatons Corp. July 1973.

Memory Card Issues: Activities & Opportunities. Conference Proceedings. Battelle Columbus Laboratories. 1985.

Prepaid Cash Card System: Japanese Market Report. PSI. 1989.

SCAT (Smart Card Industry Assoc.) '90. Conference Proceedings. Presented by the Information Exchange and Personal Identification Newsletter. 1990.

Select Card Research and Analysis Articles: Survey Work Emerging Technology Applications. CARD. 1981.

The Smart Card: The Card for the 90s. By Chou Fang Soong. Gemplus Asia Technologies. 1994.

Smart Card Forum International Symposium. Smart Card Forum. 1994.

Stored Value Cards: Technology and Implementation. Payment Systems Strategies. Summer 1994.

Takashimaya Smart Card: Loyalty Card Made Smarter. By Madeleine Long. Verifone Pte Ltd. 1994.
Value Pricing of Bankcard Services. Working Paper No. 34. Credit Research Center; Krannert Graduate School of Management; Purdue University. 1980.

Binders of Selected Articles
These binders are compiled by the Information Center Staff. The articles that they contain have been selected from a wide variety of periodicals and newspapers pertaining to the financial industry and to smart cards. They provide the user with a one-stop capability.
Prepaid Cards. 1991–Present.
Smart Cards (Banking). 1990–Present.
Smart Cards (Educational Segment). 1990–Present.
Smart Cards (General). 1990–Present.
Smart Cards (Government Segment). 1990–Present.
Smart Cards (Standards). 1990–Present.
Smart Cards (Technology). 1990–Present.
Smart Cards (Telecommunications). 1990–Present.
Smart Cards (Transportaton Segment). 1990–Present.
Smart Cards (Travel & Entertainment Segment). 1990–Present.

Periodicals and Newspapers
American Banker
Bank Automation News
Bank Network News
Bank Technology News
Card Fax
Card World
Cards International
Credit Card Management
Credit Card News
Electronic Payments International
Financial Times
Payment Systems Worldwide
POS News
Report on Smart Cards
Smart Card News
Smart Card Monthly
Smart Cards & Comments

SMART CARD RESOURCE LIST

Online Services
Nexis/Lexis
Compuserve
Internet

CD-Rom Sources
American Banker on CD-ROM

SMART CARD FORUM DELIVERABLES

Work Group	Deliverable
Financial Services	
Multiapplication	Consumer Research Top Line
	Consumer Research Final Report
	Merchant Market Research Study
Prepaid	Prepaid Business Case Model
	Business Case Model Appendix
	Stakeholder/Functionality Matrix
	Scheme Descriptions & Comparisons
Security	Smart Card Security: A Business Perspective
Technology	Standards & Specifications Document
	SCF Vendor Directory
	Applications Lifecycle Framework
	Applications Database
	Contactless White Paper
	Plastics White Paper
	Identity & Biometrics White Paper
	Glossary of Terms II
	Standards Update Newsletter
Telephony	Applications White Paper
	National Interoperability of Disposable Prepaid Smart Cards for Pay Phones
	Smart Cards for Personal Communications
Healthcare	PC-Based On-Line Demo/Contactless Card
	Healthcare Presentation
Education	Industry Status Presentation
Legal	Strawman Analysis for Issues Surrounding Issuance of Smart Cards
	Privacy White Paper
	Reg. E. White Paper
Transportation	Smart Card Use in Ground Transportation
	Current Smart Card Based Transportation Solutions
Transportation	Business Issues in Automatic Fare Collection
	Requirement Document
General	Smart Card Forum Abstracts
	Research Library
	Home Page/Web Page
	1995 Annual Conference Interactive Session

BIBLIOGRAPHY

Benton International, "TransLink Program Plan," prepared for the Metropolitan Transportation Commission, Oakland, CA, December 1995.

Charles Broshus, "Metrocard: A Migration Path from Closed to Open Systems," Conference Proceedings, CardTech/SecurTech, April 1995.

William Bushnell, Coopers and Lybrand, "Smart Cards for Transit: Multi-Use Remotely Interrogated Stored-Data Cards for Fare and Toll Payment," prepared for the Volpe National Transportation Systems Center and Federal Transit Administration, April 1995, FTA-MA-26-0020-95-1.

CardTech/SecureTech Conference Proceedings. CardTech/SecureTech Inc. 1991.

CardTech/SecureTech Conference Proceedings. CardTech/SecureTech Inc. 1992.

CardTech/SecureTech Conference Proceedings. CardTech/SecureTech Inc. 1993.

CardTech/SecureTech Conference Proceedings. CardTech/SecureTech Inc. 1994.

CardTech/SecureTech Conference Proceedings. CardTech/SecureTech Inc. 1995.

Candace Carlson and the IBI Group, "Regional Fare & Technology Coordination for Central Puget Sound," Phase I Feasibility Study Final Report, January 15, 1996.

Floyd Diaz, "Implementing Smartcard Projects in Transit: A Comparative Study of Hong Kong and Manchester, UK," in Conference Proceedings, CardTech/SecurTech, May 1996.

Michael Dinning and John Collura, "Electronic Payment Systems in Public Transit," Intelligent Transportation: Realizing the Benefits, the Proceedings of the 1996 Annual Meeting of ITS America, June 1996.

Russell Driver, "TransLink Regional Fare Collection System," presentation at Electronic Payment Systems: The San Francisco Bay Area Model and Applications Around the World Workshop," Metropolitan Transportation Commission, Oakland, CA, February 1996.

Daniel Fleishman, et. al., "Fare Policies, Structures, and Technologies," Transit Cooperative Research Program, Transportation Research Board, Report 10, 1996.

Frost & Sullivan Inc., "Smart Cards: A Technology Impact Report." 1990.

Groupement Carte Bleue, Bank of America, The Royal Bank and VISA. "Report on the Integrated Circuit Card: A Joint Study." 1985.

Terry Griffis, "Stored Value Cards: A Transit Perspective," in Conference Proceedings, CardTech/SecurTech, May 1996.

Peter Harrop, "Prepayment Cards. The Electronic Purse Becomes Big Business." Financial Times Business Information. 1991.

The Information Exchange and Automation Working Group, "The North American Trade Automation Prototype, Report to the Heads of Customs," June 1995.

Institut International de Robotique et d' Intelligence Artificielle de Marseille. "Healthcare Card Systems International Conference: September 1993." 1993

Benjamin Miller, "1990 Biometric Industry." Warfel & Miller, Inc. 1990

Multisystems with NuStats, Inc., "Chicago Transit Authority Stored-Value Card Pricing Survey and Ridership/Revenue Model," December 1995.

Ray Rebiero, "Transit Smart Cards in Ventura and Lompoc Counties," presentation at the Electronic Payment Systems and Fare Integration Workshop, Seattle Metro, Seattle, WA, June 1995.
Retail Banking Research Ltd, "Future of Prepayment Cards: Market, Technologies and Opportunities." Retail Banking Research Ltd. July 1994.
Atefeh Riazi, "MetroCard," presentation at the Institute of Transportation Engineers District 1 Annual Meeting," May 1996.
Randy Schafer, "Electronic Payment Systems in Transit: A Financial Institution Perspective," presentation at the Electronic Payment Systems in Transit: the San Francisco Bay Area Model and Applications Around the World Workshop," Metropolitan Transportation Commission, Oakland, CA, February 1996.
The Schuler Consultancy, "The Advanced Card Report: Smart Card Primer," 1993.
Smart Card Forum Deliverables
Applications Lifecycle Framework, Technology Work Group, 1995.
Applications White Paper, Telephony Work Group, 1995.
Business Case Model Appendix, Prepaid Work Group, 1995.
Business Issues in Automatic Fare Collection, Transportation Work Group, 1995.
Consumer Research Final Report, *Financial Services* Multi-ApplicationWork Group, 1995.
Consumer Research Top Line, *Financial Services* Multi-ApplicationWork Group, 1995.
Contactless White Paper, Technology Work Group, 1995.
Current Smart Card Based Trans. Solutions, Transportation Work Group, 1995.
Glossary of Terms II, Technology Work Group, 1995.
Healthcare Presentation, Healthcare Work Group, 1995.
Industry Status Presentation, Education Work Group, 1995.
Merchant Market Research Study, *Financial Services* Multi-ApplicationWork Group, 1995.
Prepaid Business Case Model, Prepaid Work Group, 1995.
Privacy White Paper, Legal & Regulatory Work Group, 1995.
Reg. E. White Paper, Legal & Regulatory Work Group, 1995.
Smart Card Forum Abstracts, 1995.
Smart Cards for Personal Communications, Telephony Work Group, 1995.
SCF Vendor Directory, Technology Work Group, 1995.
Smart Card Security: A Business Perspective, Security Work Group, 1995.
Smart Card Use in Ground Transportation, Transportation Work Group, 1995.
Stakeholder/Functionality Matrix, Prepaid Work Group, 1995.
Standards & Specifications Document, Technology Work Group, 1995.
Standards Update Newsletter, Technology Work Group, 1995.
Strawman Analysis for Issues Surrounding Issuance of Smart Cards, Legal & Regulatory Work Group, 1995.
SCAT (Smart Card Industry Assoc.) '90. Conference Proceedings. Presented by the Information Exchange and Personal Identification Newsletter. 1990.
Stored Value Cards: Technology and Implementation. Payment Systems Strategies. Summer 1994.
Jerome Svigals, "Smart Cards: New Bank Cards." Macmillan Publishing Company. 1993
U.S. Congress, Office of Technology Assessment, "Making Government Work: Electronic Delivery of Federal Services," OTA-TCT-578, U.S. Government Printing Office, Washington, D.C., September 1993.

U.S. Department of Labor, "Applications of Computer Card Technology." U.S. Department of Labor. 1989.
Warfel & Miller Inc. "Advanced Card and Identificaiton Sourcebook." Warfel & Miller Inc. 1993.
World Trade Organization, "International Trade Trends and Statistics," June 1995.

INDEX

ABP; *see* Adler Boschetto and Peebles
Access keys, 10, 24–25, 154, 156, 241
   management of, 144, 148, 255–256
   public, 253–254
   shared, 252–253
Activity chain analysis, 86–88
Addressing, 100
Adler Boschetto and Peebles, 58
Advantage, creating, 84–89
Advertising, targeted, 105–106
AEI; *see* Automated equipment identification
Agriculture, Department of, 175
AID; *see* Application identifiers
Airlines, 206–207
   paper/plastic transactions, 200–201
   security, 207
   ticketing pilot programs, 201–203
Algorithms, 138, 252–256, 259, 261
Allen, Catherine A., 2–20, 57–78
Alliances, 44–45, 46
   banking, 37, 227, 229, 231–232
   electronic community, 61
   entertainment/travel, 199–200
   market share and, 58
   private/public, 175
   retailing, 221
   service provider, 36–37
   telecommunications, 37, 128, 129, 230–231
   transportation, 179–180, 187, 195, 196–197
American Airlines, 203
American Banker, 14
American Express, 231
American National Standards Institute, 246
American Personal Communications, 135
Ann Arbor Transportation Authority, 187
Anonymity, in payment process, 96, 108, 189
ANSI; *see* American National Standards Institute
Application identifiers, 244
Applications, smart card, 10–11, 23–26
   campus, 225–227, 228, 233
   consumer interest in, 27–33
   financial services, 119–120
   in government, 173–176
   healthcare, 158–167
   multiple, 12–13, 26, 30, 31–33, 61–62, 64–67, 172–173, 226–228, 259

Applications, smart card (*continued*)
   retailing, 215, 217
   strategic marketing and, 38–39
   telecommunications, 130–143
Archives, publications, 104
Asia, smart card growth rate in, 8
AT&T Universal Card Services, 53
Atlanta Olympics (1996)
   collectible smart cards and, 13
   VISA Cash and, 52
ATMs; *see* Automated teller machines
Australia, 8, 52–53, 54
Authentication, 109, 143, 252, 258–259
   vs. confidentiality, 254–255
   UIM cards and, 138
Automated equipment identification, 190, 191
Automated Permit Port, 192
Automated teller machines, 133
   screen-based telephones as, 134
Ayer, Kenneth, 44–56

B&B Fone Cards, 14
Bank cards, 6
   campus card systems and, 227
   French, 7, 22, 50
   transit fare payment with, 187
Banking, 51–54
   alliances, 37, 227, 229, 231–232
   home, 134–135
   standards for, 8
Banksys, 54
Barr, William J., 57–78, 90–109
Belgium, 54
Bellcore, 14, 58
BellSouth Personal Communications, 132
Benefits, government
   delivery, 171, 174
   fraud, 172
Birkmayer, Georg, 165
Blockbuster Video Card, 214
Blood bank cards, 164
Braco, Ron, 112–127
Brainerd, Lorraine, 151–168
Branding, 67–68, 84, 201
Brazil, 54, 203

303

Burke, John, 57–78
Bus systems; *see* Transportation, public

CAD; see Card acceptance devices
Caesar, Julius, 250, 252
Canadian Imperial Bank, 53
Card acceptance devices, 241–242
Carta Moneta program, 23
Cartes Bancaire, 22
Cash; *see* Currency
Cash cards; *see* Electronic purse systems
Change, accelerating pace of, 57–58, 113–114
Chase Manhattan, 17, 53, 242
Checks, 96, 212
Chip cards; *see* Smart cards
Chips; *see* Microchips
Choctaws, 251
Church, Murray, 14
Citibank, 17, 53, 242
Citicorp, 14
Clip, 54
Collectible cards, 13–14
Colleges; *see* Education
Combi-cards; *see* Dual mode cards
Commerce, electronic, 90–109
   consumer perspectives of, 99–102
   defined, 90
   opportunity in, 91
   phases of, 92–98
Commonwealth Bank of Australia, 52
Communities, electronic, 60–62
Competition; *see* Advantage, creating
Complexity, hiding, 99–100
Comptroller of the Currency, Office of, 72–73
CompuServe, 100
Computing
   home, 142, 216–217
   mobile, 139–140, 143
Constitutional rights, 262–263
Consumer loyalty programs; *see* Loyalty, consumer
Consumer market; *see* Consumer/supplier relations; Market, smart card, consumer; Smart cards, consumer perceptions of
Consumer/supplier relations, 93–95, 97–103; *see also* Service providers, smart card
   in financial services, 112–113, 116–117, 120, 122–123
Contact/Contactless cards, 181–184, 187, 194, 196, 238, 239
   ISO standards, 243, 245–246
   in travel industry, 202–203, 206

Contracts
   consumer, 76
   multimedia, 105
Convenience, 27–28, 115, 125
   in airline industry, 207
   electronic couponing, 216
   of telephone cards, 131–132
Copier machines, 226
Corporation, virtual, 104–105
COS; *see* Systems, card operating
Costs
   airline, 206–207
   government service, 173
   infrastructure, 149
   medical care, 151, 152, 161, 165–166
   smart card, 119
CouponRadio, 215–216
Coupons, 212
   electronic, 106, 215–217, 220
CRC; *see* Cyclic Redundancy Check
Credit cards; *see also specific cards*
   American, 7, 95
   authorization of, 212
   fraud, 95–96
   on Internet, 143
   standards for, 8, 202
   universities and, 231
Crook, Colin, 16, 59
Cryptology; *see* Encryption
Cunningham, Dan, 224–233
Cunningham, Danyl, 224–233
Currency, 96, 146
   handling, 219
   stored value and, 119, 120
Cybercash, 18, 126
Cyclic Redundancy Check, 259

Danmont, 7
Data alteration, 250
Data Elements, 244–245
Data Encryption Standard, 253
DCL; *see* Dedicated Commuter Lane
DE; *see* Data Elements
Debt Collection Act (1996), 170
Decryption; *see* Encryption
Dedicated Commuter Lane, 192
Defense, Department of, 66, 157
Delivery systems, 97
   proprietary documents and, 105
   smart cards as, 11
Delta Airlines, 203
Dependent identification, 161–162

INDEX

305

DES; *see* Data Encryption Standard
Devices, card acceptance; *see* Card acceptance devices
DigiCash, 18, 126
Digital Signature Standard, 254
Dinning, Michael, 177–198
Directories, 100–101, 144
Document delivery, proprietary, 105
Driver's licenses, 174, 190–191
DSS; *see* Digital Signature Standard
Dual mode cards, 183, 188, 193

EBT; see Electronic Benefits Transfer
EDI; *see* Electronic Data Interchange
Education, 46, 171, 224–233
   motivations of, 230–231
   multifunction cards and, 63, 226–229, 233
   transportation and, 180–181, 187
EEPROM; *see* Electrically Erasable Programmable Read Only Memory
800 cards, 133
Electrically Erasable Programmable Read Only Memory, 238
Electronic Benefits Transfer, 66
Electronic Data Interchange, 154
Electronic Money Working Group, 72–73
Electronic purse systems; *see* Stored value systems
EMV; *see* Europay/MasterCard/Visa specification
Encryption, 109, 136, 138, 139–140, 143, 250–255
   decryption and, 251–253
   history of, 250–251
   in interactive television, 141–142
   modems and, 147
   of patient data, 159
   public key, 253–254
England, 53, 157
Ensor, Eric F., 132
Entertainment/Travel, 46, 199–208
   alliances, 199–200
   home entertainment, 140–142
   paper/plastic transactions, 200–201
   stakeholders in, 199, 202–204
EPROM; *see* Erasable Programmable Read Only Memory
Erasable Programmable Read Only Memory, 238
Error messages, 101
Escheat, 76–78
Europay International, 54
Europay/MasterCard/Visa specification, 8, 48–50, 52, 54
Europe
   collectible cards in, 13, 14

Europe (*continued*)
   GSM systems in, 135
   smart card growth rate in, 7–8
Everything cards; *see* Applications, smart card, multiple
Evolution path, 261
Exeter Care Card Project, 157

FCC; see Federal Communications Commission
FDIC; *see* Federal Deposit Insurance Corporation
Federal Communications Commission, 135
Federal Deposit Insurance Corporation, 18, 72
Federal Reserve Board, 70
Federal Trade Commission, 73
Financial Management Services Division, U.S. Treasury, 14
Financial services, 22, 32, 45, 59, 112–127; *see also* Bank cards; Banking; Stored value systems
   deregulation and, 112
   educational institutions and, 230–231
   in government, 171
   predictions impacting, 126
   smart card implementation in, 123–126
   stakeholders in, 116–118
Financial Services Technology Consortium, 96
Financial Services Workgroup (Smart Card Forum), 39
First of America Bank, 229
First Union, 13, 14, 52
Five Forces Analysis, 86
Florida State University, 13
Food stamps, 174, 212
France
   healthcare smart cards in, 55, 152–153
   smart card growth rate in, 7, 22
   telephone cards in, 130–131
Fraud
   airline, 207
   credit card, 95–96, 218
   government benefits, 172
   health insurance, 151, 166
   scenarios, 260
Freight industry, 179, 181, 189–191
FSTC Electronic Commerce Project, 108
FTC; *see* Federal Trade Commission
Functions, smart card; *see* Applications, smart card

Germany
   chip technology integration in, 202–203
   health insurance cards and, 55

Global System for Mobile Communications, 24, 48, 66, 135–139
Golden Card, 18
Government, 45, 169–176
  documentation, 172–173
  technology and, 169–171
  transportation, 190–191
Government Applications of Computer Card Technology, 170–171
Graphics, smart card; see Branding
Group Administrator, 165
GSM; see Global System for Mobile Communications

Hackers, 257–258, 259
Health access card; see Health insurance cards
Health Insurance Association of America, 151
Health insurance cards, 55, 152
Health services, 32, 45, 55, 151–168
  emergency, 164
  facilities for, 162–165
  providers of, 153–154, 159, 162
  security, 55, 156, 160
  specialty, 163
  spending, 151, 152, 161, 165–166
Hoff, Ted, 4
Hongkong & Shanghai Banking, 53
Honold, Frederick J., Jr., 90–109
Host computer, in security systems, 256
Hotels, 203–204
Hubbard, Gerald, 21–40, 79–89
Hybrid cards, 237

IATA; see International Airline and Transportation Association
Ichikawa, Bryan, 248–264
Immigration, 191–192
Implementation, smart card, 15
  barriers to, 35–36
  campus, 228–230
  financial services, 123–126
  government, 173
  rapid, 167
Income; see Revenue
Industries, 9, 16–18
  shifting boundaries of, 58–59, 112, 113
  with smart card potential, 21–22, 45–46
Information age, 128
Information-backup, 145
Information managers, smart cards as, 10–11, 25, 28, 144–145, 156–157

Information Security Handbook, 248–249
Information services, 58–59
  consumer relationship management and, 64
  corporate, 104–105
  in electronic commerce, 93–94, 102–106
  library, 103–104
  mobility and, 108–109
  telecommunications as, 129–130
Information superhighway; see Internet
INSPASS system, 191–192
Installation, smart card; see Implementation, smart card
Insurance, health, 151, 160, 161–162, 165–166
Integrated Circuit Card Specifications for Payment Systems; see Europay/MasterCard/Visa specification
Intel, 4, 18
Intelligent agents, 106
Intelligent Buildings, 25
Intelligent Transportation System, 177–178, 180
Intermediation, 91–92, 118
Intermodal Surface Transportation Efficiency Act (1991), 178
International Airline and Transportation Association, 201–202
International Organization for Standardization, 48–49, 137, 193, 242–246
Internet
  electronic commerce on, 91, 143, 220
  public access to, 142, 143
Interoperability, 47, 48, 189, 242; see also Standards
  in telecommunications, 145–146
  in travel industry, 202, 205–206
ISO; see International Organization for Standardization
Issuer Profit and Loss Statement, 41–43
Issuers, smart card; see Service providers, smart card
ISTEA; see Intermodal Surface Transportation Efficiency Act (1991)
ITS; see Intelligent Transportation System

Jacksonville Jaguars, 14
Jamaica, 204
Japan, 55
  collectible cards in, 13–14
  strategic pricing and, 88
JAVA, 18, 67, 126

Kars Unlimited, 14

INDEX

Keenan, William, 21–40, 79–89
Keys; *see* Access keys
Kutler, Jeffrey, 2–20

Labor Birkmayer Blood Laboratories, 165
Legal issues; *see also* Regulatory issues; *specific legislation*
   escheat concept, 76–78
   privacy, 74–76, 262–263
Liability, for lost/stolen cards, 69
Libraries, 103–104
License, driver's, 174, 190–191
Lifecycle of A Smart Card Application, 262
Life cycle, smart card, 84–86, 238, 239, 240
Lisimaque, Gilles, 248–264
Lout, Jim, 151
Loyalty, consumer, 24, 86, 132, 214
Ludwig, Eugene, 72, 73
Lufthansa, 202
Lutz, Ken, 128–150

Machiavelli, Niccolo, 91
Magnetic stripe, 5–6, 200–201, 226, 227
   vs. contactless cards, 181–182
   future performance requirements and, 9
   memory and, 237
Malpractice, medical, 162
Management, 98
   access key, 144, 148, 255–256
   information, 10–11, 25, 28, 144–145, 156–157
   UIM capabilities, 137–139
Manufacturers; *see* Material providers
Manzi, Jim, 18
MARC; *see* Multi-technology Automated Reader Card
Marine Corps, U.S., 176, 251
Marketing, 11; *see also* Advantage, creating; Market, smart card; Propositions, business
   traditional vs. intelligent, 79–84
Market, smart card
   consumer, 26–34, 76, 80–82, 99–102, 204
   expanding, 63–64
   horizontal vs. vertical, 87–88
   projected size of, 21–22
   service provider, 34–37
MasterCard, 9, 17, 52–53, 242; *see also* Europay/MasterCard/Visa specification
MasterCard Cash systems, 52–53
Material providers, 117–118, 240, 243
Matson, Beverly, 209–223
Mcard, 187

McKenna, Jean, 44–56
Meal plans, 231
Medical Device Safety Act (1992), 161
Medication, tracking, 163–164
Medici project, 67
Memory cards, 4, 237
Merchants; *see* Retailing
Merging, industry; *see* Alliances
Metropolitan Transportation Authority, 185
Michigan, University of, 187, 228–229
Microchips, 4–7
Micropayments, 96
Microsoft, 67
Midland Bank, 53
Military, U.S.; *see also* Defense, Department of
   smart card trials, 172, 176
   transportation, 190
Mobility, 108–109, 135–137, 139–140
Model, business
   for electronic purse cards, 39–40
   for financial institutions, 121–123
Modems, encryption and, 147
Mondex, 18, 53–54, 134
Money Card program; *see* Carta Moneta program
Moore, Gordon, 5
Moore, John, 169–176
Moreno, Roland, 4–5
Motorola, 18
MTA; *see* Metropolitan Transportation Authority
Multiple application cards; *see* Applications, smart card, multiple
Multi-technology Automated Reader Card, 18, 66, 157
Murray State University, 228

National Institute of Standards and Technology, 254
National Security Agency, 254
National Westminster Bank, 53
NationsBank, 13, 52
Native Americans, cryptology and, 251
Natwest Group, 53
Negotiation, electronic commerce, 94
Netherlands, 54
Networks, 9
   security, 256–257
   telecommunications, 24, 130, 143–144
New Banking Technologies Task Force, 72
New Zealand Banking Group, 52
Nippon Telephone and Telegraph, 14
Nissan Car Life program, 25
Nonrepudiation, 252

Nursing cards, 164
Nynex, 14, 22

Oahu Test, 157
OCC; *see* Comptroller of the Currency, Office of
Olympics, summer (1996); *see* Atlanta Olympics (1996)
Ontario Ministry of Health, 159
Operation Time Saver, 178
Ownership, 148–149
  of information, 104–105
  multiple cards consolidation and, 67–68

Parris Island, 176
Partnerships; *see* Alliances
Patients, 153, 158–161
  eligibility verification of, 154, 161
  insurance for, 151, 160, 161–162, 165–166
  personal records of, 55, 151–152, 156, 159–160, 167–168
  tracking, 163
Pay Ease Food Stamps, 174
Payment, 10, 23–24, 94–96, 146
  electronic vs. paper based, 91, 96, 200–201
  healthcare, 154, 157–158, 166
  retailing, 212, 213
  security of, 107–108
  transportation, 177, 178–179, 181–189, 194–196
Pay phones; *see* Telephones, pay
PCMCIA; *see* Personal Computer Memory Card International Association
PCS; *see* Personal Communications Service
PDA; *see* Personal Digital Assistant
Personal Communications Service, 129, 135–137
Personal Computer Memory Card International Association, 156
Personal Digital Assistant, 101
Personal identification number, 69, 134, 138, 230, 258
Personalization, 102, 106, 109, 135–137, 141
Phillips, 18
Phones; *see* Telephones
Physicians, 160, 161–162
Pilot programs; *see* Implementation, smart card
PIN; *see* Personal identification number
Point of service, in security systems, 257
Portability, 115, 139–140, 160
Porter, Michael, 86
POS; *see* Point of service
Post Telephone and Telegraph, 130–131

Prepaid Subcommittee (Financial Services Workgroup), 39
Prescription routing, 165
Pricing, 8, 88–89
Privacy, 73–76, 262–263; *see also* Encryption; Security
  consumer concerns, 33–34, 74, 76, 196, 205, 221
  technology, 107, 108
Privacy Subcommittee (Smart Card Forum), 263
Processing power, smart card, 115, 237
Promotions and International Cash Cards, 14
Property, escheat concept and, 76–78
Propositions, business
  consumer concerns and, 32, 38, 64–65, 81–82
  electronic purse cards case model and, 39–43
  strategic considerations of, 38–39, 121–122, 222
Proprietary information; *see* Ownership, of information
Proton, 54
Proximity cards; *see* Contact/Contactless cards
PSI study (1995), 29–30, 34, 36
PTT; *see* Post Telephone and Telegraph
Publications archives, 104
Public key cryptography, 253–254

Radio, 215–216
Radio Frequency Tags, 246
Railroads, 190
RAM, 237–238
RBOCs; *see* Regional Bell Operating Companies
Rea, Martha, 21–40, 79–89
Refundability, smart card, 34
Regional Bell Operating Companies, 129
Regulation E, 70–72
Regulatory issues, 69–72
  campus, 231–232
  retailing, 221
  telecommunications, 147–148
  transportation, 195–196
Reloadable cards, 132–133, 184
Research, market, 80, 123, 204, 218
Retailing, 45, 209–223
  alliances, 221
  goals, 117, 211, 217–218
  infrastructure, 212–214
  opportunities in, 211–212
Revenue
  fare systems, 185–186, 195
  sharing, 68–69, 230–231
  smart card issuers, 123

INDEX

Revenue *(continued)*
  stored value and, 120
Reward cards, 24
RFPs, 18
Rivest, Shamir, and Adelman, 253–254
Roaming, 137, 138
ROM, 238
Royal Bank, 53
RSA; *see* Rivest, Shamir, and Adelman

Saks First Card, 214
Salt Lake City, Utah, 66
SAM; *see* Security Access Modules
San Diego, California, 176
Schlumberger, 14, 55
Search engines, 101
Security, 6, 33–34, 118–119, 144, 148, 248–264; *see also* Privacy
  airline, 207
  attack scenarios, 260
  basic elements of, 248, 251–252
  CAD selection and, 241
  campus, 232
  electronic payments, 107–108
  in government, 171–172
  history of, 250–251
  of medical records, 55, 156, 160
  in mobile communications, 136
  television and, 141–142
  transportation, 194
  UIM cards and, 137–138
Security Access Modules, 241
Serial numbers, smart card, 261
Service Encounter Card, 159
Service providers, smart card, 34–37, 116; *see also* Consumer/supplier relations
  alliances, 36–37
  locations, 30–31
  opportunity areas, 35, 36, 76
  Regulation E and, 70–72
  revenue/expenses, 123
Short Message Service, 139
Signatures, 254–255
SIM cards; *see* Subscriber Identity Module cards
Simplicity, consumer perceptions of, 99–101
Smart Card Forum, 5, 14–16, 46, 175
  studies by, 26–27, 33
Smart Card Privacy Issues-An Overview, 263
Smart cards; *see also* Applications, smart card
  collectible, 13–14
  consumer perceptions of, 27–34, 60, 64–65
  cost of, 119

Smart cards *(continued)*
  defined, 3–4, 45, 237
  future of, 2–3, 12, 93, 95, 97, 98, 126, 167–168, 176, 217, 263–264
  history of, 4–7
  life cycle of, 84–86, 238, 239, 240
  lost/stolen, 34, 69
  manufacturers of, 117, 240
  memory of, 4, 237–238, 261
  portability of, 115, 160
  processing power of, 115, 237
  reloadable, 132–133, 184
  security features, 260–262
  terminology, 236–237
Smart TV, 215, 216
Smith, Michael, 224–233
SMS; *see* Short Message Service
Society for Worldwide Interbank Financial Telecommunications, 25
Software companies, information services and, 130
Specifications; *see* Standards
Sprint Spectrum, 135, 136
Stakeholders
  education, 230–231
  entertainment/travel, 199, 202–204
  financial services, 116–118
  healthcare, 153–154, 155
  in smart card life cycle, 240
  telecommunications, 129–130, 140, 142
  transportation, 180–181, 188–189, 190–191, 192
Standards, 242–246
  encryption, 253, 254
  international, 8, 47–50, 137, 201–202, 205–206, 242–246
  lack of, 125, 149
  transportation, 193
St. Louis, Missouri, 230
Stored value systems, 8, 9–10, 50–54, 119–120
  benefits of, 122
  business case model for, 39–43
  campus, 226–228
  consumer interest in, 30
  interoperability and, 146
  multidimensional marketing and, 83–84
  Regulation E and, 70–72
Subscriber Identity Module cards, 24, 48, 136–140
SUN, 18
Supplier/consumer relations; *see* Consumer/supplier relations; Service providers, smart card
SWIFT; *see* Society for Worldwide Interbank Financial Telecommunications

Swindon, England, 53, 134
SWOT analysis, 86
Systems, card operating, 241
   open vs. closed, 46–47, 124, 183–184, 197

Takashimaya Visa Card, 24
Tarbox, Andy, 248–264
Tarbox, Judy D., 151–168, 169–176, 236
Technology
   entertainment/travel, 205
   government and, 169–171
   information, 59–61, 68
   innovations in, 16–20, 113–14
   intermediation and, 91–92
   retailing, 219–220
   security, 107, 108, 147
   simplifying, 99–101
   transportation, 192–195
Technology Committee (Smart Card Forum), 247
Telecom, 22
Telecommunications, 21–22, 32, 45, 128–150
   alliances, 37, 128, 129, 230–231
   applications, 130–145
   boundaries of, 128
   entertainment services, 140–142
   French, 7, 130–131
   information services, 129–130
   networks, 130, 143–144
   simplicity of, 100
   ubiquity of, 101
Telecommunications Reform Act (1996), 128–129, 141, 148
Telephone cards, 130–135, 147–148, 231
Telephones; *see also* Telecommunications
   GSM, 136–137
   pay, 32, 131–132, 146
   screen-based, 134–135
   sharing, 138
Television
   cable, 130, 140–141, 142
   censorship of, 141
   interactive, 141–142, 215, 216
Terminals, 32
   defined, 49
   manufacturers, 117
Terminology, smart card, 236–237
Third-party intermediaries; *see* Intermediation
Thomsen, 18
Toll collection, 171, 188–189, 194–195
Torts, privacy, 263
Transit, public; *see* Transportation, public
Transportation, 45, 177–198

Transportation (*continued*)
   alliances, 179–180, 187, 195, 196–197
   international, 179, 191–192
   motivations of, 180–181, 184–188, 188–189, 190–191, 192
   payment for, 177, 178–179, 181–189, 194–196
   public, 177, 179, 180, 181–188
   ridership data, 186
Travel; *see* Entertainment/Travel; Transportation
Traveler identification, 191–192
Treasury Financial Management Service, Department of, 170–171
Trillin, Calvin, 73
Trucking, 179, 189–190
TV; *see* Television

UBI consortium, 25
Ubiquity, consumer perceptions of, 101–102
UIM cards; *see* Subscriber Identity Module cards
Uniform Unclaimed Property Act, 77
United States
   consumer reaction studies in, 26–27
   government smart card trials in, 172
   GSM systems in, 135–136
   healthcare spending in, 152
   smart card growth rate in, 7
Universities; *see* Education
USDA; *see* Agriculture, Department of
User Identity Module cards; *see* Subscriber Identity Module cards
US West Communications, 22

Vaccinations, school, 164
Value, cash; *see* Currency
V-Chip, 141
Vehicle operations, commercial, 179, 181, 189–191
Ventura County Transportation Commission, 184
Villages, electronic; *see* Communities, electronic
Viruses, 259
Visa, 9, 17, 24, 52, 242; *see also* Europay/MasterCard/Visa specification
VISA Cash systems, 52
Vitale, 152–153
Voltaire, François Marie Arouet de, 69

Wachovia, 13, 52
Warehouses, Transaction, 104
Washington University (St. Louis, Mo), 230

Wells Fargo Bank, 53–54
Wesley, Robert, 199–208
Westpac Banking, 52
Wilke, Cliff, 199–208, 209–223
World Wide Web
   addressing, 100

World Wide Web (*continued*)
   advertising, 106
   change on, 57–58

Zimmerman, Joseph R., 169–176